The
Book
OF Roads

A Life Made from Travel

The
Book
OF Roads

A Life Made from Travel

Stories and photographs by
PHIL COUSINEAU

Foreword by
LARRY HABEGGER

VIVA
EDITIONS

Published in the United States by Viva Editions, an imprint of Start Midnight, LLC, 375 Hudson Street, Twelfth Floor, New York, New York 10014.

Printed in the United States.
Cover design: Scott Idleman/Blink
Cover photograph: iStockphoto
Text design: Frank Wiedemann

Second Edition.
10 9 8 7 6 5 4 3 2 1

Trade paper ISBN: 978-1-63228-019-0
E-book ISBN: 978-1-63228-025-1

Library of Congress Cataloging-in-Publication Data is available on file.

First edition published by Sisyphus Press.

Phil Cousineau wishes to acknowledge the following publishers of the stories included in this volume: *Journey Magazine*: "Sudden Chartres," "The Marrakesh Way," and "The Galloping"; *Fan Magazine*: "The Splintered Night," "Playing Catch in the Dark," and "Reading Box Scores with Pythagoras"; Conari Press: "Bach in Brazil" and "The Marrakesh Way" from *Prayers for Healing*; Harper San Francisco: "Blue Mosque Reverie" from *Prayers at 3 A.M.*; Conari Press: "Sudden Chartres" from *The Art of Pilgrimage*; Harper Collins: "The Gift of Bread" from *Prayers for a Thousand Years*; Reputation Books: "The Marrakech Way" and "The Bazaar Request," from *Vignettes and Postcards from Morocco*; Viva Editions: "The Night I Drove Kerouac Home" from *Burning the Midnight Oil*; Snickerdoodle Press: "The Night I Drove Kerouac Home" from *Jan Kerouac*; and Travelers Tales: "The Magicians of Prague," from *Prague* and "The Oldest Road in the World" from *The Best Travel Writing: 2006*.

To my Brother in Arms,
Paul Stanley Cousineau,
fellow traveler,
against the wind
and into the mystic,
on the long and winding road.

ITINERARY

xi   Foreword: Frozen Footsteps and Shared Roads
     by Larry Habegger

1   I
2   Conestoga Wagons
5   The Royal Road
9   Cardboard
12   Playing Catch in the Dark
14   Flying Lessons
18   The Ghosts of Birmingham

25   II
26   The Long Acre
28   A Shot of Cutty Sark
31   London Graffiti
34   The Running of the Bulls
37   Pure Kalinga
40   The Path through the Rice Terraces
43   Southeast Asian Train Ride

47   III
48   Blue Mosque Reverie
49   The Marrakech Way
51   Sudden Chartres
53   Bach in Brazil
55   The Splintered Night
57   The Galloping
59   Verne's Volcano
61   The Gift of Bread

65   IV
66   The Oldest Road in the World
69   Taloned Tracks
71   The Red Road

74   The Peyote Road

77   La Ruta Maya

81   The Road to Konya

86   Night Walk

88   The Last Journey

91   The Road Dogs of Dublin

97   V

98   Waiting for Himself

101   Ovid in Exile

105   Looking for Walt

108   Poe's Last Drink

110   The Bazaar Request

117   VI

118   The Tycoon

121   Out of Step in Odessa

124   Sharpshooters

126   Elegy for Yugoslavia

129   The Knock

132   The Ruinistas

136   Rainforest

141   Favelas

143   Pantherine Dreams

146   The Caves of Cappadocia

149   The Shadow of Ancient Ruins

151   Drunk at Midnight at My Father's Grave

155   VII

156   Cougars

158   The Trunk

161   Turtle Beach

163   Barracudas

165   The Philosopher of Tulum

167   The Mysterious Messenger

169   The Long Blue Road

173 VIII

174 The Columns

176 Reading Box Scores with Pythagoras

180 The Magicians of Prague

182 Krakatoa: East of Java

185 Vermeer's Desire

188 Carver in Paris

192 The Night I Drove Kerouac Home

196 Les Voyageurs

201 IX

202 The Way That Is No Way

204 Night Train

207 A Parable about Lamplighters

209 The Dangers of Reading All Night

215 Blue Pearl

221 Opening Day

223 Miniatures

230 The Chauffeur

234 Who Stole Her Arms, Mama?

237 The Bull Catchers

243 Catch as Catch Cannes

250 The End of the Road

256 Last Exit Before Paradise

271 X

273 Notes on the Photographs

275 Passing Thanks

279 About the Author

FOREWORD
FROZEN FOOTSTEPS AND SHARED ROADS

WHEN I WAS A KID growing up in Minnesota, I loved walking in a fresh winter snow in my buckled rubber boots and snow pants, tromping through city parks, across frozen lakes, and into deep woods. The biting cold, glowering winter sky, or even heatless sunshine on a below-zero day couldn't suppress my pleasure. I'd march along, kicking snow forward with every step, and pause from time to time to look back at where I'd been. The trail of footsteps in the snow marked my passage. I knew they were my steps alone.

I didn't realize it at the time, but my impulse to look back in admiration at my trail suggested a broader desire to leave a mark. In my child's mind, those footsteps were visible proof that I had been there, just as the rabbit tracks and squirrel prints showed me what animals had been out foraging since the snow had stopped falling. But I learned later that this impulse to leave a mark walks hand-in-hand with the desire to see where you've been and to tell others about it, whether to impart wisdom, share what matters to you, or simply entertain.

We are all storytellers, and for me, the roots of my storytelling stretch back to those winter ramblings as a boy. But why is this important? Why does it matter where we've been and what we've done, seen, and experienced?

Phil Cousineau, in *The Book of Roads*, goes a long way toward explaining that. He travels down one road and up another, chronicling life in our time with a poet's grace and filmmaker's vision. His travels take him from the rough streets of Detroit to the stony paths of Connemara, from Rumi's tomb to Chichén Itzá. He goes with a hunger for knowledge and a thirst for connection, to see the long thread of human history in the world around him and the earthy wisdom of shepherds and touts and countless other souls who share these roads with us.

By taking us along, revealing what he learned simply by showing us what he saw and felt and lived, Phil grants us a new perspective on our lives and world. We follow his lead and discover new connections with people and places and reflect on our own experiences so the tapestries of our lives extend beyond their usual borders and we are made richer for it.

We are here now. This is our world, our time. When we speak to each other, entire universes open up.

Thanks to Phil, I can look back on those childhood tracks in the snow and see that they were the beginning of something bigger. His stories have helped me understand that leaving a trail, making a mark, sharing our own hard-won wisdom helps create the human story and is vital to our shared history.

We all lean on each other. We are all connected. And with Phil as our guide, we see farther and deeper, and walk with a lighter tread down these roads, one step at a time.

Larry Habegger
Executive Editor, Travelers' Tales Books

I

"Life is a journey, the universe an inn."
—GAUTAMA BUDDHA

"What can we do?
We were born with the Great Unrest."
—CARIBOU ESKIMO TO KNUD RASMUSSEN

"Man, is the past a long and twisty road."
—SATCHEL PAIGE

CONESTOGA WAGONS

CHRISTMAS EVE, 1956. The snowdrifts pile up against our small brick house, impossibly white, rising with the moon, and shrouding the cars in the street. The wind bends the evergreen trees in the front yard. The cold night leaves frost feathers on the windowpanes.

I am four years old. My family gathers around the Christmas tree that we cut down at a tree farm out near Ann Arbor. The silver tinsel shimmers, the crisscrossing strings of popcorn smell fresh and salty, and the hand-me-down ornaments that came all the way from Ottawa glitter and glow in the reflection of the green and red lights.

It's time for the presents. My heart is beating jackrabbit fast.

My Grandpa Louis LaChance gets down on all fours on the living room carpet and offers me a firm man-to-man hand-shake, my hand disappearing in his. I notice the long gray hairs on the back of his hand, and then something cool against my palm. He has slipped me a silver dollar, telling me to look at the date. I try to read the numbers, and he helps me: "1896," he says proudly. It's a grand flourish, more for my mother than me. I can tell by the way he looks at her, pleadingly, as if asking for forgiveness for hurting her feelings in some way I'm too young to figure out. How could I have possibly understood what it felt like for her to lose her own mother in childbirth—the very act of bringing her into this world—and how he blamed her and asked his sister to raise her?

All this captured in a single furtive glance.

In the soft glare of the tree lights, my eyes grow large and curious. My forehead is already creased from the tension of trying act older than I am. The pattern is set. I am trying to look as serious as my father when he heads off to work at the big Ford Glass House, in Dearborn. I am practicing the poses of the man who will cultivate his worries and look like a deep thinker, which would please him no end.

Eagerly, I tear off the wrapping paper of his present to me. All eyes are on me. A book opens out like a rare flower. On the cover is a brightly colored painting of a Conestoga wagon with a tall mast rising out of the canvas roof, billowing with canvas sails. A pioneer family is in the driver's seat of the magical wagon—mother, father, son—as it jounces across the prairies. The background is teeming with buffalo herds and Indian hunters riding bareback on white horses.

I scratch at my red wool pajamas. It is my first enchantment. Something surges in me, a longing for the marvelous. Turning the pages of my new book, the contours of my life take shape. I want to climb inside that wagon and glide across the Great Plains with the white sails unfurled to catch the winds hurled down from Canada, wild winds that will propel the wheels for thousands of wild miles.

Later on in life, whenever the mannish boy in me heard the call to explore the world, it wasn't been because of the usual goads, a vision of a sleek red Corvette careening along "Route 66," or the lure of a travel poster for steamer ships heading to remotest Borneo. What has stirred my road-dark blood again and again has been the returning dream of gliding across America in a Conestoga wagon powered by prairie winds. To this day, my heart races with seven-league boots every time I remember the moment my grandfather sat me down on his knee and began reading from my first book of adventures in his raspy Ottawa accent, his grizzled whiskey breath warming my cheeks.

"*The wind came howling down from the north, Philip,*" he began and never stopped. I can still hear his voice in my third ear: "*And they lifted the sails to catch the wind.*"

That is how it begins; that is how it always begins. At the

end of the beginning appears the luminous moment that never ends, the boyhood memories that prove as inexhaustible as the wind off the prairies pushing us forward to a new world.

Wayne, Michigan
September 2001

THE ROYAL ROAD

"Give me back the soul I had as a boy."
—FEDERICO GARCÍA LORCA

LATE ONE FRIDAY AFTER school, Mom tells me that Grandma Dora's been having one of her lonesome spells, so we're going to spend the weekend with her at the little yellow cottage on Steele Street, near St. Alphonsus. I'm ecstatic, since I love Gram's cooking and her lion's-foot bathtub and her old RCA radio that is taller than me.

The next night, after our feast of pot roast, glazed potatoes and carrots, caramelized onions, and Johnny bread, Gram gives me a warm bubble bath. She hums one of her favorite old English dance hall songs, "The White Cliffs of Dover," which makes me think she's happy enough. I screw my face into an unasked question about her being so lonely we had to drive all the way into Detroit to make her a little less lonely. Humming to herself, she wraps me in a white terrycloth towel and leads me to the yellow brick fireplace in the parlor where my mom is waiting for us.

"Ma, I haven't heard you sing that in forever and a day."

"Makes me think of Sydney," my Grandma says. "Now don't get yourself all in a fret. Look, Rosie, he's all squeaky clean." Gram sits me down on her thick throw rug in front of the yellow-bricked fireplace. She offers me a cup of hot chocolate and Mom a cup of Earl Grey tea and flops down in her easy chair and sips her nightly sherry from a tulip-shaped glass.

"Frankie," she says to me, "can you flip on the TV? I think it's time for *The Lawrence Welk Show.*" Mom is about to correct her for calling me Frankie, but I shake her off and gladly flip the black plastic dial of the big console TV. On flickers the Polish prince of polka and soap bubbles. Gram and Mom talk right over the show, pausing for the flourishes of his waving wand and when the the Lennon Sisters come on, then slip into gossip about the Hatfield-and-McCoy-like family feuds. I pretend that I'm watching TV but keep sneaking glances at Gram's face. "One wrinkle for every heartache," Gram says when she catches me watching her. She's had two glasses of sherry now and is getting frisky, and revels in her stories about Grandpa Syd, like the way he used to snap his suspenders, or disappear into his leather-bound volumes of old English poetry, or tell Mom funny riddles each night before she went to sleep.

As they talk, my eyes explore her house, roving over the Early American furniture, the bric-a-brac from Birmingham and London, and back to the hypnotic fire in her yellow-bricked fireplace. On the mantel is an old clock, a Hummel doll, a leather-framed photograph of my Grandpa Syd, and a miniature royal carriage. I've looked at the mantel a million times and never noticed it before. The gold-painted royal seal gleams in the lamplight, and its four white enameled wooden horses look as they've just been brushed down by the royal guardsmen.

"Well, bless my soul, Frankie," Gram says, noticing my interest out of the corner of her eye. "Maybe you'd like to play with my little carriage." She gives me one of her great Grandma chuckles, lifts herself gingerly out of her easy chair, and walks over to the mantel. Her legs and ankles are so swollen it's a wonder she can walk at all. With two hands, she takes down the carriage and gives it to me with trembling hands. Until that moment, I'd never thought of her as old, just as my Grandma. Her blue serge dress with the crisp white apron over it ruffles gently in the heat waves from the fire. She pats my head, and says, "Close your eyes, little man, and now stick out your hand." She presses the tiny carriage into my hands and tells me she brought it back from England, "donkey's years ago," as she puts it.

"It's my one and only souvenir of Queen Victoria's jubilee," she says. I can feel her chamomile tea-breath on my cheek.

Then she calls me "Frankie" again. This time my mom can't help correcting her.

"Oh, Ma," my own Mom says, "you're all discombobu-lated. This is *Philip*. Philip, Ma, not Frankie."

My Grandma stares so intensely into the flickering fireplace I'm afraid she is going to drift away, like one of those old boats on Lake Huron that lose their moorings and are never seen again.

I feel awful for her. I'm only seven, but I'm old enough to know Frankie was the name of her dead baby boy. I know he's dead because his bronzed baby shoes are on her bed stand. I've seen them, held them, wondered how a baby could wear such heavy shoes. They're the saddest things I've ever seen. All worn and shriveled. They smell of death.

"Frankie," Gram says softly, calling heaven to see if he'll answer. "Put down those shoes. They're not worth a farthing. I didn't tell you that you could touch them."

Hearing herself pronounce the forbidden name, she shakes all over, then reaches over and hugs me, hard, in a wordless apology. I smell lavender coming off her dress. Her flashy earrings bump against my cheek. She's got on so much hair spray it scratches my cheek when she grips me. She starts to cry as she presses the metal carriage deeper into my hands. I can smell the sherry on her breath when she whispers, "Here's our carriage, my boy."

Now it's my turn to stare long and hard. She gently takes my hand and shows me how to push it down the slickly waxed floor. The carriage rolls and rolls until it bumps up against the hearthstone like the enchanted carriage in a Grimm's fairy tale that shape-shifts at midnight. I pick it up and turn it over and over, spin the black metal wheels, open the gold and red crested doors, place it back on the floor and hitch up the white plastic horses. I look around Gram's parlor and see roads everywhere. I see them between the folds in the rugs, over mountains of pillows, under the oak cabinet radio, and across the flatland hardwood floor. I turn couch cushions into drawbridges for grand castles, shirt cardboards become highways, dustpans make handy bridges. I twist old *Life* and *Look* magazines into tunnels, shoeboxes into country inns where I can water the queen's horses. No boy ever felt a greater joy. Gram seems transported by my transport as she watches me playing with that carriage through that long winter night.

Out of the blue, I ask her, "Gram, why did Frankie die?"

There's no reaching her now. She's lost in her own world, just watching me roll the carriage back and forth over my imaginary roads.

She just says, "Take me home with you, my prince."

I'm young, I'm confused. *You are home, Gram*, I want to shout out.

My mom puts her finger to her lips and whispers *shush*. My grandmother weeps softly. A strange beauty flickers over her face, an odd ache in her voice as she reverts to the French of her youth, "Mon garçon," she cries, "my boy," to which boy I'll never know.

Years later, I asked my mom about the miniature royal carriage. She swore by all that's holy she couldn't remember it. Not for the life of her. But in my mind's eye I can still see it on the mantle in Gram's parlor. I can still feel the otherworldly tenderness in her beautifully wrinkled hands as she places it like a charm in my hand and gently steers my hand to help get it rolling.

I learned early on that travel means moving down real roads in imaginary carriages.

CARDBOARD

MY FAMILY IS FULL of escape artists. My great-great-grandfather Cyril fled a shootout in western Canada to save his skin and start life over on the French River in Northern Ontario under a dead man's name. My great-grandfather Charlemagne was a *voyageur*, paddling his canoe seventy-five miles a day for six months every year, from Ontario up to the Yukon and back again. Grandpa Horace evaded a hard-scrabble life on the Lake Nipissing farm by riding the rails across Canada to work the harvests in the summer and fall, and the mines of British Columbia as a dynamiter over the winter. My father broke away from a backwater town outside Detroit on weekends to travel to distant museums, antique markets, and car shows. Later, I would find his receipts for the down and out motels he holed up in so he didn't have to come home until late Sunday night. At dawn, he was up and singing along with the latest songs on J.P. McCarthy's radio show on WJR. On the button, at 7 a.m., he was slamming the front door behind him and leaving a trail of Mennen's aftershave in his wake. I would lean on my elbow against the cold metal windowsill, and listen for the sound of the engine turning over, then watch him roar away in the family Ford Falcon, wondering where he was bolting off to this time, and when he would be back.

Secretly, I was relieved. His freedom was my freedom.

Whenever he left town I had the run of the basement, that strange underground kingdom of tools and spare car parts, scrap wood, hubcaps, army gear, old radios and busted television sets, stacks of *National Geographics*, and shelves of the *Encyclopedia*

Britannica. Our basement held the promise of other worlds, a reprieve from the world upstairs.

Every summer of my youth my friends Mark and Tim and Steve and I conjured up escape plans to rival those of our fathers. Nineteen-sixty-two was the hallmark year. That July, we crowded around the old stand-up Philco television to watch John Glenn slingshot into outer space. Inspired by his voyage, we found two old refrigerator boxes near the Howe Road railroad crossing and hauled them across Forest Park and two baseball diamonds, down Eastlawn Avenue to our house, and slid them downstairs into the cool confines of our basement. Every day for the rest of the summer of '62 we spent a few hours building our cardboard spaceships, getting ready for blast-off.

Finally, over the Fourth of July holiday, my buddies and I took turns crawling inside our cardboard ships, strapping ourselves in with my dad's army belts for the mighty moment of blast-off. First, we had to check all the dials, which we'd drawn with crayons on the pull-down the end-flaps of the refrigerator boxes, pretending they were retractable consoles. Then we checked our path to the stars on shirt cardboards I'd pilfered from my dad's drawer, on which we'd drawn maps of the solar system copied from the astronomy volume of my Golden Book Library. After agreeing on some remote corner of the galaxy, we turned on the vibrating throttle of the train set, flipped hairpin dials we'd copied from war comics, and loaded toilet-paper-roll howitzers with tinfoil bombs. We checked the cache of old Halloween candy stored in a Converse shoebox to fortify ourselves for the long mission into outer space, then argued about who got wear the leather flight goggles that Mark's dad had brought back from flying fighter planes in World War II.

We took turns shouting out, "Ready for take-off," as we'd heard in a million movies, and then switched on the portable record player that had recordings of space ships that Steve's dad had brought home from a work visit to NASA.

With that telltale rumble, we'd blast off, flying out the basement door and over the maple trees in the yard, beyond the sandlot baseball fields and over the Michigan Central railroad tracks, high into the hot summer sky.

On the last day of summer my buddies drifted home for supper, leaving me alone in the corner of the cool basement. From inside the sanctuary of my cardboard spaceship, I could hear the roar of the incinerator, a castaneting cricket that must have snuck through an open window, and the purring sound of Tigers baseball game on old Leo Hutman's radio next door.

I was most home when most alone.

And then came the ominous sound of my dad coming home from his mysterious weekend odysseys, the Falcon downshifting as it came up the driveway. Upstairs, I could hear my mother shouting to my sister to turn down the volume of the old black-and-white Philco so my father wouldn't be upset when he came in the door. The door opened, the shouting began, and the TV volume went up again. My sister, I imagined, turned it up so the Kochers next door wouldn't hear them shouting about where he'd been and how his supper was cold.

I slipped in the earplugs of my transistor radio—my hookup with Cape Canaveral—and begin the grave count-down: *Ten, nine, eight...*, and flicked the volume switch to "High" to simulate the roar of NASA rockets. With one hand on the hubcap steering wheel of my customized ship and the other on the tuning dial of my crystal radio, I took off for a destination light-years away from the battles at home.

It was a terrifying solo flight. My skinny arms bled from the wounds inflicted by enemy fire. The quick, short razor cuts on my rubber-band-thin biceps echoed the two red chevrons on my father's army shirt that I wore on the secret missions.

I twisted the paper towel tube of my periscope and saw an old wood-framed photograph of him taken at Fort Jackson, South Carolina, where he was lecturing on electricity to a roomful of crew-cut GIs studying to be radio operators on the battlefields of Korea. His handsome young face is already chiseled with the mordant wit and corrosive anger, the fierce desire to always be *somewhere else* that marked the rest of his restless life, and mine.

Playing Catch in the Dark

THE LONG SUMMER NIGHT crackles with lightning. The ghostly branches of birch trees twist in the wind of the oncoming storm. The blue light of television screens flickers in front windows up and down the street. On a dark porch a lone man sits in a lounge chair smoking a cigarette and drinking the last bottle of his nightly case of Stroh's while he listens to the Tigers ballgame on his transistor radio. Telephone wires hum with neighborhood gossip, lawns rasp with water sprinklers, and back gates clang shut for the evening.

Summer sounds.

Underneath the light pole, where Eastlawn and Gertrude streets converge, two young brothers play catch in the dark. The older brother hurls the battered leather baseball high over the spidery extension pole, imagining he's the graceful right-fielder Al Kaline throwing a runner out at home. He loves how the seams feel against his fingertips and how the ball rolls so easily from his grip and takes flight through the bright cone of light. His heart races as he watches the blurring ball disappear into the dark sky for a few taut seconds—

Standing alone in the sweltering darkness on the far side of the street, the younger brother imagines he's the Tigers catcher Bill Freehan waiting at home plate for Kaline's long, low throw from the right-field corner. The tow-headed boy circles and circles under the street lamp, covering his head with one hand and extending his gloved hand as the ball begins its descent from darkness and through the flickering white light. Grimacing, he plants his feet, braces himself for the *thump* and *sting* of the tumbling ball dropping into his glove. Triumphantly, he ignores the sting in his hand and yells with a voice that breaks like a Sandy Koufax curveball, "I've got it!"

Waiting in the lazy evening, the older boy gazes at the stars overhead, slaps at a mosquito on his arm, smells the pungent fire starter from the neighborhood barbecues, hears the moaning whistle of the Michigan Central freight train chugging through town. He glows with summer sweat and the love of a good game of catch with his younger brother.

Waiting in the darkness, the younger boy flexes his old fielder's glove, anticipating the booming shout of "Great catch!" from his older brother lurking in the shadows underneath the streetlight. Words that will resound in his head for the rest of the night, and will be there when he wakes up the next morning to go to practice.

Waiting, their hearts grow bold.

FLYING LESSONS

*"I have been searching for a whole lifetime for only one
thing, the essence of flight...flight, what happiness!"*
—CONSTANTA BRANCUSI

GROWING UP IN THE relentless flat lands of suburban
Michigan I was haunted by fever dreams about flying away, like
a manic Icarus fleeing the labyrinth, feeling no less inventive
than the Wright Brothers, as single-minded as Phileas Fogg, the
hero of Jules Verne's *Around the World in 80 Days,* the movie my
father insisted I see with him at the State Wayne Theater every
Saturday for a month.

The summer before my freshman year of high school, I
hauled sand in an old wheelbarrow from the woods near the
railroad tracks to the open field behind our house so I could
build a long-jump pit. All summer long I practiced my jumps
by doing wind-sprints down the crude dirt runway, then
launching off through the air, flailing my arms and legs, before
crashing sixteen, seventeen, eighteen feet away in the warm
sand. Thousands of jumps that prepared me for the hot summer
day at the All-City Track Meet when I broke the city record for
seventeen-year-olds, and earned my name on the big wooden
scoreboard at the Wayne Rec Center.

And so the muscle memory of being airborne burrowed into
my young body until it sank into my unconscious. Each night
that summer I dreamed of flying through the air, windmilling
my arms and legs through the air, and through sheer willpower
soaring into flight. Only to wake up right back in bed, disappointed, embarrassed, earthbound.

In the last restless days of that sweltering summer, my friend Steve and I scribbled a design for a flying bicycle on the back of my father's Ford Motor Company pay stub.

Deep in the cool confines of our cement-walled basement, we leaned earnestly over the green Ping-Pong table and drew up plans for an airborne bike built for two with helium balloons over each wheel. The idea was that our pedaling would turn gears that would turn paddlewheels suspended over the handlebars and fenders. Steve was convinced we could achieve liftoff, if only we could pedal fast enough, and I was sure that by fall we would be taking our dates to the Homecoming Dance in our newfangled contraption.

Emboldened, I confided to him, like the rocket planners I'd seen on an episode of *The Outer Limits*, "Imagine our entrance, Steve!"—knowing full well I sounded like Mickey Rooney rousing his buddies to put on a summer play. "We'll land in the parking lot in front of the gym to the music of 'Fly Me to the Moon,' playing on the portable record player we can carry in the sidesaddles!"

I didn't dare tell my buddy that I'd heard my dad sing the Sinatra song to my mother late one night as they danced in the living room, thinking we kids were fast asleep. Nor did I tell him it was only tender moment I ever heard pass between them.

"Sounds cool," Steve said, cool as ever.

My face lit up like the dashboard of my Uncle Cy's '57 T-Bird convertible. For weeks I fantasized about soaring over the rooftops in my hometown, then following the Michigan Central railroad tracks beyond the smokestacks of the River Rouge foundry, to my date's house in nearby Dearborn. With heart pounding, I would descend on her front lawn in our whirligig, whisk her away to the high school gym, and with her ever-lovin' arms around me make a glorious entrance before our astounded friends.

We wrote away to a helium company in Troy, Michigan. To my utter shock, they wrote back. Though dubious about our plans, they said we could have the tanks for forty bucks apiece. I winced when Steve, a human slide-rule, if there ever was one, did the math in his head and frowned: "That's two weeks' wages at the pizza shop, Cousineau." The pay stub blue-prints were stuffed into a box under my father's work bench, next to the tangle of two-by-fours that had been our Soap Box Derby car, the twenty-foot-long balsa wood dragon kite, the tin-can telephones that connected our tree forts, and the plastic model of the Levacar that my Dad used to drive around the Ford Rotunda.

We went out for track instead.

Fast-forward to the late seventies. I'm living in Berkeley with my girlfriend Cynthia, who has a pilot's license. Over the summer she insists on paying for me to take a co-pilot's course. She tells me she wants to give me wings. I earn my certificate, and she takes me up in a Cessna 150. The moment we pass over the span of the Golden Gate Bridge is a rapture. Clouds scud by like skyborne swans. The sunlight all around us is silky. She lets go of her controls, her laughter chiming above the engine roar, then shouting that it is all up to me now, that it always was, if only I would listen to her, learn to steer for myself.

For the first time in my life I'm truly flying.

My heart is beating hard enough to bruise my ribs, a sweet pain.

"Where would you like to go?" she shouts above the din of engine. I hear an offer like the one by the shopkeeper in the bazaar in *The Arabian Nights Entertainment* when he handed the brass lamp over to the restless Aladdin, a book my family had read out loud together the winter before.

For a held-breath moment, we hover motionless over the sparkling waters of San Francisco Bay, just as I had dreamed of doing in the helium-powered bicycle. I smile at the memory but say nothing to her, just feel the wonder at the loose spools of memory. The dials and lights before me glow like the eyes of skulking creatures in a dark forest. We're engulfed in a halo of gold light.

Then a marvelous thing happens. Gliding through the sea of sky, I suddenly realize that to the west of us in the deep blue magnificence of the Pacific Ocean, and 2500 miles away to the east waiting in an unworn groove of time is a shy high school girl with auburn hair, still staring into the sky, waiting for her prom date who'd promised her a ride she'd never forget. I am caught in the vortex of a dream, spinning and annihilating time and space. For one glorious moment anything seems possible if I can hold fast to the time when my heart seethed with dreams of flight and love, and I trusted the suction of infinity pulling me onward.

"Which way?" she asks again.

A smile swoops across my face.

I pull gently on the throttle, thrilling to the roar of the engine and the shimmying wings. Gripping the U-shaped steering wheel, I feel a rush of euphoria as the plane rises, gaining altitude, her silver nose aiming straight for the blue heavens, silvered light glittering on the wings.

I veer east, pressing on against the unknown.

THE GHOSTS OF BIRMINGHAM

MY GREAT-AUNT FLOSS THORNYWORK lives in the North Country. On the train ride north from London I read a Dickensian description of her hometown of Birmingham as "frightful and sooty-tentacled." I'm here to visit her at the request of a raft of relatives from all over America, none of whom have ever been to Europe.

Her doting neighbor, Geoffrey, greets me on the stoop of her house, and as he leads me down the dark hall and into the kitchen, he confides that I'm her first guest from the States since my grandparents visited decades ago, "back when God was in knickers."

Despite her show of nonchalance, "Aunt Floss," as she asks me to call her, has primped a little for us. She bothered to have her hair done, though she says "it was no bother," and baked a pound cake and made watercress tea sandwiches, which Geoffrey tells me is the first time in ages she's stepped foot in the kitchen.

She's also retrieved old family photos from wood and leather steamer trunks, which she shows me with great pride as she plies me with cups of Darjeeling tea set down on lace doilies "made in Belfast," she says proudly. As she adds more and more branches to the family tree, she twines her fingers nervously, speaking in a thick Lancaster accent, sounding oddly like Alfred Hitchcock, who just happened to grow up down the street. Her angular features have grown into an unnerving likeness of her brother, my Grandpa Sydney England. *My Grandpa England from England*, I used to joke with my friends, who never believed me, until I introduced them to my Uncle Lonny, short for *London*, as in *England*. I can't help but feel he's in the room with us, smiling at the reunion, and if he were alive I would ask him, "How in heaven's name could you name your first-born *London England?* "

"Your grandfather moved to America just in the nick of time," she says. "Shortly afterwards, the Great War broke out and most of his childhood friends were killed at Verdun. Did he ever tell about the time he suffered through a mustard gas attack? Near Bruges, I think it was."

She pauses in disgust. "Lordy, lord," she says, then returns to her narrative, like a BBC announcer recounting the tales of a typical English family during the Great War.

"During the Depression I almost followed him to America," she recounts bitterly, "but family responsibilities kept me in England." By the time the Second World War came around travel was impossible, and she had her own family to raise. It is strange to hear how arbitrary a life can be, turning this way or that, depending on the winds of war.

Mulling over the ship not taken, she gasps, "California." She pronounces it with a curious twist of her chin, an uncanny reminder of the grandfather I adored. "I always wanted to see California," she says to no one in particular.

Her neighbor looks all Pecksniffian, haughty and impatient, saying, "Nothing there that we ain't got here, mum." But she's not having any of his sanctimoniousness.

Slowly, I warm to her. Casually, I open my camera bag. "Do you mind if I take a few 'snaps,' Floss?" I ask her, using her brother's favorite word for photographs.

She smiles as I imagine she hasn't for decades, warmly. I'm charmed beyond words. It's a blown-glass moment, beautiful, fragile, liable to break apart at any moment. I want to hold on to it, but not too tightly. I look down at my backpack, knowing my Yashica is in there. Do I pull out the camera or stay in the moment?

In between sips of tea and nibbles from the plate of cream cakes, I snap a few shots of her flipping through her albums, chatting with her neighbors who keep arriving. All the while

I'm thinking of the family response back home at my chance to have a few fugitive moments with an "England in England," as my Aunt Shirley had joked before I left. I'm sure they'll be as enamored as I am with Floss's resemblance to my grandfather.

After pouring the last of the tea, she asks Nick, her caretaker, to bring her an envelope from her dresser drawer. With palsied hands, she pulls out my Grandpa Syd and Grandma Dora's marriage license and a handful of yellowed photos. Tears cloud her eyes like cataracts. "How long *has* it been you saw Grandpa Syd?"

Snap.

"No one's visited from America since my brother came," Floss replied through a sepia haze, "and brought Dora home for the family to see. They came across in steerage, even though she was pregnant. Couldn't have been easy, but life was hard then. Seventy years. Not since 1910 has anyone been to visit."

Snap.

Saying those words out loud shattered the delicate spun glass of memory. Through the cracks oozed her long-held bitterness. Her brother left home to become an opera-loving, baseball-enamored, book-devouring pharmacist, living first in Ottawa, then later, a long train ride away, in Detroit.

Snap.

Her anger startles her neighbor and me. "Sydney promised to visit me one more time, but he never did." Her only memories of him are in the form of letters from his children, and now grandchildren. She takes one from the red-ribboned stack, and adjusts the ruffled sleeves of her calico dress. It's from my Aunt Jacqueline, her main correspondent, a sweet ramble about their family business doing so well her husband plans to retire—at thirty-seven. Floss shakes her head in amazement, and takes a proper sip of tea, her pinky finger slightly crooked, out of long habit. She casts a cursory glance at several others, and decides on one last one from my grandmother, dated 1933.

Snap. Snap. Snap.

"My dearest Floss," it begins. "The Depression has hit us hard. Life is very difficult for us now. We have seven mouths to feed, and every day there is a knock at the back door from some poor man who is wandering around with nothing to eat. Just last year we took in my brother's little girl, Rosemary, after her mother died in childbirth. Poor thing…"

Snap. Snap.

I'm shocked to hear my mother's name mentioned. Floss shakes her head and dabs at her mouth with a lace handkerchief, long enough for me to appreciate her genteel manners, and then with heartrending deliberateness packs away her family treasures. I get the feeling she will never open the box again.

Snap.

Her anecdotes segue into sweet rambles about the wasted years since her husband died, her own lack of usefulness. I finish out the roll, scrolling the images in my mind that I'll print in my darkroom back in California.

"Hope you didn't mind the camera, Floss," I remark as I rise to leave. "Everyone at home will be thrilled to see a few 'snaps' of you since you were never able to send any of yourself."

She shrugs. But she isn't paying much attention. She's drifted away. I'm thinking that as far as she's concerned I've already left. Is that how the elderly deal with memories that are too painful, I wonder, just shunt them into the attic of their mind like an unwanted trunk?

"No bother," she finally says with a tight smile.

Outside on the stoop, an afternoon drizzle grays the skies. She shakes my hand with nineteenth-century formality.

I turn crimson with embarrassment at what feels like exactly what my English friends have been accusing me of for years, being the ever-optimistic Yank, Undaunted, I promise to see her again, even to bring some of our sprawling family over from America. But the offer garners little response. I ask if she has any message for the family back home.

She steps forward again and in a strange gesture, as if from someone else's life, she holds her palms out in front of her, then turns them over, fingers splayed, open to the heavens. It is the gentlest sign of resignation and acceptance I have ever seen.

"Tell them I'm ready to die," Floss says without a scintilla of self-pity. "Tell them I'm eighty-nine years old and ready to die."

Sometimes a voice is a soothing thing, sometimes a disturbing one. I feel like the man who spent a night reading about the uprising in the Warsaw ghetto, and woke to find his hair had turned white overnight.

I have no idea what to say. My mouth feels sewn shut.

Floss surprises me again, this time with a tincture of tenderness, "Remember me to your family, won't you? Tell them I forgive them for not visiting me before I die. Can you pass that on for me? Can you describe our visit?"

It's an elliptical question, swinging like a lantern that appears out of nowhere, revealing shadow and light, shadow and light.

Then Floss looks down at the camera hanging around my neck with a kind of old-world consternation.

I feel unmasked.

I cover it up by muttering, "Of course, you can count on me." Yet what I'm really thinking is that I can do better. The thought that heroes through my mind is that *I'll show them my photographs*. Smiling uncomfortably, I shamble away.

Halfway down the street leading toward the train station, I'm suddenly struck by the way the slate-gray sky is being parted by fingers of crepuscular light that gleam on the chimneypot roofs. Instinctively, I grope for my camera and flick the film advance lever with my thumb so I can capture the image. But the lever won't budge. I hit the shutter button but it's stuck.

I feel my heart seize up as if in sympathetic response with the frozen lens of my camera.

The film hadn't spooled. No film had advanced all afternoon. I had captured nothing but ghosts. My fingers are phantoms, moving nothing, remembering less.

My face flames. I play back the events of the afternoon like someone trying to retrace a lost object, and faintly recall a kind of twinge, a muscle memory in my hand of the advance moving too freely, without its usual resistance. Did I just block it out, neglect to check it, overwhelmed with the vanity of my dramatic appearance in her life, all the way from "California"?

I stare out over the drizzling sky and feel exposed. In search of the missing half of our family, I had come halfway around the world, but was only half there. There would be no resurrection of my grandfather through the time-looping maneuvers of photography. There would only be my spectral words to describe the fragrance of her regret.

Again, she summons her most plaintive voice and asks, "Remember me to your Grandma Dora, will you? Can you set her mind at rest, that I have fared well all these years? Can you describe this to the family back in Detroit?"

"Not yet," a cavernous voice within me answers.

I slump to the curbstone, and feel the rain drizzle down my neck, and say to no one in particular, "Not yet."

Paris, France
August 1989

II

"*Tout est le chemin.*"
(Everything is a road.)
—ALEXIS DE TOCQUEVILLE

"*What is more beautiful than the road? It is the symbol and image of an active, varied life. Each of us should make a map of our lost fields and meadows.*"
—GEORGE SAND

"*The Open Road. The great home of the Soul is the open road.... It is a wayfarer down the open road.*"
—D.H. LAWRENCE

THE LONG ACRE

ONCE IN AWHILE THE feeling comes back, the craving for the whiskey-and-soda air of Connemara, the walks at dusk across the bog and down the long acre, the stonewall-lined roads along the seaside, past the coral beach to Kehoe's pub for a revivifying pint of stout.

Winter 1974. Guinness twenty-three pence a pint. Bed and breakfast rooms for five pounds a night. Vagrant memories. Irish fry breakfasts, potatoes and beer, the melancholic swooning of rosewood fiddles and bodhrán drums. Nothing like it, yer man said, to raise the blood in a man. Lusty nights along the twilight edges of the Celtic world. Hitchhiking under slate-gray skies, picking blackberries along the side of the road, longing for the unmet friend. Scrying the meaning of sullen megalithic stones. Fathoming the fabled melancholy of the ancient land of my ancestors.

On I traveled through "soft days" of gentle rain, with my *soul clapping,* as Yeats wrote from his stone tower. Rambled on under *heaven trees that hung with nightblue fruit,* as Joyce rhapsodized in cunning exile. *Ventured into the slipstream,* as Van sung from Hynford Street. Searched for the lost chord, like Edna O'Brien, *Inebriated of love, shadows of love, fantasies of love, but not the one true love.*

Each night, in a different inn along the road, drunk with

words and feeling eloquent with *the drink*, I wrote postcards filled with cryptic messages to friends and family, callow efforts to convey my astonishment that I had escaped the hellhounds of the hometown factories and been blessed with the chance to live as if I were truly *alive*.

Those cards and letters, dropped into magic lantern mailboxes, and franked with brilliantly colored stamps, revealed a heart bursting with happiness I'd never known in the steel factories of Detroit, a conflagration of joy like the sudden rays of sunshine exploding over the turbid seas around the Aran Islands.

My words flew across the *whale roads*, as the old monks called the sea, shaped like the seagulls riding the thermals over the cloud-high Cliffs of Moher, winged words flying back to the home I couldn't wait to get away from and have never been able to forget no matter how far I wandered, how far I roamed.

A Shot of Cutty Sark

IT'S SPRING 1975, and I'm living in the West End of London, working construction by day, playing ball at night, when a friend from my recent kibbutz days in Israel stops by my Hammersmith flat on his way to Africa. Jeff and I celebrate his departure for a four-month-long safari with a pub crawl around London in his '68 Volkswagen van. After eleven pints of Guinness at a local Irish rebel bar, The Hop Poles, our voices are raspy from travel conversation. On our drive back to my digs near Marble Arch, we get deliriously lost, making two hours of wrong turns, as the night gets longer, foggier, less funny.

Suddenly, we're sobered up by the specter of creaking masts and the sound of groaning halyard ropes from a tall ship looming in dry-dock. We're nowhere near any of the old piers of London, but thirty miles away, in the parking lot of the Greenwich Observatory.

As we edge closer to the ship, I think of the story of the long-lost nineteenth-century sailors who were seized by the strange vision of a ghost ship crusted with ice, riding atop a towering blue iceberg. But this weird apparition looks familiar, like something I've seen on the labels of whiskey bottles and billboards around the world. That's when silhouetted ship reveals itself as the Cutty Sark, the fastest ship of its time, the last of the great tea-trading clippers.

Slowly, we slip through the fog-drenched parking lot, and come to a quiet stop. For half an hour we sit there, trying to sober up, as the cool air rushes in through the open windows of the van.

A security car making its rounds rakes the darkness with

a searchlight before spiriting off into the night. Our eyes turn to the ship straining against its moorings, its emptiness ringing loud in our ears. Dark river water splashes against the side of the ship.

Finally, I shout, "Hey, buddy, isn't that something?"

He burps and laughs. "If we were a little younger, a little drunker—"

I raise an eyebrow expectantly, a subtle challenge, a move I'd learned from my father, who learned it from his.

"Well, we'll never be any younger," I add groggily.

"And I doubt if we'll ever be any drunker," he says, finishing my thought.

His mischievous words startle me into action.

A split second later, we nod at each other and simultaneously fling open the van doors, leap over the guardrails, scamper up the gangway and onto the ship. The smell of fresh oak stain on the hand-rubbed deck fills my nostrils, the salt air coming off the Thames fills my lungs. Within seconds I'm caught up in boyish dreams of buccaneers and pirates. My eyes scan the soaring masts, then I roguishly blurt, "If I were a little older and a little soberer—" As if trying to talk myself into an adventure.

The word *climb* clings to my lip like rum from an old cask.

Simultaneously, we nod, smile, then seize the ropes. We begin climbing hand over hand up the catwalk rigging to the moon-dusted crow's nest. My mind is a tumult of images. Hanging there with trembling fingers, I think of wind-burned sailors who holystoned the decks, turned windlass ropes, and survived storm-wracked voyages to bring home darkly contoured stories of sea monsters, cities of gold, spice-rich islands, and sun-spangled tea plantations.

We hang in the air for a small eternity, until Jeff says, "Same pub, ten years from now?"

I grin to beat the night, reveling in the feeling of the spidery rigging in my hands and the wind in my hair. "Sure. It's a deal."

At that instant anything seems possible as the stars shimmer overhead and the fog trembles over the Thames and I seem to hang there over all of England. Nothing matters more than the tang in the air and the glimmer of dawn on the observatory, the amber lights twinkling on the river, and the feeling of climbing halfway into the sea of the sky.

The task of tasks is to move the world through our souls like a lantern slide and gaze in wonder at what is illuminated.

Ballyconneelly, Ireland
April 1980

LONDON GRAFFITI

NIGHTTOWN KILBURN, splintered cries of a working-class neighborhood. Shrieking subway trains across the trestle tracks. Windows rattling, plaster falling, bricks cracking every time another train rumbles past. I'm in a trance-deep exhaustion from sixteen-hour days working construction, demolishing old clubs in Soho for posh new apartments. Powdered pea soup and grilled cheese sandwiches cook on a two-burner stove while I look sullenly at BBC1 late-night news. Mid-stupor, I realize I'm staring at live footage from Vietnam. The words tremble across the screen like a hallucination:

DATELINE APRIL 30, 1975: LAST GI'S LEAVE SAIGON.

The room presses in until my temples hurt. I see camouflaged tanks rumbling through the charnel house of Saigon as the humiliating evacuation unfolds. Women and children convulsing with cries in the burning streets. Dark-green helicopters hovering in the apocalyptic sky over the American embassy, their dreaded rotor blades *whump, whump, whump* over the shouts of terrified marines pulling up rope ladders with screaming people who slowly corkscrew in the turbulent air.

I'm roiling with them down the vortex of memory. The dread of waiting for my draft number, year after year. Car caravans to antiwar demonstrations in Ann Arbor, Washington, Chicago. Years of watching the carnage scoreboards on the evening news. A threat from a war hero uncle to disown me if I run off to Canada, followed by a threat from my college girlfriend to leave me if I don't. Combustible images of school friends who came back from the war lamed, crazed, and ready for more battle.

A kid I'd played ball with came home to a ticker-tape parade and the next day was shouting from his rooftop with an M16. Everyone laughed. The next day he parked his red Camaro in the woods behind the Clark Gas Station on Michigan Avenue, and crawled on his belly through the mud, then dragged his sorry ass across the parking lot where he charged the gas station attendant like he was back in Khe Sanh. Never even recognized him as one of the guys we both played ball with every day, dawn till dusk, as if there were no tomorrow. Robbed him blind. Bumped into the next morning down at Brownie's Diner and bought him breakfast. Still didn't recognize him. Ended up at Eloise Hospital for the insane for a few months until he was invited onto "The Dick Cavett Show." Said something like he'd left his soul behind in the foxholes. Others said that's what you get for pretending nothing's happening to your war heroes when they come back home.

On my tiny black-and-white television, a shrapnel-edged montage of war images unwinds from the BBC archives: My Lai, Bien Khuet, Haiphong. Mahler's adagio plays underneath, achingly beautiful, like a song of Orpheus from the bowels of hell. Peace conferences, downed warplanes, disinterred bones, incinerated rainforests, and coffins loaded onto cargo planes.

The rancid smell of burnt cheese in the old flea-market skillet yanks me to the reality of my room of exile. Subway car wheels screech as they brake for the tube stop across the street. Neighbors across the brick-walled yard bellow at each other about unpaid bills. Holding the charred sandwiches in my hand, I turn up the volume of the small television as the droning voice of the narrator recounts the last moments of the grievous war.

Whump, whump, whump....

Suddenly, I'm whirled back to the hellhole factory on the ironically named Freeland Street where I spent a thousand nights during my college years, my skull thumping from the relentless noise from the monstrous steel presses. It's the dead of winter. Icy winds are slashing through the jagged glass of broken windows. I'm training a guy to drive a forklift who's only seventy-two hours out of the sultry jungles of Vietnam. Daryl has eyes as hard as onyx, sharp-pointed boots he calls his "shit-kickers," and a Brilliantined haircut he sweeps back into a pompadour with a gritty comb every chance he gets. He's very angry and very jumpy. Near midnight, a shot rings out—the backfire of a truck—and Daryl is jolted into action, instantly dropping to one knee and transforming his shovel into an M16 that's aimed right in my face. For a shaved second I'm in 'Nam with him, looking over my shoulder for a hidden sniper. Quivering with terror.

Then I see Schick, my foreman and an ex-Green Beret himself approach us from behind, saying, "Easy does it, fellah. Ain't no problem, here, soldier."

Daryl casts a 1000-yard stare right through us. Slowly, the shrapnel-like words bore into him like the relentless steel drills pounding, pounding, pounding all around us. Moments later, he realizes where he is—shivering in a dark puddle of oil on a cold concrete floor. He starts to sob.

Lying in bed, I feel like I've been lowered into a coffin. I'm smack dab in the middle between two jungles, 8,000 miles apart, I chew the horror, not knowing the difference.

London, England
October 1987

33

The Running of the Bulls

SLEEPING FITFULLY ON THE rough wooden bench, I'm rudely woken by the 8 a.m. ceremonial rocket explosion and the Santo Domingo corral gates opening like a loud slap, and seeing the seven outraged bulls stampeding through the barricaded streets as I dash like a crazed halfback through the bellowing crowd toward the bullring half a mile away. In my fever dream I can feel once again the steaming breath of the bull on my legs that forced me to lurch inside a doorway and suck in my gut to avoid its slashing horns.

Over and over, I wake up in a cold sweat, doubled over with stomach cramps, startled to find the raucous bands of the San Fermin Fiesta silenced, the fireworks spent, the wineskins empty, the pandemonium of the *encierro* only a memory. Then I look down the twisting railroad tracks, waiting for the *hiss* and *whoosh* of the steam locomotive as it approaches this remote station high in the Pyrenees.

Near three in the morning, I'm jolted awake by the shouting of an angry student in a white shirt, red beret, and scarf around his neck. One of the fiercely proud bull runners, he squeezes a long arc of wine from his bota bag into his mouth. With a flourish, he then unfurls a stained banner that says *Down with the Fascists!* The last of the revelers from the fiesta, desperate for some rest after around-the-clock partying, yell at him to keep his mouth shut. Instead, he stomps up and down the platform like a man possessed, cursing the government, and plastering incendiary posters on the station walls: *Down with the Dictator! Franco Must Go!*

I collapse again, beyond weariness after five days and nights of revelry. Hours pass before I wake up to a sleep-strange procession. Are these stilt walkers from the Pamplona Fair impersonating Franco's soldiers?

The goose-stepping is chillingly real.

In heart-raking panic, I look for Steve, my traveling buddy, who's fast asleep on a nearby bench. The six soldiers, in dull grey uniforms, march directly toward the rowdy student, who backs away from them, then cowers behind a pillar. In one swift motion, they lift him up by his armpits. The fierce move sucks all the wind out of him, catching his fury and his curses in his throat, leaving him livid as a meat-hooked animal. The expressionless soldiers march him to the end of the platform and disappear behind the station, silent as stone.

I'm unsure if I'm dreaming or awake. I look quickly up and down the platform for a clue. Everyone is pretending to be asleep.

Then, thunderbolts. Or was it the sudden clanking of train cars, the backfiring of a car, the snapping of bones in a nearby shop, a hunter's early morning warning shots in the distant hills? Or an execution?

When the soldiers return a few minutes later without the demonstrator, their eyes look hollowed out. Their hobnail boots slam down on the railroad platform in eerie unison, their rifles pointing like foul exclamation points to the starless sky.

Across the tracks, a withered peasant woman in black mantilla fingers a rosary of white crystals, and crosses herself rapidly, as if stitching herself up. She mutters a defiant prayer as the stone-souled soldiers pass by. My rosewater memories of lovely Spanish girls in flouncy white skirts with scarlet handkerchiefs in their hands as they dance the fandango are crushed.

The soldiers cross through the station, spreading fear like a scythe. By the time they reach the camouflaged military trucks, I've fallen into a precipitous sleep out of sheer exhaustion.

Lost in the fever dream again, I'm darting down the *Calle Estefeta* of Pamplona, in and out of the rampaging crowd of red-scarved runners, like Night Train Lane, my boyhood football hero, leaping over fallen runners, pushing past stragglers, evading the pursuing bulls a few steps behind me. I'll never be able to reach the bottlenecked entrance to the stadium before the bulls. In the peculiar logic of dreams the enraged bulls know that—and with deadly speed they turn to charge the nearest runners. I can feel their fury. It has its own metallic smell. I can see the horror before it happens – and try to wake from the nightmare, clawing in a windstorm of fear....

Instead, there is the fleeing man running for the barricades, reaching out for a saving hand—but he is shouted at and pushed back by police and crowd, who are furious at his cowardice. Two burly men hurl him down to the ground, shouting, *Run! Be a man! Take your chances!* In their faces I see that some ancient mystery will not be completed if the runners do not lure the bulls into the ring: The sacred bull will not be sacrificed, the world will not be renewed.

It is like peering into a mirage to see the runner lifted off the ground by the snorting bull, its horns goring his thigh, sending a gush of blood in long red arcs into the morning air.

It is the silence that wakes me, as sound and life drain out of the streets of white-spired Pamplona.

At dawn, the moaning train pulls into the station, snuffling like an old animal. Black plumes of smoke rise into the sky. Not a passenger speaks as we straggle on board. The conductor swings his red lantern and blows a shrill whistle. I lean out the window, straining for a view of the fields behind the station. I see less than nothing. It is like looking into negative space and trying to sketch in charcoal the dark lines of what is real. The travelers in my compartment press up against the window in morbid curiosity as we grind along the rails and out of the village.

The doubt haunts me. It's the not-knowing, the dull fury, that hurts. I sense the others staring at me, furtively trying to read my face for what I know but cannot say.

PURE KALINGA

LATE-AFTERNOON SUN POURS molten heat into our rumbling Jeep. Dust devils raise hell on the narrow mountain road behind us. Through the front windshield I see the old warrior running effortlessly along the precipitous trail that winds through the rice terraces.

Near the metal girder bridge spanning the gorge outside the village of Bontoc, the driver slows for the checkpoint. As we pass him, I catch a glimpse of him through a tear in the canvas that drapes the back of the Jeep, spear in hand, sun-bronzed, sweat-streamed, his craggy face fixed on the ground in front of him. The spiral tattoos on his arms and legs, evidence of headhunting days, swirl hypnotically as he runs at a pace beyond time.

At the border we downshift to a gear-stripping stop. Military guards scrutinize our faces. I gaze back over my shoulder into the bright sunlight and see the mirage of Stone Age long-distance running dissolving in the distance.

"Pure Kalinga," snaps the young Filipino across the aisle, startling me out of my reverie. The kid's been squirming in his seat since we left Bontoc, strutting his city stuff for the benefit of the nervous village couple seated next to him and the tribal kids crammed in around him. He's trying to convince us that his blue and gold UCLA warm-up jacket sets him apart from this strange world in the mountain provinces. But his stories about his self-described sophisticated life at the university in Manila find little sympathy out here in the boondocks, a word that just happens to come from *bundok*, the tribal word here for mountains.

"Pure fuckin' Kalinga," he says condescendingly, shaking his head. The warrior's tribal name, so melodic to me, is a joke to him. Yet he can't help from craning his neck for one last glimpse of the hunter as the jeep lurches ahead.

Behind us, the warrior is poised at the trailhead that leads up the mountain to his distant village, as if knowing we would glance back at him. His mica eyes are sparkling, his sun-crinkled mouth widens into a wizened smile as he turns to climb the steep switchback path, and is gone.

The moment the warrior disappears from view the kid is unsettled, as if he wants to leap out of the speeding Jeep to follow him into the mountains, which is an unexpected turn of heart.

"I thought his kind were all taken care of by Marcos's army," he says. His cockiness vanishes. He looks confounded, and asks me, as if I would know, "Where do you think he's going?"

I shrug, say, "Home."

The kid nods, his show of bravado somehow stymied by the hunter's enigmatic smile. The wounded look on his face suggests that he's just realized to his horror that the hunter knows things he doesn't.

The kid sneers, squints out the back of our juddering Jeep into the bright sunlight. He seems desperate for a sign from the first person who has seen something in him that he's never even guessed at: the hidden trail, the way out to the way in.

The mist clears for a moment and we can both see the old warrior reappear for a moment on the crest of the receding mountain. The blade of his spear glints in his leathery hand, his crusty red loincloth flaps in the breeze.

The kid blurts out, "Who would want to live like *that?*" and turns down the canvas flap. He can't hide the longing in his voice. I have a strong urge to say, *You do*, but resist, sensing this is a revelation he has to come to on his own.

I turn up the edge of the wind flap for my own glimpse. The last thing I see before we careen out of sight is the old warrior watching us watch him.

Something cold seems to sting the back of my neck, the long sigh, the last breath of a world fading away.

Luplupa, Kalinga Province, Philippines
September 1984

THE PATH THROUGH THE RICE TERRACES

THE STONES HAVE A PERFUME of their own, a mix of storm, heat, buffalo dung, tropical rain, pine air, and the ancient breath of the mountain gods. I tilt my face to the sky, and raindrops asterisk my glasses. Through the draping fog, I see tier after tier of rice terraces, rising 1000 feet into cotton clouds. While Stonehenge was being calibrated, the Giza pyramids configured, and the Incan emperor's vast estate Macchu Picchu was still a glint in the third eye of his architects, Filipino peasant farmers were coaxing these stone-braced terraces out of the stubborn Cordillera Mountains, in Northern Luzon.

Halfway up a precipitous cliff, I stop to catch my breath. A leather-faced, g-stringed Igorot farmer steps gingerly along the stone walls straddling lime-colored pools of rice. Beyond him stretches ten thousand miles of rice terraces carved out of the mountainsides long ago by his ancestors. He is leading his young boy to their ancestral rice paddy. A bamboo sluice pole balances precariously on his sunken shoulders. A grey sheet of rain advances ominously as I follow him discreetly down the terrace paths to a village of nipa huts, pig corrals, and a clothesline flagged with foreign T-shirts. But he's disappeared, so I quickly find a sari-sari store and order a simple dinner of fish, rice, and beer. I'm restless from weeks of solo travel through remote mountain villages, and weary of trying to make myself understood to people I'll never see again, so I fend off the usual questions about where I'm from and why I'm alone.

On my way back along the washboard road into Banaue, I hear the faraway sounds of flutes and drums. At the dark crossroad between the brightly lit tourist hotel and the ramshackle

Traveler's Inn where I'm staying, I surprise myself by following the music in hopes of a little human contact. Inside the hotel I find a folkshow in progress for a group of scientists from the International Rice Institute who are inhaling dozens of bottles of San Miguel beer, and laughing raucously at the performance. I slip inside, silent as smoke, trying to blend in with the crowd, a move born out of the half-baked desire to end the months of road loneliness and find the unmet friend.

The performance is embarrassingly neo-colonial: a medley of treacly folksongs, skits about the coming of the missionaries. I stand to leave, but am held back by a traditional clashing bamboo stick dance. It's led by the same rice farmer I saw earlier in the day. I'm impressed at his dexterity—but put off by the racist comments of the daytrippers from Manila. I bolt in disgust.

Outside the hotel, a mango moon rises over the valley. The ancient stone paths through the rice terraces are speckled with the red lantern lights of villagers ambling home. A little girl approaches me with a basket of orchids for sale. An old woman with brocades of snake bones in her still-black hair passes by, smiles, and bows.

Slowly, I head down the mountain road to the inn. On an utterly dark stretch of road beyond the glaring lights of the hotel, I pass the farmer and nod silently. I want to slip by him, but he recognizes me. He smiles sheepishly, then mumbles in his mountain staccato, "You want photograph? I famous actor."

He lifts a flashlight so I can see his face. All I can manage is a stare of disbelief as he tongues the one craggy tooth in his betel-stained mouth.

"No, no, that's all right," I mumble back.

"In 'Pocalypse Now," he says percussively. "I one of chopped heads—last scene with Brando. Very hot. Very strange man."

The old farmer forms an arcing "T" with his two wildly tattooed arms to create a picture of an umbrella like the one used to keep the flies and tropical sun off his head while he stood buried up to his neck in the ground in take after take after take of the notorious "temple scene."

"Yeah, I've seen the movie," I say, then add something stupid effort to make conversation. "I think I remember you."

I keep staring, waiting for reality's jump cut. As he describes the film, I hear the soundtrack of Wagner's "Ride of the Valkyries" and napalm bomb attacks. The grisly fight at the end of the movie just doesn't jibe with my Stone Age image of the rice farmer earlier in the day when he was sludging through his fields teaching his son the secrets of the rice gods.

While I'm trying to splice together the warring images, something amazing comes my way. A conflagration of fireflies lights up the dark night. It's a miracle of incandescent flight flickering on and off. In one long blinking necklace of light they stream away toward a tall pine tree down the road, circle it several times, then settle in as if a pointillist artist was busy dotting the tree with thermoluminescent light. Slowly, the tree seems to swoon as thousands of male fireflies synchronize their mating calls.

The sky crackles with green-gold light and a monsoon pours down its thick black night rain. The towering pine tree is snuffed out like a candle. In the sudden darkness a silent motor-cycle with sidecar edges past us and glides to the bottom of the hill.

The old Igorot smiles knowingly and tugs at my arm. I cringe, and back away. His words trail after me as I hustle away, "You see movie, Joe?" Streams of red betel-nut juice dribble down his chin. "You want photograph or not, Joe Boss? Cheap. One dollar!"

Banaue, Philippines
February 1984

Southeast Asian Train Ride

FOR SIXTEEN TEETH-GRINDING HOURS, we ride the train from the papaya-colored skies of Chiang Mai near the Laos border to the purple-flowered banana groves and green comma palm fronds of the coconut plantations in the south. The smoke from the rickety huts thickens the sky, and peasants returning from the rice fields appear like silhouettes in a shadow play. The dragon wings of Buddhist temples are etched like charcoal against an emerald and coral sunset.

Darkness falls slowly, the sigh of nightfall, and I'm filled with the familiar longing of one too long on the road. The serenity of this ancient landscape evokes a lacerating loneliness. The isolation is intensified by the singsong conversation of the Mandarin astrologer next to me on the wood slat seat, the low murmur of turbaned Indians praying, or the gossip of my fellow travelers.

Near dawn, the train stutters into a ramshackle station in a nameless village. In the ruby shadows of an abandoned temple I see an orange-robed monk. He bends down over the edge of a lotus pond and flicks his thumb against a single lotus flower, sending it like a prayer that floats on water. His calm demeanor reminds me of a teaching I received in a temple near the Laotian border the week before.

"Watch and listen, then listen again," the young monk told me as he applied gold flakes to a statue of a revered master. "Anything that wakes you up has Buddha nature inside it."

I lean out the train window as we pull out of the station and over the slow, lurching curves of track. The rush of sweet country air fills me with wonder as we languorously make our way toward Bangkok.

The wheels of the train squeal, the whistle blows, and the food sellers on board scurry away across the platform and down a road leading to a humble temple filled with wood smoke. There, a single silhouetted monk ascends the lone tower to pull the rope on a great brass bell. I close my eyes to listen better, to focus on the necessary, the faint pealing of a monastery bell from the village calling everyone's attention to the miracle of the moment.

Nothing is more real than those bells.

Bangkok, Thailand
Autumn 1984

III

It runs up the hill,
And runs down the hill,
But in spite of all,
It still stands still.
—ENGLISH RIDDLE

I have no legs and cannot move,
but I can run up and down mountains,
across plains, villages, towns, and cities.
What am I?
—CAMEROON RIDDLE

He accompanies you constantly,
and you pay him nothing.
—ARABIC RIDDLE

Answers on page 273

Blue Mosque Reverie

A WHITE CRESCENT MOON passes behind the long slope of Sultan Ahmet's mosque, glazing ancient Istanbul with silver light. The medieval stone archway in the pine-bowered garden frames the six needle-shaped minarets and twenty-four blue tiled domes like a border in an illuminated manuscript.

In and out of the god-source dark night, great white streaks of seagulls fly around the minarets and domes as if retracing the arabesque patterns painted on the mosque.

Near the jasmine-scented garden walls a peacock cries like a sleepless baby, a cry, the ancient Sufis believed, for the soul to dance. From the distant cafés along the labyrinthine lanes of the old city echoes the percussive sound of slapping dominoes and the haunting melodies of Turkish folksongs that crackle on old radios.

In that deep pool of listening, I heard the dark consonants of long-forgotten tongues, and the sultan's horses scraping prayers on old cobblestones wet with rain.

It was long ago that this would happen again.

The Marrakech Way

DEEP IN THE THROBBING heart of the covered bazaar, the last of the weary shopkeepers are closing their doors for Ramadan. The dusty maze of streets is so quiet I can hear the shuffle of my own sandals. Near the Djama el Fna plaza, I find four blind drum-makers on a bench next to the door of an old music shop. They are shadow-striped by the afternoon light coming in through the slatted roof of the market, which intensifies the thrilling shadowplay of their music. One man plays a wooden flute, another a slender-necked rebec, a third shakes a jangly tambourine, and the fourth thrums a goatskin drum. All while singing folk songs as old as the desert. Their self-assured smiles are strong enough to prop up the crumbling walls of the *medina*. The oldest musician is a Bedouin nomad with a dusty beard and a rhythm that sounds like an approaching sandstorm. His head sways back and forth, in and out of the slanting light, as if he's listening to the bells of a distant caravan juddering across the desert. He gestures for me to come out of the shadows. I lean down to hear him.

"With hands, is Marrakesh way," he says softly. "No feeling with sticks. Just with hands comes feeling, for drumming."

His own sun-burnished hands dance over the taut drum skin as if they're circling God. His voice yearns, finds Him. Higher and higher he pushes the prayer high into the impossibly blue skies above the towering red walls of the city. Smiling, he invites me to join them for some moist wild figs and glasses of tea with floating mint sprigs.

"And you, kind sir," he asks, pouring the steaming tea for me in a long graceful arc. "What do you feel, with your hands?"

One, two, three sugar cubes fall into the hot glass, splashing in the hot tea, and dissolving bead by bead.

"What is your way through the world, for feeling?" he asks.

My hands wind tight around the glass, absorbing the heat. The sugar vanishes, becoming indistinguishable from the tea.

Far below me, below the cool sand, below the ancient city, below the fossils laid down long ago, a rumble begins. It is the sound of words said long ago, prayers lifted from a very great distance, and now knocking on the door of my heart, waiting for an answer that needs more music.

Sudden Chartres

STORMS OF SUNLIGHT STREAM through the stained glass windows. My heart surges as I enter the ancient labyrinth. Each step I take slows time as I follow the ancient winding way over the white and black flagstones. Each step on this path has been worn smooth by pilgrim sandals over the last 800 years. A strange tension builds as the turns tighten and I close in on the center, then slip inside, as if in a dream. My feet rest on the restless center where once was bolted a bronze relief of Theseus slaying the Minotaur until the church deemed it pagan and yanked it from its stone mooring. Now the center of the labyrinth is blank, empty, yawning.

A cool clarity comes over me. The knot inside me begins to loosen. The voices in the cathedral fade away, and I hear nothing but the sound of my own bloodsurge. An utter stillness. A thousand hearts beat as one in the vast cathedral.

I am poised on the still point of the world.

Unwinding, I follow the meandering path back out of the labyrinth. As I emerge, an old Frenchman in a black felt beret is waiting. He taps me on the arm with the crook of his oak cane. He has the eyes of a court jester, the weariness of the wayward pilgrim. With the riddling power of a traveling bard, he asks me, *Do you know where I can find God?*

He is listening hard to what the philosophers here regard as the *l'appel du vide*, "the call of the void."

A cool shiver rivers down my spine, the back of my neck prickles, something winged flutters in my heart.

The old man's eyebrows arch expectantly. Is he a mad theologian? A sardonic existentialist? A dubious philosopher? His slantwise gaze suggests I am being tested about my knowledge of sacred architecture. He squints, waits impatiently for the words lurking in me that might surprise us both.

A ray of blue light slants in through the brilliantly bright rose window above the choir loft and finds my face, warms my soul. It is like those visions of beatitude I was forced by the nuns to read about in the lives of the saints. I didn't even know it, but I've been waiting for this moment of lucid light all my life. With my right thumb, I point backwards over my shoulder to the whirling pattern in the stone floor.

The old man touches the edge of his beret, and bows elegantly. Letting a long Gallic sigh out of the corner of his crinkled mouth he steps across the threshold and disappears inside the labyrinth, his cane keeping the time beyond time, in this space beyond space.

BACH IN BRAZIL

THE GRACEFULLY CURVING WOODEN bridge leads to a small lake in the old granite quarry. Two white swans glide across the still water, their long necks curling into feathered question marks.

As the morning sun crests the treetops, I am startled to hear the rumbling of Bach's Toccata and Fugue coming from loud-speakers attached to the soaring stone walls. I sit on a carved bench at the edge of the water, watching the play of light on the lake, listening to the deep organ drone until it slowly fades away and transforms into the joyously conversing violins of the Brandenburg Concertos.

Abruptly, the spell is split by the shrill cries of a chainsaw at the edge of the park. Metal teeth gnash the air. Motors growl. White-flashing blades bite into ancient bark. The forest moans as great branches crash to the ground.

An unseen hand turns up the volume of the music, producing a strange syncopation of falling trees and soaring violins.

A dusty trunk in the attic of my memory opens wide and I recall a legend about Bach. One brutal winter a frost destroyed all but one of the apple trees in the great composer's grove. Desperate to save his last tree, the composer ventured out into the stricken field to offer it the only protection he could think of—the life-preserving pages of his Brandenburgs. With those parchment-bandages, he tenderly wrapped the bark of the dying trees and kept them alive until spring.

Out in the middle of the lake, the two white swans twitch to the last snarls of the chainsaws, then stretch their lovely necks, their question marks turning into exclamation points.

The interlude is brief, the swans poised like patrons at a concert waiting for the first notes of music.

Hearing nothing, they glide on, moved from below by the unseen.

Effortlessly, they crisscross the canyon lake, making the mildest of waves, riding the waves of their own sound.

Curitiba, Brazil
August 1993

The Splintered Night

STRANGE DAYS WITH THE Doors in Tokyo. After years of contractual disputes, Warner Brothers has finally agreed to release their music, fourteen years after the group disbanded. I'm here for a week of research and interviews for a book on the shamanic band in between a soft parade of press conferences, during which they announced that rock and roll, not politics, is what saved America during the volatile sixties.

When asked by the awestruck media if the Doors had a message for the Japanese people, Ray, the legendary keyboard player, pauses oracularly and hands down his prophecy: "What Japan needs is LSD and Doors music. It could save you from working yourselves to death."

On the last night of the tour, I'm ready to *break on through* the bars of the velvet cage hotel and on to the other side, even I'm not sure what. For nine hours I roam the neon-crazed streets of the Ginza, and meander through the maze of Kabukicho's love hotels, pachinko parlors, karaoke bars, and kung-fu cinemas. Around three in the morning, I meander back to the hotel and am stunned to hear the *thwack, thwack, thwack* of baseball bats splintering the night. I follow the percussive sounds until I find a towering three-story batting cage, ablaze with light and alive with the shouts of insomniac businessmen cursing their missed swings and the blisters on their hands.

Standing on the curb, I gawk at the strange vision of an all-night batting cage floating above me in the night sky. The reverie is broken by the arrival of a long white Mercedes limousine with black-tinted windows that pulls up next to me. Out of the front seat leap two *yakuza,* a deep-bowing chauffeur and a burly bodyguard with jet-black pompadoured hair. Out of the back bounce two more, dressed in jade green Armani suits with glittering gold chains around their necks. Now the stretch is surrounded. A pit bull of a man emerges, sporting a white fedora, white suit, white leather shoes, and the requisite bad-ass black shades. Over one muscled shoulder is a 42-inch baseball bat.

Gazing anxiously, he limbers up with a couple of left-handed practice swings, as if standing in an on-deck circle. He rolls his shoulders, then tries another get-the-kinks-out swing. Grimacing, he pulls two white patent leather batting gloves out of his hip pocket, and slips them over each hand. He grips the bat again, and the little finger of the right glove hangs limp under the handle. Only nine fingers clutch the bat as he swings at an imaginary pitch. My blood ices over. I try to turn away and look at the batting cages, but can't help myself and keep snatching glimpses of the empty finger of the glove, and watching the replay in my mind's eye of the ritual *yakuza* punishment for some business betrayal—or was it the last vestige of some arcane initiation?

With his snarling entourage following behind him, the slugger passes me, his bat slung over his shoulder, like a samurai and his sword as he trudges toward battle. He grunts and mumbles to himself as he heads for the cages to take his practice cuts high in the Tokyo sky.

The Galloping

I'M LOST IN THE world of an old travel journal at an open-air Greenwich Village café. Late summer light scallops the sidewalk. What are my maundering reflections on the fugitive truths of life compared to the fleeting beauty of this moment? T. S. Eliot warned me: I had the experience, but lost the meaning somewhere along the road. Discouraged to find nothing worth salvaging in the journal, I stuff it back into my road-burnished leather satchel.

Feeling nervous without a real book in my hand, I reach back into the satchel and pull out a tattered copy of Moore's *Care of the Soul*. For a few lazy minutes, my eyes roam over the pages, then trip over the exposed roots of an idea. The wild line demands a cuff on the forehead and several focused rereadings: *"When the divine shines through ordinary life, it may well appear as madness and we as God's fools."*

Leaning over the book, I underline the sentence and draw a thick asterisk in the margin. No sooner do I mark the page when the moment is thrown out of joint by the hollering hoof-beats ricocheting off the last of the Village's cobblestones. A runaway police horse gallops within arm's reach of where I sit, beads of sweat from its flanks and rippling back tossed in the air and landing on my table. I look up just in time to see the terror in its marble eyes, steam rising from its nostrils like locomotive smoke, its tail swishing through the air.

Seconds later, a horseless cop races past in red-faced pursuit, punching his fist in the air, swinging his truncheon with the other, yelling a long, dopplering *"Ssttooppppp!"*

Astonishment leaps like an acrobat from face to face of passersby and shopkeepers up and down the street. A young woman in a bright red dress and black hat pauses mid-stride, dazzled by the sight. The old baker next door leans out of his doorway and smiles at the sight of the runaway horse, thrown back decades to when horses were an everyday sight.

Every moment contains the possibility of eternity breaking through into time. A sword rises from the lake to save a kingdom, fossils dug out of the ancient seabed seize the imagination, or a package of spices from a distant bazaar rekindles a memory of lost love you thought was gone forever.

Exalted moments. As now, when the sweat of the runaway horse falls to the hot asphalt street, hisses and turns to mist. Time stops, the soul pauses. The movie of my life freeze-frames this late autumn afternoon, in Greenwich Village, 1991.

Verne's Volcano

MY EYES ROVE OVER the darkness to the holy rage
spewing out of Stromboli. The volcano roars like an infernal
furnace, streaming molten fury into the cold, hissing sea.
Here is the surprise the ship's captain had store for us when
he called us out on deck during the middle of dinner. Far off
the starboard side of the ship is the Island of the Winds in the
Odyssey, the fiery entrance to the underworld in Jules Verne's
Journey to the Center of the Earth. On we sail, through a world of
ancient paroxysms, past incandescent magma and whirlwinds
of fire from the earth's core. Spindrifting spumes of fire, redri-
vertongues of lava snaking down the riven side of the myth-
molded island.

All around us, in a dozen Babeling languages, voices shout
out in joy at the sight of the old spark-fling volcano setting off
its fireworks.

Turning to embrace you, I lose myself in the silky web of
your hair, feel the strength of your hands interlacing mine. Your
face is utterly luminous. In this way you never fail to touch me.
Opening my heart, you remind me that to be alive is to be on
fire, to know that some nights ask us to take our wonder outside
and marvel at the unexpected beauty of the world.

Tonight, the ship rolls like a cradle in a soft summer breeze,
but my dreams smolder: The world is ablaze and trembling in
the diabolical light of a sudden eruption. Boulders ricochet
deep within a crater. The coal-black night that covers the sea is
broken up by a red tracery of fire and filled with a hailstorm of
pumice. A bristling sulfuric smell overwhelms the spices in the
air off the island's coast.

Near dawn, I wake with you clasping me tightly, as if we've just fallen a great distance through the coiled night. Your breath is soft on my face. Blissfully I breathe in the ravishment of your sweet almondy hair. You are lovelier than anything I have ever known. You move closer. The magnetic field shifts. My heart leaps like the gallivanting needle of a compass rose. It points to the north of you in me.

Everything has to do with heat and darkness, the terror of love, the volcanic eruptions of beauty, dangerous elements forged in the voluptuous workshop of night.

The Gift of Bread

AFTER HIKING ELEVEN MILES along mountain ridge paths, I arrive weary and hungry in the village of Colares. Immediately I head to the local bakery for a warm loaf of *terra do pao,* the Portuguese bread of the earth. The shop is suffused with the sweet aroma of fresh baking. The owner has flecks of flour on her hands as she wraps the bread in newspaper. Her face is crinkled with weariness, but leavened with pride. She offers the small package to me with a knowing smile. Heat rises in waves to warm my chilled hands.

With this gift in hand, I hurry down past the medieval stone pillory where villagers were publicly scorned during the Inquisition, and beyond the outdoor café where the locals vehemently argue rural politics, to the cobbled road that will take me home. Along the way I break off pieces of bread to fortify myself. I taste wheat, millstone, rain, sun, and the paths left by kneading fingers. I savor a passion that binds together farmer, miller, baker, and traveler.

Beyond the village is a narrow flagstoned path that meanders through fields of sunflowers. I pick up the pace, walking briskly, morseling out the bread, step by step. Each waft of aroma, each mouthful, takes me back to a delectable moment on the back roads of the world. I remember a chunk of dark pumpernickel bread in Russia, a bannock of soda bread in Ireland, holy bread in Israel, pandesal in the Philippines, thin slices of aromatic rye in Bavaria, ruginé duona in Lithuania, cornpone in New Orleans, cinnamon rolls in Sault Ste. Marie, round loaves of oak-fired sourdough on the Rue du Cherche-Midi in Paris, focaccia in San Francisco—and the loaf of carbonized bread in front of the baker's oven in the ruins of Pompeii.

I rest under the shade of a lemon tree. The air is sweet and good. I twist the crust in my fingers, marveling at the mystery of dough, the smell of wood smoke, and the sound of the oven's song of bread. I roll one last morsel around my tongue before heading home down the last stretch of cobbled road.

In this brief curve of time I realize if I don't savor the joyous rasp of the moment, I'll never know what the poet meant when he said, "I like reality: It tastes like bread."

Penedo, Portugal
February 1991

IV

*"Some revile me, others applaud.
I am simply following my incomprehensible road."*
—MIRABAI (THIRTEENTH CENTURY)

*"Few such moments of exhilaration can come as that
which stands at the threshold of wild travel."*
—GERTRUDE BELL

*"Strange travel suggestions are
dancing lessons from God."*
—KURT VONNEGUT JR.

The Oldest Road in the World

ON THIS MOONFLED NIGHT what I've learned while looking up something else is that the oldest road in the world is in danger of being lost. I'm hunkered down over a glass of Chianti at Mario's Bohemian Cigar Store, my local North Beach café, riffling through the pages of an old magazine when my eyes bulge under the weight of the following words:

"A project is underway to preserve a 90-foot-long trail of human footprints in northern Tanzania that, scientists say, provide the only proof that man walked upright as many as 3.5 million years ago."

I read on to learn that in 1977, on the barren plain of Laetoli, two archaeologists on a team led by paleoanthropologist Mary Leakey were "larking about"—hurling dry elephant dung at each other—during a playful camp fight. One of the scientists tumbled to the ground. By sheer chance he noticed some peculiar indentations in the ground around him. Thousands of years of erosion had exposed the imprints of plants, animals, even raindrops that had hardened to stone through the millennia. Further excavation revealed that the animal prints had been made when they tramped over fresh ash from the nearby Sadiman volcano while the ground was still wet with rain, and over the millennia the ash set like concrete.

Two years later, Leakey herself discovered an even more tantalizing print—a single heel print she was convinced belonged to a hominid. Eventually she uncovered a veritable trail seventy-seven feet across the Laetoli plain. Two or even three individuals had walked this way millions of years ago. Leakey surmised that the two larger ones were ambling side by side shortly after the violent blast, unwittingly leaving a few prints behind them in the wet ash. The prints of the third, evidently a child, were laid, in places, over the larger tracks.

Ingeniously, Leakey noticed that one of the prints left by the female turned outward, a single stutter step the scientist interpreted as a brief pause when the female looked over her shoulder. But why turn when running for your life? To listen to the rumble of the volcano while the ash fell all around her? To check on her child as lightning sundered the sky? To better hear the growl of a predator?

What moves me most about this serendipitous discovery is Leakey's own description of what she saw through the scrim of time, what she read through her own fingerprints when she touched those antediluvian footprints: "This motion, so intensely human, transcends time…a remote ancestor—just as you or I—experienced a moment of doubt."

In the hopes of preserving this eerily human moment—and the compelling evidence of transition from "four-limbed arboreal life" to "two-legged travel"—Leakey's team covered the fossil trail with polythene and river sand. But over time termites have chewed through the plastic. Acacia seeds hidden in the sand have grown into trees. Their roots are destroying the trail. Twenty years later, twenty-nine of the original sixty-nine footprints have eroded. The rest remain buried under river sand. Plans for the surviving roadbed range from surgically excising the tree roots and injecting acrylic into the prints, to covering it over with concrete, or even transferring the entire road to a museum in the shadow of the Sadiman volcano.

I finish the article and am overcome, as if I've swerved back and forth several million years in a matter of minutes. Why am I feeling such a cascade of emotion? Why all the concern over a trail left by unknown ancestors while Africa reels under relentless cycles of famine, slave trading, and warfare? Is it the "genetic memory" that Richard Leakey has suggested is the source of our fascination with prehistory? The intellectual pleasure in the idea that the "unambiguous evidence for upright walking" means that *locomotion* may be the adaptation that set our ancestors apart? Or is it due to some vague sense of nostalgia for the original home of the whole human race?

I gaze through Mario's fabled red and yellow neon-lit window and across the Union Street to the soul-soothing vision of tree-lined Washington Square Park. In one corner looms a statue memorializing the firemen who have saved San Francisco time and time again. In another corner looms a monument to Juana Briones, the poor shepherd woman who fed the hungry after the 1906 earthquake. In a small grove lies a time capsule, not to be opened until 2079. Relaxed by the ruminations, my mind moves slantwise to an interview in which Laurens van der Post asked Carl Jung why we should be concerned about the fate of ancient cultures.

"Everyone has a two-million-year-old man inside," Jung replied. "If he loses contact with that he loses himself."

Before I can figure out what he meant, I'm split in half by strange dislocations of time. I'm back on the beach at Camp Dearborn, a boy of four or five. My hand is in my father's. He is pulling me forward, yanking me, insisting I keep up with him. I try not to fall behind, and then figure how to keep up. All I need to do is walk in the footprints he leaves behind in the hot sand as he strides toward the cool lake water.

My father is pulling me forward—or is it the torque of time?

Forty years later, I still feel the force of being flung by time. Now I am the father walking with my boy Jack, holding his hand, leading him not down to a lake, but to the ocean. I'm pulling him forward as my father pulled me. I'm looking over my shoulder and seeing him try to walk in my footsteps. He has to leap from one footprint to the next, and somehow he does, though the sand nearly swallows his tiny feet, and his prints disappear into mine.

Isn't that the way it's always been between fathers and sons?

At the water's edge my boy looks up to see if I'm watching him. How can I not? I can't take my eyes off him. His own eyes leap with joy watching me watching him.

It means everything to be able to remember whose footsteps we walk in, and who walks in ours.

TALONED TRACKS

A STRANGE LIGHT LURCHES around this old Portuguese farmhouse outside Sintra, Byron's favorite town in Europe, where I'm living for a few months. Shadows from my evening fire shuffle along the thick stone walls. Surf thrashes against the cliffs a mile away. A wildcat wind blows open the tall, shuttered windows, and rattles iron bolts on the doors.

The candle in the lantern, the only light in a house without electricity, sputters out. Cursing the shades of night, I leap up from bed and step gingerly over the cold flagstone floor to the balcony, where I feel the wings of the hawk-shaped night. Gnarled clouds pass in front of the full moon, turning the night sky as livid as El Greco's "View of Toledo."

Restless, I slip into my leather jacket, and dash out into the blustery night for an evening walk to the bodega. At the fork in the road, I change my mind and scramble down the high-walled paths of the village to the path overlooking the Atlantic. A hundred feet below, the sea makes odd snicking sounds along the beach.

Lit only by the zodiacal light, I edge my way down the slippery boulder steps, steadying myself with a hand on the towering limestone wall. Halfway down the stone staircase, the moon appears, illuminating the cliff like a spotlight.

Suddenly, I am not alone. I am walking with dinosaurs.

The rainpocked rock is imprinted with fossilized dinosaur tracks that soar straight up into the night sky. I stare open-mouthed at the petrified footprints of hundred-ton beasts held fast in limestone for the last sixty-five million or so years. The night seethes with ancient voices. I'm unsure for a dizzying moment if I'm still in bed—or lost in a primordial dream about tracking dinosaurs, like one of Ray Bradbury's time travelers.

I reach out to touch the sea-sprayed wall. I want to make sure it's real and I'm not back in bed dreaming. The hair rises on my arms as my hand disappears inside an oval footprint. The taloned footprint is so long and deep I have to strain to trace it with my fingertips. Every inch is an eon. Inside it is the rumble of an ancient story before stories came to be.

The lurid light turns the world upside down. Time is moving in both directions at once. Scudding clouds part for a brief moment and moonlight flashes on and off like a mad strobe light that casts moonshadows onto the wall, revealing now the entire wall covered with a fifty-yard-long fossilized migration of shrithing, slope-shouldered beasts climbing high into the sky.

I swear I can hear a distant thunder. Is it the pounding sea or the pummeling sound of a blood memory surging to the surface of my life?

I wedge myself between the giant rocks, and feel a wild urge to clamber up the face of the wall, in the footsteps of lumbering dinosaurs. The wind off the Atlantic blows like the bellows of an angry sea god. The surf rips along the beach, and far out at sea strange lenticular clouds pass in front of the moon.

For this layered moment, as stratified as the wall I am leaning against, nothing is happening, but everything is changing.

Something ancient and holy is watching over me.

Penedo, Portugal
March 1991

THE RED ROAD

THE NIGHT BEFORE THE filming began, I dreamt of gray-eyed Quanah Parker telling stories around the fire in wind-whipped canyons, a buffalo rumble of images about how troubles had come to the Comanches after they had controlled the Great Plains for five centuries.

While the camera operators load the first roll of film for our documentary, I take a walk in the woods around the Star house, where the legendary chief lived a hundred years ago with his seven wives and twenty-one children. Warrior and medicine man, then diplomat, railroad owner, and movie actor, Quanah bridged two worlds. But as the screenwriter on the project I'm torn about *which* Quanah to portray. It's a combustible question among his descendants, so I'm clawed by anxiety about the upcoming interview with his grandson, Baldwin.

The leather faced old Indian leans against the steps, eyes pitched far into the distant past. He knows about the factionalism in the tribe, the fight for power and influence among the descendants, and wants no part of it. The coyote in him listens for sounds from another time and place, hears everything that moves on the wind. Watching him prepare for the first interview, I recall the words of another Comanche chief, Chased-by-Bears, who once told a roving reporter that before they spoke of holy things his people made offerings. They lit the sacred pipe, raised it to the sky and lowered it to the earth before smoking holy tobacco together.

Only then would they be ready to talk.

My gaze wanders over to the tepees erected for the powwow held in Quanah's honor. The noon light shimmers on the canvas. I'm haunted by Crazy Horse's vexing question to a stunned photographer a hundred years before: *"Why should you wish to shorten my life by taking my shadow?"*

Cagey old Baldwin pulls his Stetson down over his eyes, and stares at the ground for a few moments, measuring his words like a surveyor before he speaks. "Whenever our family honors Grandfather," he says, looking over his shoulder and round the old wooden porch, "I come to this house and pray. I know he listens to my crying heart."

With Crazy Horse's troubling words in mind I carefully ask Baldwin what he thinks Quanah would've wanted to get down on film about his life, his people.

"Grandfather," Baldwin tells me softly, "used to say that it's not *what and where,* but *how and when* that's important. I think that's why he agreed to play that part in *The Great Bank Robbery* way back there in '05. He wanted to show how powerful us Indians could look in the movies." Baldwin holds his right hand up like a wary hunter, breathes deep. "Now you fellahs may know a lot more than me about books and that there intellectual stuff. But I just want to tell you one thing 'bout Grandfather." Tipping the brim of his hat, he goes on. "More than anything else, more than him being chief, the leader of the Comanche Moon Raids, the first Indian millionaire, a railroad owner, or a film star, Quanah was an honest man. He loved his family and he trusted his heart."

Baldwin glances over at his son, Vincent, his "Hollywood Indian," as he calls him, who has flown in from his job at a major studio in L.A. to be sure that the filming honors the spirit of his family. Vincent checks his own notes and nods approvingly, sweat beading his silk shirt.

"If you smart fellers are going to go outta here with anything," Baldwin says, "go with that, will you?"

I see before me an elder of the old ways, a *sacred dreamer,* as they've been called out here on the Staked Plains for centuries. A man who sees farther than others. One who has cultivated his memory like a farmer his field. One who knows that understanding comes from knowing where to put your eyes, where to place your heart, when to be the lamenter, when to be the praise-singer, when to be the faithkeeper. Something holy is moving down through the seven generations of his face, glowing like the fires in the translucent tepees of his ancestors.

"Baldwin," I say, playing a hunch, "do you remember what Iron Jacket said to Quanah when he was a boy?"

Looking bemused, Baldwin glances up.

"Tell me if I wrong, sir, but I think he said, 'Someday...when you begin to know who you are, you will seek a vision.'"

Baldwin gives me an avuncular pat on the knee and winks.

Smiling, I gesture to Ivan, our cinematographer, to roll 'em.

One flip of a switch and something simple and strange, something wonderful happens. The camera whirs. The long tongue of the movies, hundred then thousands of feet of film move over metal sprockets and then across small glass windows, allowing enough light into the darkness to capture the elusive and the sacred. It is a movement I've come to believe in, one that lengthens our lives by stretching, not stealing, our shadows, as the old stories are seized from the past and move across the flickering present and into the future.

"My grandfather, Quanah," Baldwin begins, "once told his best friend something about his vision quests that goes right to the mystery. 'When your regular eyes fail you as you go down into the valley, use the eyes of your heart. Those eyes will never fail a good man.'"

I live for these flickers of truth.

La Reno, Oklahoma
June 1988

73

The Peyote Road

THE SKY IS ASWARM with white bee stars. Night-shy by firelight, macaws sleep in round wire cages. Wild horses stomp and neigh at the river's edge. Flamingos stand on reed-thin legs, as if posing for wandering sculptors. Old Huichol women roll blue flour in stone troughs until their hands turn livid. Mud-black coffee burbles in iron vats. Curls of red peppers dangle from palm fronds. Peyote pilgrims from twenty distant tribes, including Mohawks, Navajo, Lakota Sioux, Winnebago, Pawnee, Cherokee, and Tarahumara, gather round all-night fires to pierce heaven with their full-hearted cries to a common grandfather, the sacred cactus.

This is where the long red road has led you.

You are at the windy juncture between the sacred and profane worlds, smudged by sky-climbing smoke and scoured by the bitter drink of green peyote tea until the god of the waiting vision finds you either wanting or worthy. Which is it going to be, pilgrim?

Long after midnight, weary but peaceful, you lie down on the fire-warmed earth, inside the ceremonial arbor of palm-thatch. You watch the constellations cartwheel overhead. You hear the heartbeat of old drums, eagle whistles, gourd rattles echo through the night, like rainstorms pouncing on the parched fields of your heart. Nine mighty drums sound while the white-smocked dancers who ran two hundred miles in tire-tread sandals to participate in this ancient rite trace the pilgrim footsteps of the gods.

The simple tin bowl of peyote tea you drink from through the long cool night startles you with its cavern roar every time you sip from it. A vision of a shimmering blue shaman hovers above you. Who is she? Where did he come from? Her eyes glow like rubies. She is the jaguar woman of sweet blue laughter who is there to drop you down the nine levels of your soul you didn't know had been carved into you. Only now might you speak with the lords of the underworld. The jaguar woman is suspended by quivering lines of light. She throws lightning bolts from his ample belly. Her hands trace phosphorescent birds in the black air. Without speaking, she summons you back to the fire blazing in the center of the arbor.

Around the fire, warriors caper in a deer dance. Are you seeing this—or aren't you? If so, *which* you? Something that has been purring in your veins since before you were born, the time after the first hunt, but before the rush of the god into your prayer-swollen soul. The thundering drums and sacred medicine are pushing your heart to the outer edge of every road you've ever wandered, and yet you feel as if you've never traveled before you set out on the peyote road.

Beside the fire, the shaman sits listening to the voice within the flames. She begins to chant and you follow her pulsing songs into the darkness, mouthing words you didn't know you knew as she leads you like her own brother down the peyote road.

At the crossroad, Grandfather Peyote asks, *Will you follow further, to Wirikota, the sacred land of the night journey? Can you stand the vision? Can you carry it home and not call it yours?*

Near dawn, the breath of an unknown god rouses you to a barely recognizable world. The forest is a shimmering emerald. The blood red roosters raise the sun with soul-waking cries. The indefatigable Huichol and Tarahumara drummers push the stone of night high into dawn's waiting hand while you stretch for the longest quest, the one lingering beside your deepest desire. And with that dark, side-slithering move comes the sublime moment when you see everything you've ever turned back from, the shimmering invisible world pulsing behind the visible one.

Who knew?

The holy medicine is teaching you about the black-and-blue

depths of your many-chambered heart. Either that or the secret of the beginning of the world is about to be revealed, if only you can stay awake, and listen to what the tongue of God is saying in the dancing flames before you.

And then the Winnebago Road Man with eyes ablaze whispers to you, "Everything you need to know is in that fire."

If only, if only.

Tresbol, Old Mexico
March 1992

La Ruta Maya

FIVE HUNDRED YEARS AFTER the once great city of Chichén Itzá was plundered, on an afternoon white with bright sunlight, I wander down an ancient *sacbe,* a road of jagged and glistening stones that leads through a sparse forest.

That the road has endured at all is an unexpected solace for me. I walk on, attempting the oldest traveler's trick in the world: trying to visualize the ancient world we tread on. I hear nothing but the crunch of my own footsteps, see nothing but my thinning shadow. The emptiness gnaws at me, as it sometimes does when I'm riven with those inevitable travel twinges about worthiness, such as *Who are you to deserve such beauty, such encounters?*

I reach a crossroad of radiating paths where I'm surrounded by yelping Mayan children wanting to touch my cameras, and mournful elders selling carvings of long-dead kings and velvet paintings of leaping jaguars.

Which way to go? One road leads to a serried row of hawkers, another into the deep velveteen green of the forest, the third to the *cenote,* the sacrificial well, the site of current excavations. The one path to the right leads to the crevice-shaped *bom,* the ritual Mayan ball court, believed to be the very entrance to the Underworld. Ahead of me is another *sacbe,* the old white road leading to the aquamarine sea a hundred miles away.

How does the old joke go? When you come to a fork in the road—*take it!*

I travel to be surprised, and as a kid from the mean streets of Detroit, a city proud of pouring the first concrete road in history, I am thrilled to discover this road, which is, oh, about a thousand years older, and that in turn is humbling. I had no idea the Mayans laid out roads as rigorously as the Romans or the Greeks, or that they played a ballgame curiously similar to our basketball crossed with our volleyball. Seeing it for myself makes me feel like just one more bumptious stranger laden with ignorance about native ways, tourist as conquistador stumbling through the jungle in sweltering suits of armor.

I sit down by the side of the road, swig from my water bottle, and simply gaze down the road that trembles with sunlight and bends with odd shadows. When I stand up again I stagger and lose my balance, wondering if sunstroke has overtaken me. I'm floating into a fugue state, neither alert nor unconscious, feeling oddly enough like the man in de Chardin's story who was walking and talking with a companion in the desert *"... when the Thing swooped down on him."*

If nothing else, I'm stepping through the smoking mirror of history. The old chronicles tell us that the elders of the Yucatán believed their land was settled by a strange race from the East, "whom God delivered by opening for them twelve roads through the sea." Ancient Mayan travelers walked these white-stoned roads that connected their far-flung temple complexes for 1000 years, carrying copal incense and burning plates. Wherever the pilgrims stayed they would erect an altar of three small stones, burn incense, and pray that their god Ekchuah deliver them safely home.

In the time of the conquistadors, the furrowed *milpas* were trampled, the villages of the ancestors burned, and "many edifices of great beauty" demolished. The nefarious Bishop Landa helped ignite the 400-year-old war of extermination by burning their books, fields, and bodies. He was much conflicted. Contemptuous about the Mayans' "deluded beliefs," his reports are also studded with praise for their "generous spirit" and their "hospitality and amity." His descriptions of their "savage" sacrifice rituals are hauntingly ironic considering the vengeance exacted in the torture chambers of the Inquisition back in Spain. But the observation that startles me most is about their exquisitely painted history books made from simple bark pulp and lime. Maddeningly, the bishop wrote these words before lighting the bonfire of the codices, "It may be that this country holds a secret that up to the present has not been revealed, or which the natives of today cannot tell."

The shrill whistle of a roving guard pierces the quiet day.

"*Vamanos, vamanos,*" he shouts from the open plaza. Let's go, let's go. "*Cerrida, cerrida!*" Closing time!

I suppress a laugh, wanting to ask him how you can enforce a closing time in a place beyond time? What would that prove? Instead, I pretend I don't hear him and keep walking down the ancient way. Landa's words haunt me as I stroll past the last rickety shacks of trinkets and postcards. What secret was he referring to? The arcane discoveries of the astronomers in their nautilus-shaped observatory where they learned how "the gods weave the mat of time"?

If so, why demolish their observatories, and burn their intricate maps of the heavens? Why hurl their priests into bottomless wells?

Dusk deepens. Squawking parrots streak across the sky. The air is redolent of burning leaves from nearby villages. I listen deeper, want to know more. In the forced reverie of the desperate traveler, I try to imagine the cries of victims hurled into the nearby *cenote,* the conch shells trumpeting warnings of invading armies, and the exuberant cries from astronomers in their stone domes.

But I hear nothing but the words of a wise old friar in Mexico City who once consoled me by saying, "As it was in the past, so it is now."

A thunderclap rips apart my reverie. The skies open like a sluice gate, releasing torrential rain from the heaven, cooling the air, raising steam off the jungle floor. I walk on through the afternoon sauna, wiping the sweat off my brow every few minutes. Beyond a grove of strangler fig trees I catch a tiny comma of an old peasant woman hunched over with a load of rolled-up shawls. She sees something I can't make out through the sheets of rain. She stops by the side of the road and pries an old stone out of the ground. She walks a few yards deeper into the woods, leans over, and places her stone atop a cairn of pilgrim's stones. Bending painfully, she murmurs a prayer that is bounded by her sense of reverence and gratitude. She caresses the stones as she braces the pile around its base, occasionally lifting her eyes to the heavens. The ritual seems to have shaped her worn-out body like the words that have shaped her soul.

Have the mute stones broken their code of silence?

If the moment is to be believed, the rituals here were never extinguished. Pilgrims never stopped traveling along the ancient paths, adding their stones to the sum of things. Silent as shadows, they slipped into sacred sites known only to them and the weavers of time, carrying the "secret" that the dreaded bishop knew of but dared not speak about. The old woman staggers to her feet, then slowly slips down the ancient road as dusk falls like a shroud and the white hands of the stars reach down to guide her home.

Night here rises from the ground, rather than falls from the skies. I meet it halfway, alone on the ancient road, then make my way to the tall cairn and add my stone to the pile. It is a humbling gesture that lifts my heart as the pile rises impercep-tibly toward the ancient heart of heaven.

The past is never dead if we live outside of time, *live* being the vital word here, there, and everywhere.

Chichén Itzá, Yucatán, Mexico
March 1992

The Road to Konya

"Time is a powerful lion."
—MEVLANA RUMI

ON A ROAD CUTTING through the same wheat fields Genghis Khan thundered across nine hundred years ago, I drive a rattletrap rental car two hundred kilometers south of Ankara. I'm risking life and limb to visit the tomb of the poet Rumi in the ancient city of Konya. Admittedly, this is a strange vehicle for a holy pilgrimage, but there you are. After a few hours of bone-rattling driving I stop at a roadside *lokanta,* a Turkish restaurant, and more, a kind of modern *caravanserai* for travelers. Centuries ago merchants from China or Damascus would have stopped here to trade silks for spices, ebony for gems, camels for rugs.

The Sufis say there are two kinds of hunger, one for the stomach, the other for the soul. Right now all I want to order is a *meza* of salad, eggplant, yoghurt, bread, rice pudding, savoring each mouthful. The soul can wait, right, and I vow to attend to my spiritual hunger when I arrive in Konya. On the wind is the smell of persimmons mixed with gasoline fumes. I am as happy as I've been ages. On the sputtering radio above the freezer comes the haunting voice of a Turkish folksinger. When I ask my waiter who is singing, he says in halting English, "Livaneli—he is, how you say, Turkish Woody Guthrie."

Lurking over my coffee, I liberate my leather journal from its temporary sentence in my pilgrim's satchel and begin to jot down a few observations from the long drive, such as U.S. Air Force fighter jets flying overhead, and the camels I saw.

After a few pages I realize that my fulgurating fingers have caught the attention of the five bored waiters who have nothing else to do but wait on me and slap dominoes down on the old wooden tables near the entrance. Feeling their eyes on me, moving toward me between their domino moves, I look back and nod, smile. Within seconds, I'm surrounded.

"*Roman?*" one of the waiters asks, not of the content of my writing, but of the *script*. They lean over me, fascinated by the swirling, crisscrossing motions of my hand. Wings of black ink fly across the blank page like crows through a bright white sky. Their sighs of admiration surprise me. The headwaiter arrives, graceful in his burliness. He murmurs to the others about the mechanics of my writing style, his elbow going this way and that. I imagine him describing my pen as something like a "beautiful writing machine." He asks to hold it, which I'm oddly reluctant to do since it's a beautiful chromium Schaefer model given to me years ago by a friend while on holiday in Yorkshire. I've loved it so much I've carried it with me to dozens of countries around the world and used it ritualistically, to write my stories and my *par avion* letters. Still, the request is so elegant I offer him the chance to hold the pen.

While he is twirling it around in his hand I wonder if I should try to tell him that my buddy gave it to me while intoning that originally it was advertised as featuring an "Exclusive Pneumatic Down-stroke Filler." Or better yet, that the first "reservoir pen," one that carried its ink within, was invented around 973 in the Arab Maghreb region of Morocco, by Caliph Ma' d al-Mu'izz, who demanded a writing instrument that would not stain his hands?

His admiration knows no bounds, so much so that it's not out of the question that he would ask for it as a gift. Quickly but gracefully, I ask for the pen back. He smiles with embarrassment, then reluctantly surrenders it. A busboy sidles up beside me with a fistful of locally produced pens. The head waiter suggests a trade, but I demur. Any traveler in remote Turkey knows that the homegrown variety is filled with disappearing ink and shrivels up after a postcard, or a customs card.

While we're bartering, the owner of the *lokanta* drives up in an old rustbucket Mercedes, and I hear his name muttered by the head waiter like a spell, *Bedri*. He walks in with hands on hips, surveying all he sees, as I imagine a *shaikh* might enter his caravanserai centuries before. He instantly reminds me of a Bedouin *shaikh* I once saw stop a bus on which I was traveling in the Sinai Desert. I remember him striding down the aisle with his right hand resting on the pearled handle of a sword thrust inside his *jellaba*. Everyone on board stood, bowed low, and kissed him out of respect.

Bedri commanded a similar respect as he strode toward me. In elegant French he tells me he lives in the nearby town of Koulour. He has tufty eyebrows and a mustache shaped like buffalo horns. Boldly, he asks where I'm from and where I'm traveling, and why I am writing, and what I have been eating and drinking in his *lokanta*. A half-dozen questions, a friendly fusillade designed to make me feel welcome, a measure of respect in Turkey I have come to love.

"I live in California, and I'm headed to Konya," I tell him in fractured French that would have scandalized my grandparents. But Bedri's eyes widen with sudden admiration.

"I have friends who live in Konya," he tells me. "The Konya of Rumi," he adds with a kind of tremolo in his voice when he pronounces the name of the still-revered poet of love. The mere mention of the beloved Mevlana inspires him to murmur a few words of what sounds to my ears like rhyming couplets. Sifting sunbeams fall on his hands. They spin like inspired dervishes as he speaks in ecstatic words about the great poet.

In the wind these are the kind of "praising sounds" that need to fill the world, as Rumi described so long ago. I smile happily as I pack my things for the remainder of the long trip south.

Consternated, Bedri asks, "Must you go *now?* What is your hurry? You must stay here so we can discuss Rumi and the dervishes. I can see you are a man of letters. You *must* stay—as my guest. It is rare for a lover of Rumi to pass by my *lokanta*. You must tell me what you know."

His earnestness startles me. It is the best offer a traveler can hope to hear. But I feel pressed for time; driving on these roads after dark is considered suicidal. I shake my head no, try to be gracious, but what I say is "I don't have time." Awkwardly, I point to my watch in the international gesture indicating *no time!*

Clearly, he's disappointed. He orders another cup of gutbucket Turkish coffee for me, plus a plate of Turkish delight. He tells me he has cousins who could introduce me to local dervishes. "To have come so far and not have time to discuss Rumi—"

It is utterly incomprehensible that someone so clearly blessed cannot find the time to talk about the things that matter most.

"The Sufi is the friend of the present moment," he murmurs like a prayer, not to me so much as to himself, and then directly to me, he says defiantly, "To say *tomorrow* is not our way."

I recognize the saying as one of Rumi's, ironically, one of my own favorites, and am rendered speechless.

"You must stay for supper," he pleads, now in English. "Do you know what else Rumi said? 'Those who know the secret of the whirling, live in God.'"

Reluctantly, I slide away. When I reach my car I pause for a moment and gaze at the great sky that seems to stretch to infinity.

I start the engine as Bedri leans through the half-cranked window. His fingers roll his maroon *misbaha*, or prayer beads, as he confides to me as if to a lost soul, "Do you not know you cannot *have* time? Time belongs to no one."

"Thanks for the offer, but I really have to go," I mutter.

But do I? Am I scurrying away out of a genuine intention to still myself for a real encounter with the spirit of the great poet in Konya, or am I just being a jerk, anti-social, an ingrate for the offered hospitality?

"I have friends waiting for me tonight in Konya," I continue. Which, of course, is not the whole truth. The whole truth is that I must go because I do not want to waste any more time. I only have so much time, three more days, and I want to spend them in Konya. In my mind's eye I can see peasants and soldiers and politicians and schoolchildren, all standing together in line to pay their respects at Rumi's tomb.

I nod back and shrug my shoulders, and jot down a few words in a tiny spiral notebook. In the light of our conversation the letters seem to flame out of my pen like the tongues of still unnamed gods.

He takes my hand in his, and says, "Rumi never wrote. He only listened to God. Then when he spoke everything he said was poetry. Others wrote it down."

As he speaks, the weight of my watch presses in on my wrist.

"Who *are* you, really?" I ask, laughing nervously, shaking his hand.

As I drive away, I think back to my time in a poetry-starved Detroit factory where I was working my way through college. Late one night, I read on the factory wall, "Make it real, or don't bother. Ain't nothin' like the real thing, brother."

Ahead of me is two hundred more miles of desert road. A ruby red light lingers on the horizon, beckoning me down the road. I follow, feeling free. I want to drive forever, until I run out of gas, until the tires go bald, until I run out of road, until I make up for all the lost time that torments me.

Night Walk

THE NIGHT CONTAINS MULTITUDES. The twisting road home from the local *bodega* winds along a serpent-back lane. The clouds forming over the raging Atlantic muscle through a turmoil of stars. Torn moonlight casts strange shadows over the cobblestones. Chilblain-cold winter rain runs down my leather jacket and off my hiking shoes. Gulls screech from their rooftop perches. Dark cypresses whisper ancient theological secrets about Inquisition trials held here centuries ago. The threnody of those nights still echoes in the dark stone walls of the church.

At the village crossroads in Penedo, an old stone barn is outlined in dark charcoal by the hand of night. I pause, slowly opening and closing my eyes to imprint the image in my mind for a sketch the next morning. Moving on, the cobbled road slopes gently, past the blue-and-white tiled wall overflowing with storm-water runoff from the distant vineyards. Alert for wandering dogs, who are notorious for attacking strangers along the village road, I clack at the stones with my gnarled walking stick, before descending along the dark stretch of country lane.

In this *S*-turn of thin road I see the shadow of eighteenth-century village life. I hear rain purling down the sand-colored cobblestone gutter that borders the whitestoned road, the night-storm gruffly rebuffed by the windbreak of tall cane in the dark mauve fields below. Like a laughing percussion player, the sea breeze plays with the chimes hanging in the windows of the red-tiled, whitewashed houses built into the side of the mountain, where the village lane follows in a graceful hairpin turn.

Reaching the lone-wolf street light, I lean for a moment against a brightly mossed stone wall. In a nearby garden, sunflowers gleam in the ivory light of the moon. A flicker of lilac gleams over an old well embossed with the date *1747*. Nearby, the scarlet petals of bougainvillea glow near the old stone bridge.

Mournful *fado* music from the *bodega* phantoms the night.

Further on down the road, I recall the words of Portugal's everyman poet, Fernando Pessoa, a nightstalking walker around Lisbon: *Everything is something besides,* words that make me pause near the old stone bridge, night thrumming in my heart like a crazed arrow.

I am all eyes tonight; tomorrow night I'll be all ears.

On the other side of the dark river is my new life.

THE LAST JOURNEY

"AT THE END HE was terribly weak," Melanie told me on the phone a few days after Tony died. "Unrecognizable. He'd lost twenty-five pounds, and was yellow with jaundice."

Her voice was remarkably calm, considering she was his closest friend at the end. "We wished him a good journey," she continued. "Elaine read from Hildegard of Bingen, and I read from the book of Yeats's poetry you gave him in Ireland. We kept touching him on the head and chest, to reassure him. I wished him well, and told him that we were sending him off on his journey with love. Then I said, 'Rest, be still. Know thou art God.' I'm not sure where that came from; maybe I read it somewhere. And then he simply stopped breathing."

After tenderly detailing our old friend's final hours, it seemed that she couldn't breathe either. A few grief-breath moments later she said softly, as if not to disturb those souls listening in on us, "He was good to people, you know. So we sat with him awhile longer, at least another hour, until we knew he had left us. An immense amount of energy was being released, so we just stayed with him. It was really blissful, a miraculous event. Almost...*severely*...beautiful, I suppose. Does that sound strange?"

"No, not at all," I told her, lost for words myself. But as she recounted Tony's last days, I remembered Sean Browne, the charming Irish bus driver who became our friend on the tour we had launched together in Ireland back in 1984. Late one night in a Killarney pub he raised his glass of Guinness high and toasted us, first in Gaelic, then in English: *"May you lads have one son for each corner of the coffin and one daughter to cry for you."* The quirky toast made me think of the way Tony and I had clinked glasses that rainy night in the Irish countryside, and allowed me to momentarily forget how he had been abandoned by nearly all his friends and family as he lay dying.

I stared out the bay window of my apartment into the gloomy winter day and thought of the last time I saw him, alone and wasted away in his dimly lit flat of 5000 books. "Death doesn't scare me, Philip," he told me. "People do. All around me young men like me are dying alone in cold apartments."

Suddenly he completely changed subjects, asking me, weakly, "Did you know I gave Joseph Campbell his first astrology reading?"

This was news to me. I shook my head, wondering if it were true, and if so, why Joe had never told me during all the years I worked on the documentary film about his life and work.

Tony seemed to glow with pride, then recalled, "Joe told me afterwards it completely changed his views on the subject, that if he could find the time he was going to investigate the connection between mythology and astrology."

I asked him about the new medicine he was taking, and whether he had any hope. He had always had a way of speaking as if behind panes of glass. The effect was doubled now, as he demurred, and started talking about his rare astrology books and the fate of his library. I joked that the labyrinthine-minded Jorge Borges had imagined death as an ascent to a better library. For the only time during our visit, he smiled.

"Hmm—a better library?" he murmured, as if he was contemplating taking out a library card.

"You know," Melanie continued on the phone, "over his last three days we all argued about his Last Will and Testament. He asked if we thought he was acting like a child, and when we answered him with silence, he kind of sighed with relief and said he should do something.

"Then I said that I would really like him to die. I mean, I told him to just accept it, go with it. That it was his time. He said he'd been hallucinating, was confused, that he didn't *want* to die, that he didn't want to *leave* until he was good and ready.

Do you know what he was mostly worried about? His papers, his library. Not just that he could donate all the books, but that they would stay *together,* as a collection. When we sorted that out, and told him that Holy Names College had accepted *all* the books, he said he thought he was ready."

There was a long pause on the telephone line. Morosely, I stared out the bay window of my apartment and watched the number 32 bus drive by my apartment building, and kids swinging on the playground across the street.

"Know what he said just before he died? He said, 'If I don't keep my books together, nobody will ever remember me. I can't go home if nobody remembers me.'"

The words hung before me like frost flowers on December's windowpanes, chillingly beautiful.

"Funny, isn't it," I finally said, "what helps people get ready for their last journey?"

THE ROAD DOGS OF DUBLIN

THE BRASS PUB BELL of The Stag's Head rings to signal closing time. Our raffish pub crawl guide, Jaz Lynch, is inspired to cadge a six-pack of Guinness from the owner for our long walk back along the River Liffey to Mrs. McGeary's bed-and-breakfast. He's determined to continue our celebration of my brother Paul's twenty-eighth birthday.

Jaz leads Paul and our ex-Marine buddy, Jimmy, through the tough backstreets of the city to the wrought iron Ha'penny Bridge. When he's halfway across, Jaz opens a single bottle of stout for us to share, which is practically a sacrilege in Ireland, but we do it for the sake of solidarity, downing the bottle quick as you can say "JimmytheJoyce." So he begins to dole out a bottle for each of us. Seconds later we're startled by the raucous shouts of a gang of Irish lads. Swaying unsteadily back and forth, they're angrily singing the anthem of the local hurling team we'd watched get beaten by the Galway side earlier in the day at Croke Park. Worse, they're lusting after the five remaining beers tucked under Jaz's arm.

One of the young revelers breaks away from the pack and lunges at Jaz, trying to snatch the beers. Jimmy leaps between them, as if blocking for him, like the grizzled ex-defensive half-back he used to be. Immediately, he's surrounded. Somehow Jaz slips away. Two of them hold broken bottles over Jimmy's head. Several others start singing a threatening ditty, "Here we go, here we go," accompanied by tossing motions, as if they're going to hurl him into the dark river below. Jimmy drops into fighting position. He nods at Paul who takes a cool swig from his Guinness bottle, and moves in to protect our flank.

"Now be a good Yank and give us a beer, won't you?" cries a reedy little voice from the back of the pack. The group tightens around us like an angry fist.

Menacingly, Jimmy says, "Hey, don't mock my manhood, man. The last guys who did that are still getting their teeth fixed." His voice pours over them like bourbon over broken glass. The lads in front of him shuffle uncomfortably.

Thinking fast, I slip in next to him and mutter, "All right, road dog, everything's Kerouac-cool," and wedge my way inside the crowd, murmuring to the lads, "Don't worry. It's cool, it's cool." Trying to keep *them* from getting hurt is the last thing they expected to hear.

Slow as a good pour of Guinness, I draw out the warning words, "You guys heard of *Rambo?* Well, this is *Jimbo.* He's armed and dangerous—look at those arms!—look at those dangerous eyes! I wouldn't piss him off if I were you. Like the song says, 'You don't mess around with Jim....'"

I'm not even sure they've seen the new Stallone movie or the ads around town, or know the Jim Croce song, but the ruse seems to work. The lads look thoroughly befuddled. They move back a few steps, arguing among themselves. One by one they warily eye our granite-muscled buddy, whose stare is unequivocal: If he goes down he's taking half a dozen of them with him.

Turning to Jimmy, I mutter loud enough for them to hear me, "C'mon, Jimbo, just a late-night mistake. Nothing to get all worked up about. Remember what happened last time...." I turn to a kid someone called Spike, who is sporting an orange Mohawk and a black-and-gold Guinness sweatshirt, and, unabashedly stealing one of Jimmy's lines, I mutter, "You lads *do* have health insurance, don't you?"

Saint Brendan himself, patron saint of travelers, must have been looking out for us because Spike breaks up in laughter. "Aye, yer man is all right. Let him go, lads. Just havin' ye on, weren't we?"

I grab Jimmy and start backpedaling with him. The leader's right-hand man, a narcoleptic little guy with a broken bottle in his hand, startles us by brandishing Jimmy's passport, deftly stolen during my speechifying. "'Ey, bloke. Forget something, now did you?" he asks tauntingly, holding it out with trembling, nicotine-stained fingers.

Jimmy snarls threateningly, ready to take on half of Ireland. Paul sidles up next to him, playing Butch Cassidy to the Sundance Kid. Using them like a screen, I quickly do a bob-and-weave move of my own, waving my right hand in front of me as if holding cash inside, and snatching back the passport with my left. The Irish guys look sucker-punched, as if challenged for the first time on their bridge.

"Ah, ain't worth the hassle," Spike says, and turns to lead the retreat back into the Dublin night. "Let's find some good *craic* before the bloody sun comes up." Feigning disappointment, they slowly scatter across the bridge, leaving the four of us, for a moment, to lean over the bridge railing and peer into the darkness of the Liffey. We watch them retreat, then head toward the safety of O'Connell Street. Halfway up the street, Paul blurts out, *"Jimbo!* What the hell was that all about?"

"Don't you get it, bro? Jimbo—Rambo? Like the mad soldier in the Stallone movie? It rhymes, plus I thought it would put the fear of God into them. Didn't you see the way they backed off?"

My brother frowns in disbelief. It's clear he doesn't think Jimmy could be that clever.

"Whatever it takes," Jimmy says in a haze. "Thanks for the backup, guys. But you know, I'd already accepted my fate and decided if I was going down I was going down fighting."

"Hey, bro," Paul says, "I had your back covered."

"Jim Croce?" shouts Jaz. "In the land of Luke Kelly and Van Morrison, you have to mention Jim Croce? And this Rambo, whoever he is, he hasn't made any impact over here yet. I'm guessing the lads thought you meant the French poet *Rimbaud.*" He pronounces the name exactly like Stallone's marauding soldier. "I think that's what confused them. They still think of Rimbaud as one of the great rebels, a prophet of poetry and the 'derangement of the senses,' and all that other rot."

Paul laughs, "Well, we've got the deranged part down flat!"

He lives for the repartee.

I ask, "So it wasn't the film reference that scared them off?"

"No, more likely it was those awful *Rocky* pictures."

At the far end of the bridge the Irish lads turned back to look at us with befuddled looks on their faces that slowly turn to needling laughter.

"Rambo? Jimbo?" Jimmy chides my brother, "Man, for a second there I thought I was going to have to swim home. Couldn't you old road dogs come with anything better than that?"

Underneath the statue of Daniel O'Connell, Jaz pops the cap on another bottle of stout. "Whatever the case, what do you say we drink from 'The Book of *Guinnesses,*' as Mr. Joyce, the Man in the Black Macintosh, put it? Either way, it was a sagacious move on your part, lads, except I forgot to mention that last week a gang of ruffians threw a couple of Yanks off the Ha'Penny bridge."

As one, the three of us stop in our tracks. Beside us the Liffey loomed cold and swift on its way to the Irish Sea. Then in one of those odd saving-grace travel moments rises the unmistakable voice of Elvis singing "Jailhouse Rock" from a distant disco. "Hey, Paul," Jim says, suddenly shifting gears. "Did I ever tell you about the church marquee back in Pensacola that read, 'What kind of country is it where God is dead and Elvis is alive?'" Without missing a beat, Paul raffishly responds, "The kind of country where Elvis is God, what else?"

Jim laughs nervously as we head back to our hotel, each of us looking out for the other in the stout-dark Dublin night.

V

"If you come to a fork in the road, you should take it."
—YOGI BERRA

"More than at any other time in history, mankind faces
a crossroads. One path leads to desperation and utter
hopelessness. The other to total extinction. Let us pray
we have the wisdom to choose correctly."
—WOODY ALLEN

"Would you tell me please, which way I ought to go from
here?" Alice asked the Cheshire Cat.
"That depends a good deal on where you want to go,"
said the Cat.
—LEWIS CARROLL

WAITING FOR HIMSELF

"To err is human, to loaf is Parisian."
—VICTOR HUGO

SO SEAN, AN IRISH friend from Dublin, a consummate *flâneur* and stringer for the *International Herald Tribune,* lures me with an offer of free beer in the cheapest café in the Latin Quarter, just around the corner from Shakespeare and Company. The streets are Sunday-night empty. The trees a cheap charcoal sketch of bare winter branches. The bells of Notre Dame ring out across the river. It's one of those instants when you know you could be nowhere else than where you are. The moment in the café is mingled with the pungent aromas of Gitânes, café crème, chestnuts, and car fumes, and the ineffably sad sound of metal doors clanging shut for the evening in stores up and down the Rue St. Jacques. Over a tall glass of Pilsner, Sean tells me of his three-year pursuit.

"I've been trying to get an interview with him for years," Sean says, pulling up his collar against the cold winds that come in through the door. "Never bloody answered me, though." He gives a good rendition of the Gallic *bof,* the angst-saturated sigh that escapes out of the corner of the mouth. Only then does he show his hand. "Finally, *finally,* last week, it was himself walking near the fountain in the Luxembourg Gardens. Doing shite all, just walking with his hands behind his back."

My hands grip my beer glass as if it's my last drink. Incredulity clots my voice as I ask, "Are you *sure* it was him? How could you tell? No one has interviewed him for years."

Showing a little French-style sangfroid seemed cooler than

admitting I'd been looking for the man on every path of the Luxembourg Gardens for months, having heard the rumor that he took his brooding walks there.

My self-exiled friend nods vigorously. "Sure, sure. I was after bracing meself to do it." His eyes glaze over with the look of the shell-shocked admirer. "And introduce meself I did."

Sean searches for the *bon mot* while the espresso machine hisses and clacks and the patrons around us argue about the latest scandal in French politics.

"C'mon, 'fess up," I say, "what was he like?"

"Oh, I don't know," he begins reluctantly, swilling his beer around in his mouth. "He looked rather cadaverous, empty-eyed, all hallowed out, if you get my meaning. When he saw me approach him he sunk into that funky old gabardine of his, then pulled that old black beret down over his eyes and just muttered something about leaving an old man alone."

Sean tips his glass, smiles wickedly. "You know what the bastard said? He said, 'I never had anything to say—and I said it.'"

Sean slumps down over the wooden table, his eyes dark as slate. "Himself—yer man Beckett—left me with *nothin'*, he did. So there you are."

"Well, if it's any consolation," I say, "remember it was Beckett himself who said, 'Nothing is more real than nothing!'"

The truth is fugacious, fleeting. Sean's scoop isn't nearly the epiphany he'd come to expect. In fact, he is unable to look at me. I grant him the space, and look away, through the old leaded windows of the café, across the street to the cloisters of Saint-Séverin. Rain is spangling the old stones. The very sight chills me, so I order a couple of warm brandies, as the lights flicker in another power outage in the café. I sit quietly ruminating on the delicious paradox of an exiled soul in search of another exile who'd spent his life creating characters in search of other lost souls. Beckett never granted quarter to any reader in search of an end to his character's quests, and he wasn't about to grant one to Sean.

"Can't quit." Sean sighs, citing one of Beckett's most

famous lines. "'Not with the fire in me now'—*my arse*." He clinks glasses with me, then downs his brandy. "Enough of this foozling along here, getting nowhere, doing nothing. Suppose I can go home now."

Outside, another winter storm is approaching. The skies are turning pewter. A dark green Citroën lurches past. A woman in a black leather coat swirls a red scarf around her neck and springs open an umbrella at a bus stop. Standing in the falling rain, she opens a book. Beckett. *Knapp's Last Tape*. To me, his words remind me of the wind rattling through the empty cloisters of the soul. If I listen hard, I can hear her voice reading, trying to make something out of all his nothingness, which I find bafflingly wonderful: "I can't go on; I go on."

He went on. I go on. I walk past Saint Severin in the Latin Quarter. It is blustery, it is cold; it is bewilderingly beautiful. The source of everything, although sometimes nothing is more than something, and sometimes less than everything.

Ovid in Exile

"Habits change into character."
—OVID

1

ONCE UPON A TIME, every change was a poem. Once, the ancients believed the soul was ignited by metamorphosis. They thought that human curiosity about the mutability of things was pleasing to the gods because it expressed their desire to understand the constant shape-shifting that swerves and curves through all creation.

Traveling through the post–Ceauçescu apocalypse, it seems incomprehensible that this land gave birth to the flying brass birds of Brancusi, Eliade's refulgent study of shamanism, the absurdist humor of Ionesco, the ethereal compassion of Mother Teresa, and the last work of the Roman poet Ovid, the master of metamorphosis, the poet laureate of change who couldn't—or wouldn't—change himself, and for that was exiled here for the rest of his days.

2

Caterina, our official state guide on this brief tour of the countryside, drones on about the rate of change in her homeland. Her quivering lower lip betrays doubt when we pass the brutally ugly concrete block apartment complexes. I doubt if the irony has escaped her that her land, which resisted change for so long, is also long identified with Ovid and his changeling heroes and gallivanting gods, who have come to symbolize the power of change for almost 2000 years. If we think of the poet at all anymore in these post-Latin days, we tend to imagine him as a whimsical philosopher in a marble-white toga spinning tales in the Roman Forum. His mythological surrealism gave the ancients exactly what the tyrants here have eradicated: gods that give a mirror for human activity, the moral and social perspective that offers human action some ultimate significance.

3

There are a million ways to lose time, a thousand to kill it, only a few to reclaim it. As usual, Ovid provides some consolation, saying, "Time is the best doctor." His statue is here in front of the dungeon-like Constanta Museum of Romanian history, a changeless land that should have read him more. His final home has become a writer's nightmare. A land where one of three adults works for the secret police. A culture without bookstores or libraries, only state-run propaganda newsstands. A black crêpe-paper world without trees or public gardens. An open sepulcher without the fresh air brought in by travelers.

"Travelers bring news, ideas of good things," admits Caterina over our banquet lunch. Despite the show of bravado, there is a bitter-pill twist to her mouth when she's forced to whisper her stories. Her land doesn't seem to be *their* land of impending tragedy, where a funereal pall hangs in the streets.

"People die still every day for lack of dream," she haltingly reminds me. "Many of my friends died in the massacre that led to the fall of Ceauçescu," she adds looking over her shoulder warily at the state guards on the bus. When asked if the change will last, her eyes cloud over. "I hope so, but how can we be sure? We are afraid if we side with change, if it does not work out after, the old guard will have their revenge on us." Then, thinking she has said too much, she excuses herself and slips away.

4

Always, we travel toward ourselves. We discover on ancient roads that we are made up of our ancestors and encounters such as this make me wonder about the consequences of trying to hold back the forces of change. Eliade was right. There is an ecstatic hope in the image of "humankind's long graduation from myth to history."

Metamorphosis, by any other name.

Ovid called himself *Naso,* the Nose, he of the magical dactyls and savage wit and subversive humor and naughty verses of forbidden love. The legend is that he left Rome in a hurry, thinking he had burned all his poems, exiled by the emperor Augustus in 8 A.D. to the farthest reaches of the empire, here in ancient Tomas on the Black Sea. Some say it was for his bawdy book *Ars Amatoria*; others for his dalliances with the emperor's daughter. But he underestimated the depth of his friends' faith in him. One of them saved a few manuscripts from the fire, guaranteeing that the rustle of his myth-caressed poetry would last for the ages. What was his motive? Could he have known that Ovid had virtually saved his cast of tormented characters—Phaethon, Actaeon, Tiresias, Echo and Narcissus, Eros and Psyche, Jason and Medea, Perseus and Andromeda, Orpheus and Eurydice, Pygmalion, and the pantheon of gods and goddesses—from oblivion? Or that his *magnum opus* would inspire more paintings, sculpture, and music, according to the historian Sir Herbert Read, than any other book?

His work was a god-graced accomplishment, revealing how, at any given moment, a tree, an animal, a god or goddess, a hero or heroine, might transform into something else.

What are we without that hope for change? That longing for metamorphosis, the secret change, the shape-shifting.

"Things don't change, we do," Thoreau wrote, moments after reading his moth-eaten edition of the master, I suspect.

Somewhere near the far eastern terminus of the Silk Road the Chinese masters wrote in *The Book of Changes:* "When the way comes to an end, then change. Having changed, you pass through." Somewhere near the western end of the ancient trade route Mevlana Rumi said, "This world is proud of those who suddenly change." What has never changed is the human will to change, and the fascination for those who do —or don't.

Strange, change. The only thing that lasts.

Constanta, Romania
September 1990

LOOKING FOR WALT

"We convince by our presence."
—WALT WHITMAN

"YOU BOYS LOOKIN' FOR Walt?" she shouts exuberantly from an upstairs window. My friend Chris and I are circling around Camden House in search of some hint of the white-maned poet. Before we can answer, she's dashing down the backstairs of the old clapboard house to meet and greet us.

Without so much as "How are ya?" she starts right in, breathlessly spreading the love. "It's all about *consciousness,* ain't it, boys?" she asks, vigorously shaking our hands. "He was so beautiful," she goes on, blushing at the sound of her girlish enthusiasm. Then she carries on like one of Whitman's own long lines, not even waiting for an answer to her question. "Taught me the meanin' and power of poetry. I lost my religion because of Walt, but I found *poetry.* Some people say it's the same thing, though. 'Spect they be right."

She runs her long fingers through her short dark hair. "C'mon, let me show you around. What'd you say your names were?" she asks as she leads us round to the front porch. "Mine's Etta. You know, I ran this here house for the Historical Society until the state ran out of money and had to close us down. Damn shame, ain't it?" She pauses reflectively, so we can have a look-see inside at the old furniture and wall photos.

Leaning back against the wooden railing of the stairs, we listen to Etta's amazing rap. "But I was getting tired of him, anyways," she went on, gnomically. "Even if he did make me *see.* But you know something? Wanna know what I really *dug*

about Walt? That he saw everything *equal*. Common. Everything was common to him. Leaves of grass, factories, people,
animals. Everything was ordinary, equal, democratic. Everything was a question of *consciousness*. He kinda asked, *'Who am
I?'* I am what I am thinking, what my thoughts are, movin' on,
movin' on. What was it he wrote?" Her eyes widen and she
recites by heart,

> *Roaming in thought over the Universe,*
> *I saw the little that is*
> *Good steadily hastening towards immortality....*

Etta folds her arms and looks over The House That Walt
Built. "That's pretty heavy, if you ask me," she says. "Do you
remember D.H. Lawrence, that English dude? Remember how
he said Walt's 'soul leaked out of him,' and that Walt's poetry
was a kind of warning about how people can rush on without
their souls?" She squealed with delight. "I *loved* running that
past school kids when they used to visit. Wonder where they are
now, if any of them still read Walt?"

A grin rides across my face as she carries on with her dithy-
rambic commentary. Walt's poetry, she says, encompassed the
young country and "made American audible to itself," quoting
some Whitman scholar I'd never read. Then she really surprised
me with the heft of her imagination. "Know those things, what
are they, glass paperweights? I think of Walt's books like that.
They're beautiful and you can see right through them and they
give off the most beautiful light—and you can use 'em on your
desk to hold down all your other papers."

While Etta recounts the gusts of pleasure she gets from
reading Whitman, I happen to look across the street. In the
cruelest of juxtapositions to the simple elegance of the poet's
nineteenth-century home is the modern stone monstrosity of
the state prison. On the sidewalk running along the barbed
wire fence, a mute show is underway. A group of wives, daughters, sisters, girlfriends, and mothers are standing in utter
silence, as if in prayer, gesturing in rudimentary sign language

to the prisoners inside. Each of them is shaping the letters of the alphabet with their bare hands, communicating as best they can, in a language Walt would've appreciated from his work with wounded soldiers in the Civil War. Their hand gestures are semaphores of seduction, a street poetry shaping sounds, emotions, letters out of the turbulence of lost communication. I recall Whitman's lines:

> *O sight of pity, shame and dole!*
> *O fearful thought—a convict soul!*

The last messages are exchanged. Storm clouds gather, casting a long shadow over the windows of the jail. Nothing can be seen behind the darkened glass or inside the prison house of language. The hands of the gesturing women hang at their sides as silent as unread poems.

Presences, that's what we remember—or else.

Poe's Last Drink

*"Men have called me mad; but the question is not yet
settled, whether madness is or is not
the loftiest intelligence."*
—EDGAR ALLAN POE

A HUNDRED YEARS OF darkness seem to leak out as I sneak a peek down into the dark basement. I look around for security guards, push back the red satin rope that stretches across the threshold, and turn the brass handle of the old door so I can peer downstairs. The steps are furrowed by ten decades of footsteps, leading down to an empty cellar with brick walls. Immediately, I feel the cold breath of terror on my neck, recalling "The Tell-Tale Heart" and "The Premature Burial," and my favorite when I was a boy, "The Black Cat," all written here by the inscrutable author with the *"strange commotion in his soul,"* as Baudelaire described him.

Strange to say, I couldn't quite remember what I was hoping for when I stood there, hand on handle, staring into the basement, mooning over the remote possibility that Poe himself had touched that door handle, gazed down into the same basement. What was I hoping to see, the root source of his terror, the old black magic that transformed him into one of our first horror writers?

A shuffle of shoes on the creaking floor and the low murmurs of the tour group I've broken away from disturbs my reverie. I listen in and hear the furtive voice of our tour guide, speaking in a mock Vincent Price voice.

"We were there in his Baltimore graveyard the other night,"

he says lugubriously, "and at precisely 5:05 a.m. a man in the long trench coat and tall black hat finally appeared. Oddly enough, he seemed at home there. You see, for the last forty-four years he's kept up a ritual birthday tribute to Mr. Edgar Allan Poe."

"Hasn't anybody confronted him?" asks a strident young voice.

"Nobody," says the guide, as if everyone should know that already.

"Out of respect," he adds. "Nine of us just watched him moving like a phantom to the gravesite, where he stood for a few moments, then left his gift of three red roses and a bottle of Martell cognac. Frankly, I was baffled at how calm he was, considering the hour."

The guide pauses at the doorway.

"Who were the flowers for?" a third voice asks.

"Funny, I've wondered the same thing. Some folks think they're for his wife, and others say his mother.

"I like to think that Mr. Poe himself would've liked the strange way the red plays off of black," he says.

At that tintinnabulistic moment, as I was eavesdropping, a gnarled cloud passes over the peaked roof of the house, casting a grotesque shadow on the plaster basement wall that rises and falls like a black cat arching its back on a white picket fence.

That's all I was looking for.

THE BAZAAR REQUEST

IN 1815 A CARAVAN of 2000 camels vanished without a trace on the old merchant route from Timbuktu to Morocco. The fear that followed gave rise to a search for preternaturally talented guides to lead caravans through the Sahara, the Lands of Fear and Lands of Terror. The legend goes that a small band of blind Berbers appeared one day who could navigate the desert by the smells of the sand and the sounds of the wind.

A host of travel legends stream through my mind one afternoon when I find myself lost in the maze of the bazaar in Marrakech. I stop at the stall of a brass and silver artisan to ask for directions back to the marketplace of Djama el Fna, and am so grateful I buy a small vase for my sister, Nicole. When I hand a fifty-dinar note to the old vendor in the white spiral of turban, he tenderly touches it to his forehead and kisses it. With the hesitation of a poor man, he takes out the only ten-dinar note left in his leather pouch, unfolds it like a prayer rug, and hands it over to me so desolately I feel guilty for taking my change. I nod respectfully, then move on, drifting through the labyrinthine world of chaffering merchants hawking their silks, Turkish rugs, spices, aphrodisiacs, sponges, lacquered boxes, scarves, and robes for desert travelers.

Everywhere I walk around the bazaar I am followed by beggars and orphans. I cannot elude them, no matter what I say or how fast I try to run away. *"Un stylo, monsieur, je vais à l'école, je n'ai pas un stylo...,"* they cry. *"Je n'ai rien, monsieur.... Gentle souvenirs? Kind gifts? Cheap, special price for you, Joe."*

I push on through the densely crowded bazaar, past touts and barkers. Women are lying over the thresholds of their homes, arms and legs splayed wide, as they're being tattooed by their servants on their hands and feet with rooster-red henna for an upcoming festival. Further on, a raccoon-eyed thief is chased by two shopkeepers flashing knives at him. A German tour group barters aggressively at the door of a Persian rug shop whose owner is not amused. A foreign journalist tugs at his meerschaum pipe in an old teahouse.

On the way back to my hotel in the late afternoon, I pause to marvel at the way the sun is raking through the slatted roof-tops of the bazaar. Twilight is approaching: "the swift hour," as Bedouins call it. A coral sunset silhouettes the minarets that crackle with the pious voice of the muezzin. The prayers of the faithful mix with the smoke from hundreds of food stands and rise entwined into the sweltering sky. White-robed merchants disappear down the dark passages of the *souks*, replaced by acrobats, dancers, snake charmers, water carriers, spice traders, booksellers, glad-handing tour guides, and skittish tourists. I make my way through the human maelstrom, pause near a mint tea stand. A storyteller draws a circle around himself in the dirt, and beckons into it a group of Berber musicians to accompany his sand-rubbed legends.

I'm transfixed. An hour passes, then another. It's dark, but for torches and gaslights, when I notice I've been followed by a handsome young man in blue jeans and Sorbonne T-shirt. He has the charming world-weariness of a young Omar Sharif. In the old reflex of the hounded traveler, I turn to go, and he grasps my arm and murmurs, "I am Zachariah. I would like to lead you through the *medina*."

I wave him away and head back to my hotel, but he persists, following me through the next eleven twists of the maze of look-alike alleyways. In contrast to the hustle lines I've heard all day, he appears elegantly subdued as he describes his father's work in the Marrakech schools, and his brother's job in France.

On the next turn, he stops, looks around for unwanted strag-glers, and grabs the iron lion's head doorknocker of a heavy oak door. He knocks firmly twice and, with a graceful wave of his arm, beckons me inside his family's house. I hesitate, tugging at my earlobe, as I do when I can't make up my mind. Nervously, I look up and down the now empty lanes of the *medina*. He tempts me by opening the medieval door just enough to allow me to see a blue-tiled oasis of softly bubbling fountains, bamboo bird cages, lemon and orange trees, and to hear the sweet sounds of Berber folk music on an old radio. Despite my skepticism that he's just another hustler, I'm fairly charmed and open to an adventure. No risk, no story. I follow him inside, immediately cooled by the gentle breeze inside the courtyard.

"You must help me, my kind American friend," he says before imperiously snapping his fingers at a young cinnamon-skinned servant. She bows and scurries off for the requisite mint tea.

"What do you mean *must* help you?" I ask, not sure if I want to hear the answer. It's uncomfortably quiet while we wait for the servant. "I don't understand."

"I am nothing here, there is nothing here for me," Zachariah says sadly. "I once dreamed of Paris, but my brother and my cousins there tell me of terrible racism toward Moroccans. It is no home for us. *C'est trop dangereux.*"

Finally the servant arrives with the tea service, bows and disappears quickly. Like a fool, I try to explain how difficult it is to immigrate to America, that we have our own problems at home, just as serious, only different. He cringes like a cosseted soul suddenly afraid of being on his own, then waves me off dismissively. Sternly, he orders the maid to bring us a brass platter of sweets. Without missing a beat of his pitch for exile to America, he brings out the family photo album. As if on cue, his mother, his sister, his grandmother all arrive, to prove his excellent stock, or prove he would be a good investment for me back home. I thank him for each round of tea and the wedges of honey and walnut pastry and the family introductions, but resolutely keep trying to dissuade him. I startle myself with my argument against emigration, my sobering tales of unemployment statistics, outrageously expensive colleges, crime in the street. But he doesn't hear a word I say.

"I will sleep on your floor; I will cook for you, clean for

you." He's so dazed by California dreamin' he won't stand for any myth-busting tales. "You won't even know I'm there," he says plaintively. "I want to improve myself. America is my last hope."

Seeing how utterly unconvinced I am, he turns on me, accusing me of being ungrateful for the hospitality he's shown and, worse, of American superiority. "Do you not think me good enough for your world"?

"No," I say, feeling claustrophobic. "I just don't believe it's what you're looking for." Yet, as the words dribble out, I'm unsure of what I'm saying.

"What do you think I'm looking for?" he asks peevishly. The servant returns with another brass platter of tea and Turkish sweets. He curtly waves her away.

"I don't know," I admit. "Let's just say it's a very lonely place for people a long way from home."

There is also a good chance he thinks I'm just a traveling fool, impervious to the obvious glories of my own country. Suddenly our little party is over. He stands up, snapping his fingers imperiously, and leads me back through the blue-tiled courtyard, past the fruit trees arching over the fountain, past the giggling servants, who bow gracefully, their hands over their mouths, past his family, who are now smiling woodenly.

In the curling shadows of the medieval wooden door that leads back out into the casbah, with the heat of the *medina* and the desert pouring through the crack in the door, he grips my hand, slipping me his father's Old World calling card. In a steely voice, he whispers, "Don't forget what I've done for you. Don't forget me. Write to me in care of my father's school." Pausing, as if reading the scroll of his future in the afternoon air, he says, *"My life is in your hands."*

I give him my address. We stand there for a few moments, awkwardly shaking hands, neither one of us willing to lose face by letting go first. The smell of orange trees fills my head like a spell. I inhale like a man who's found the path to bliss. I drink in with my eyes the arabesque patterns of the blue tiles on the walls around us. They seem to glow from within and put me into a mild trance. I don't want to leave; he doesn't want to let go. For me this is the enchanted world—for him a nightmare. I think of the blind guides of the desert making their way through the vast unknown by the genius of their keen noses and lush faith, and wonder whether Zachariah will find the guide he needs to make his way to his true home.

Old carts clatter on the cobbles beyond the thick medieval door. He is sullenly silent when I say thank you and goodbye, and good luck and, yes, I'll reply to you if you write to me.

He does not believe me because of the exasperated tone in my voice; he will not listen since I've stopped hearing to him. Something he can't yet describe is lurking inside him, seeking another kind of guide, a different way through the mirage that is his dream of escape, not mine.

I can still taste the honey and walnuts. How can that be?

And so the legend goes.

VI

"The most villainous inn in al London rode [road]."
—WILLIAM SHAKESPEARE
[First modern use of the word]

"ROAD, n., A strip of land over which one may pass
from where it is too tiresome to be to where
it is too futile to go."
—AMBROSE BIERCE

"It isn't the road ahead that wears you out—it is the
grain of sand in your shoe."
—OLD ARABIAN PROVERB

TYCOON

VEXING, THE QUESTION OF memory. Why do we remember what we do, why do we not remember things we should? *Remember* is a sacred verb, but *forget* has its own numinous function. Carl Sandburg believed in the primacy of learning poems by heart but that we should also develop a *forgettery*, a room where we go to forget, the place in our mind where we stow away all the things we're better off forgetting, things that crowd out the things we should remember but can't fit in.

Years ago I was lecturing on a cruise ship weaving its way through the Mediterranean and the Black Sea. We called on glamorous ports in the Mediterranean—Sicily, Rhodes, Santorini, Samos—and sailed up the Bosphorus Straits to Istanbul and beyond, following the path of Jason and the Argonauts into the Black Sea. The oddest of all was the decrepit, rust-bucket harbor of Constanta, Romania. It was mere months after Ceauçescu was surrounded in his palace, dragged into the streets, and executed as mercilessly as he had butchered his own people for decades.

Our private tour was the first visit to country after the tyrant fell. I felt voyeuristic just gawping at the benighted world, and embarrassed traveling with bored passengers through a country that had been asleep for decades. My curiosity about the nearly obliterated culture was curtailed by the complaints from my fellow travelers about the lack of beaches and souvenir shops.

At the end of the day the ship's staff surprised our guides with an invitation to come on board our ship. They hastily agreed and followed us in a state halfway between delirium and delight as the staff described the plush comforts accorded their passengers. Eventually the charade made me uncomfortable, and I broke away from the group to explore one of the $2000-a-day presidential suites in the front of the ship.

That's when I noticed the self-styled tycoon. He was on the foredeck of the suite next door, leaning against the polished brass railing, puffing ostentatiously on a cigar. In profile, he struck the pose of a craggy, jut-jawed New England whaling captain—or a Forbes 500 tycoon. Standing like a conquering Roman emperor, arms akimbo, tugging aggressively on his cigar, he looked like he was posing for one of Delacroix's royal portraits.

I walked outside for a closer view of the floating graveyard for out-of-commission ships.

"You just get on board?" he blurted out.

"No sir," I said, trying to be polite. "I've been the so-called Enrichment lecturer for the last three weeks. The ship brought me on board to talk about Greek myths as we sail around the Black Sea."

"Oh, it's *you*," he sniggered. "Yeah, I've heard stuff. But… what *else* do you do?"

"A little of this, a little of that," I tell him casually. "I write, I teach, I make films."

"Films?" He harrumphed. "You mean movies? What kind of movies?"

Careful, I told myself, *you represent the ship*. Then I barged ahead, anyway, unable to keep myself from goading him. "I just finished working on one on the Spanish Civil War."

He takes a long drag from his stogie and drawls, "Oh, you mean you make films about *them*." Contemptuously, he lifts his chin in the direction of the ramshackle, the ground-down town of Constanta. "They deserve everything that's coming to them."

In one motion he condemned an entire continent with his scattershot sarcasm. "If I were king," he said, his voice dripping with condescension, "I would bulldoze the whole country, just make it disappear."

It was the strangest verb he could've chosen. During Stalin's reign, the mad man employed *retooshers*, professional photographers who specialized in darkroom black magic. They were given photos of people suddenly "disfavored" and ordered to make them disappear, "burned out" or "dodged" in darkroom terminology. Politicians, soldiers, poets, even Lenin, eventually, all "disappeared" from newspapers, magazines, and books.

I take a deep breath. One rash word now could have dire consequences.

"Sir," I say deliberately, "we wouldn't quite look at it that way. It was a film about men and women who had the courage to fight fascism. If you want to call it something, call it a film about freedom fighters."

He sneered as if his doctor had just held his nose and given him a dose of castor oil, then looked away, thinking about the stock market or the price of diamonds in South Africa. Who knows? I had lost his attention, which I had not wanted in the first place. He was surveying the land of the infidels, listening to his own victory march, an embodiment of the stereotype I'd heard the guides sneering about earlier in the day. One of them confided to me her boss had made her vow before coming on the ship that she wouldn't be brainwashed by "miserably unhappy rich American imperialists."

The tycoon draws deep from his cigar, blows long, lazy smoke-rings over the side of the ship. Without deigning to even look me in the eye, he mutters, "So what you're saying is that you make films about *Communists*." He pronounces the final "s" like a curse, then looks over the dilapidated town that is covered by a pall of despair. As if vindicated, he clears his throat and imperiously lifts his head.

I feel dismissed, like a bad idea.

"Say no more," he says caustically. "No more talking."

Istanbul, Turkey
October 1991

Out of Step in Odessa

RAVENS CIRCLE OVERHEAD, unwilling to land in this sinkhole of history. For all the frenetic movement in the streets, the city is in freeze-frame, a port with rusted hulls in stop-motion decay. Shoppers line up for hours to buy a miserable little bag of chestnuts, a roll of see-through-thin toilet paper, a pair of shoes in a one-size sale, a tube of lipstick. Any color you want, as long as long as it's sickly purple. Their faces are studies in immobility and resignation. They look whupped, exhausted by the strain of everyday life.

After exploring the eerily lifeless streets and strolling through a small park where children play sullenly, my brother Paul and I look around in vain for anything resembling a café. We agree we need a jolt of caffeine to keep from falling into the stupor all around us. Finally we stumble across a miserable-looking coffee stand made of upended crates and five-gallon drums, one of the first attempts at free enterprise since *perestroika* was declared. I approach the frail young woman behind the makeshift counter, waving a dollar bill for two of the Turkish-style coffees she's brewing, expecting her to show a little surprise.

Instead, she appears insulted, vigorously shakes her head, sweeps her hair out of her eyes, tucks it underneath her *babushka*. *Nyet, nyet,* she mutters. No, no. She recoils from me, acting as if she wishes I would just go away. I open my wallet to show her I have no rubles, tell her in slow English I was unable to exchange any money, but I'll give her ten times her price *in dollars*.

My brother advances behind me like a war photographer, stealthily, the telephoto lens of his camera aimed at the counter where I'm waving my greenback in a signal of the triumph of global bartering. The Russian woman's face is weary, devoid of humor and warmth, as if emotion had been excised like a cancer from her long ago. She drums her fingers nervously on her single metal cup.

Behind her sits a dour man in his late twenties with a three-day stubble, a scar above his lip, and a bandaged hand. He is reading aloud from a thin volume of Akhmatova's poetry. He looks up with utter disdain. I figure him to be an ex-soldier not long home from Afghanistan, from the look of his war-phant-omed face. He stares threateningly, then explodes with curses, his words buzz-sawing the air. An ex-soldier himself, Paul nods apologetically, as if to calm him down with one of his patented "Cool down, fellah" gestures. In an inspired move, he leaves a pack of Wrigley's chewing gum on the wooden counter as a peace offering. Then, slowly, he retreats, one hand over his heart in an inspired gesture of friendship.

The woman relents, as if accepting his peace offering. She brews us some coffee in an old tin can. Without looking up, she pours it like crankcase oil into a cup cruddy with old grounds. I hand over my dollar, expecting her eyes to light up. Instead, she's spooked and harshly demands, *Rubles!*

We are right back where we started.

I protest that I don't have any rubles, edging my eyebrows up in exasperation, as if to say, *C'mon, we both know how valuable dollars are now.* But she's not impressed.

This time the soldier leaps up and snaps his own wad of rubles down on the counter to pay for us. He violently grabs the gum and slams it back down on the counter in defiance, hatred flaring in his eyes.

Thinking *No sudden moves,* I back away in slow motion, caught in the crosshairs of an impenetrable gaze. His face grows dark. His unforgiving eyes travel down the length of Paul's camera, raking the gaudily expensive lens. A soldier who is reading Akhmatova does not tolerate fools gladly.

Is he afraid the secret police are watching him cut some kind of deal with two foreign hustlers, trying to catch them accepting black market money? Does he see a sunflare of burning images of his friends or family imprisoned for taking bribes, foreign money? Has he been jailed for merely having a conversation with a foreigner—and not reporting it to the secret police within twenty-four hours? Does he despise us for seeing him reduced to brewing coffee on a street corner? Do we remind him of war, of friends he's loved and buried after drinking vodka with them from dusk till dawn in those savage outposts?

Suddenly spooked, my brother and I quickly drain our cups of coffee, nod thanks, and leave the dollar on the counter, anyway. We slip away quietly, trying to remember what was desperately crying out to be forgotten.

An intimate moment.

Odessa, Russia
September 1990

SHARPSHOOTERS

"A journey is a fragment of hell."
—MOHAMMED

NEVER AGAIN IS HAPPENING again. The soul-anesthetic has not worn off. I'm on the Balkan Express from Istanbul to Budapest and must stop over in Belgrade. I've been waiting for interminable hours in the gloomy crypt of a train station when my eyes are drawn to a crumpled copy of the *International Herald Tribune*. Dateline Sarajevo—only an hour away. Bread, fruit, and the daily paper have been rationed, schools and hospitals bombed, orchards torched, and newspaper offices destroyed. One local author has had to burn his own books to stay warm through the icy winter. A soldier reports that he is willing to fight to the death, but he doesn't believe the country is ready for peace—because it isn't even ready for truth. Snipers have been using trolley passengers for target practice. One combustible story after the other, but I'm still not prepared for the next one. Not numb enough, not cynical enough.

My gaze closes in like a fist on the final paragraph. Soldiers have been gunning down the abandoned animals in the National Zoo for food supplies, so a group of animal lovers has responded to the pitiful hunger cries that trumpet across the pitiless Sarajevo night. They have been crawling across the concrete floor of the pen, clutching straw in their outstretched hands, to feed the last living elephant in Yugoslavia. One by one, these holy-fool heroes are being shot by snipers. According to witnesses, their "metallic laughter" echoes through the empty streets of Belgrade's end-of-the-world blood-and-circus games.

For centuries they used to say, in the villages of this land roweled with terror, whipsawed with revenge, words I read on tattered billboard: "A distant future awaits you."

I look up from my newspaper to the huge clock on the station wall. It does not move; it is frozen. The old proverb presses in on my ribs. The world is tilting at a strange new angle. The conductor's whistle pierces the night air like an ice pick. The train jolts backwards out of the station, like history trying to back away from the stacked evidence of madness.

Lurking outside Belgrade, our train is shunted off to a side-track where we wait for five hours in clotted darkness on an arc of rusting train track running parallel to the only one that leads in and out of the city. For five hours war convoys convulse the air with fearful lamentations of impending doom.

The trains are crammed with war refugees, like grainy black and white documentary footage of cattle cars clanking their way to death camps. Another riptide of refugees is dragging Europe under. This is the world's dark luster: thousands marooned like the glass-shattered faces in Käthe Kollwitz's lacerating wood-cuts. Faces pressed up against the steaming windows, flattened like children playing with contorted circus mirrors, the result, bruits the *Herald Tribune*, of "prying apart political amalgamations that never should have been amalgamated."

We wait until dusk in the Gothic tracery of twisted railroad tracks. As we finally jerk free of the station, my eyes wander outside to a boarded-up wooden shed with a rusted padlock. We're riding the train line where compassion is sidetracked with a view that shows some people are pain with skin, that there is more than one kind of madness, as the sign outside the station indicates by pointing straight down to hell: THIS WAY OUT.

None of this prepares me for what the wild-eyed female Croatian soldier hisses to me while watching the refugees pass by in cattle cars: *I feel best when I sleep with a hand grenade.*

I carve parables out of broken lives.

Belgrade, Yugoslavia
October 1992

Elegy for Yugoslavia

THE WHISTLE FROM THE Balkan Express splits the air three times, and the train staggers out of the station. There is none of the usual joy of waving and wishing travelers a safe trip. This train is ripping apart refugee families. Weeping people leap aboard the moving train at the last possible second, then stumble down crowded aisles into smoke-clouded compartments. The door to mine is shoved open. A family falls in like tumbled dice. They are furious, stringent in their speech. The old women are wrapped in dull brown headscarves. They push past me and open the window with a sobbing shove, then lean out to touch the hands of groping friends and relatives on the windswept platform. The old men huddle into their wooly coats and threadbare gloves. Stubbornly, they push back the tears with work-gnarled hands.

Their lifetime's possessions are inside strap-breaking baggage that they shove into the overhead racks. The youngest man among them is combustibly wordless. With his disheveled hair and cold adamantine eyes, he looks like he just checked out of Hotel Hell. He crashes down onto the seat in front of me, sits motionless next to the window, and begins to smoke a night-long chain of cigarettes. Flinching and scowling, his eyes register a stealthy retreat into a minefield of nightmares.

At every stop for the next fifteen hours railroad workers check underneath the train for bombs. In our compartment we have our own skirmish flaring. My traveling companions relish the blowsy heater despite its nauseous mix of smoke and steam. I'm crippled by a cough and a debilitating road fever that has dogged me for weeks. Between the heat and the cigarette smoke I am gasping for breath. Angry and not a little self-righteous, I lift the window to let in a whiff of fresh air. When I close my eyes in a vain attempt to sleep, I can hear them cursing me, and the second they think I'm asleep someone grumpily shoves it back down, as if they are afraid to let the world inside the train.

Then I get it that they fear more than the rush of ventilation. They're skittish about the United Nations soldiers who stalk the compartments, checking identification papers. For the next several hours, the older peasant women carve garlicky meals out of sausage, bread, onions, alternating vicious curses with bitter jokes. When other war-raked faces peer into our compartment the family regards them suspiciously as we descend into the mad silence of the subfusc world that is their life.

At the border with Hungary the land weeps. The forests are disappearing for winter firewood. We're shunted onto a siderail so a cordon of trains loaded with luridly painted tanks can pass by. They are headed for the front near Sarajevo. They are so close I can count every rivet. Counting them, it is not difficult to imagine the gunfire, the convulsions of the coming battles. The rails sigh beneath the slowly turning train wheels.

There is a haunting vacuum with this picture, like the *shadow acoustics* described during our own Civil War. Then, besieged towns heard nothing—though they could see the battles from behind their own hastily built walls. It's as if the gods had turned down the thunder so they might more clearly see the tragic folly being played out below.

I ratchet out of my seat and jerk open the window again to release clouds of putrid cigarette smoke. Two tracks away, a long train is crammed like the cattle cars of the condemned that shunted people off to concentration camps during World War II. The faces of the refugees are pressed hard against the filthy windows. The fear in their eyes is like a barbed hook. A death fugue hovers in the air. Then another supply train clanks its way between us. I strain to see into the window slits of the tanks for a glance into the eyes of a soldier. But their faces are a blur.

When the last trains have gone, I feel a strong finger

jabbing my shoulder. An economics student from Novi Sad has squeezed into our compartment. Leaning over me, he scratches a single word in the air like a writer with sanded fingertips, pronouncing it slowly with matter-of-fact horror contouring his voice: *"War."* He spreads his hands out flat, as if to say, "That's all, nothing more."

From the dungeon of memory comes my college philosophy professor's voice asking us: *Why is there evil?* No one in the class dared an answer. He waited until the bell rang, then said, *To thicken the plot.*

Nis, Yugoslavia
October 1992

THE KNOCK

THE NIGHT TRAIN HURTLES along the rain-stained tracks, tumbling deeper into the land of darkness. The miles click and clack underneath. Across from me in the cramped compartment, an old couple lean against each other, breathing softly. Their hands are knotted like old olive branches. Their faces are lined with kindness. For a muted moment I see myself and my lover forty years from now traveling to an unknown destination, and am lacerated with longing.

Around midnight, I start to doze off, lulled by the gentle rocking of the train. Suddenly there is a rap on the compartment door. No one moves. Another knuckled knock. We feign sleep, pretending not to hear. When our midnight visitor won't go away, I reach for the light switch but it won't flip on. The latch on the sliding door is also stuck. On the other side, I see the red glow of a cigarette. Waiting, I hear wind whistling through cracks in the window, and the lamentations of the locomotive.

I rub my eyes and glance at my father's old Timex wrapped tightly around my wrist. I can't make out the hands, though it feels like half-past late, silly o'clock, as my English friends say. I don't remember what border we're crossing, what threshold we are being tested for.

"Passport, s'il vous plaît, passport, bitte!" comes the uncompromising command from the other side of the door.

I reach for mine and open it for the officer, who holds it up to the dim light. A long whistle, then darkness and a deafening roar as we pass through a dank tunnel. On the other end, I can only make out a shadow where my face should be. I know I have to be confident when the door slides open and the customs official asks me in curt tones how far I am taking the night train. I know the routine.

Waiting, my mind slides back to an encounter a few nights before, when the secret police stopped my train at the Yugoslavian/Bulgarian border.

Wrenched, that's the only word to describe the violence with which I was pulled out of my seat and hurled outside into the numbing winter night. There was only one other man on the platform. He was alone, trembling. We had both been informed we didn't have the proper papers we were never told we needed. For several minutes we stood outside in a flurry of snow, confused. We shivered in silence while the police checked our passports in the warmth of the brick station. The other man told me to be careful, that border patrols don't like vague answers to their no-nonsense questions.

"Well, what do they want to hear?" I asked. He was paler than the snow all around us. He clutched his briefcase, and paused for a moment as the police approached, escorted by the stern stationmaster. They were carrying only one passport. The falling snow muted their footsteps. The other man glanced at me, measuring the moment.

Under his breath, as if he were a ventriloquist for his own soul, he told me exactly what I needed to know in case I was the one allowed to leave.

"They want to hear," he said tremulously, "that you are just passing through. Tell them that you are not staying long, that you have seen nothing. Tell them you are heading home."

Moments later he was led away to a rust-riddled Trabant that wobbled and shimmied as it sped away into the dark forest.

The locomotive moans. The compartment door creaks open, a flashlight rakes the room as I hand over my passport to the silhouetted figure in the corridor and we pass deeper into the night, listening to the rain on the roof of the train.

Destiny is a tangled world. It is the third presence, fate with attitude and vision. Ordinarily, it is enough to get some of us home in the strange hours before dawn. But there is nothing ordinary about the knock on the door in the dead of night.

Nis, Yugoslavia
October 1990

The Ruinistas

DEEP IN THE GREEN heart of Guatemala, cinders of black smoke from a burning *milpa* field float over the ruins of the ancient Mayan kingdom of Aguatea. It is high noon, the time of the sun's white hiss. Rampaging plants and lichen have overtaken the mounds that hide ancient temples. Fresh trenches are visible in the sides of long-destroyed palaces. Our intrepid guide, Michael Guillén, has brought us here, along with Ian Graham, an expert in glyphs, so we might witness an actual archaeological dig. But the most dramatic thing to see is in the center of the ancient plaza.

Surrounded by a peppery cloud of mosquitoes, Ian kneels down beside an ancient stela that is covered by a protective hat of thatch. He describes it as a kind of stone history book that has been intricately carved with the royal history of the kingdom that once ruled here. Revealing a surgeon's precision, he runs his hand along its rough edges, as if into a gaping white wound that gleams perversely in the scattered light. Ian regales us with the stone's story of distant Mayan kings wrestling with immortality, the all-too-familiar tale of dynastic wars. With his hand exploring the mutilated section of stone he tells us that, only a few days before, armed gunmen had descended from helicopters and, within minutes, they had cut a single glyph away, using a stone-cutting power saw. In a finger snap, he adds, they were gone, climbing back into the cobalt sky. In some dim backroom in Guatemala City, he continues with increasing anger, they'll sell off 1000 years of history that had been rediscovered only a few months before.

I ask the archaeologist what story was told in the missing glyph.

"Oh, probably just the image of a captured king," he replies. "But that's enough for a couple of million bucks in *El Norte* or on the continent. Some fancy antiques catalog will declare only that came from a private collection somewhere in Central America."

An intensely interested member of the group, a history teacher from Kalamazoo, asks how the huge stones were moved here. Before Ian can answer, Pedro, our Guatemalan boatman, chimes in, "Don't you know these people were in touch with the gods?"

Ian smiles noncommittally.

Later that night, we make camp under a luxuriant canopy of giant mangroves and towering trees flagged with red-flowered epiphytes and silvery vines. All around us birds are flashing through the trees—wild macaws, egrets, swallows, woodpeckers, parrots—and my spirits are lifted just watching them for a few minutes.

The dinner fire is started, and we gather around, alternately enthused about the beauty of the forest and distressed over the desecration. I ask Pedro how he deals with it.

"*Everybody's* a looter here," he says bitterly. He wipes stinging jungle sweat from his dark brow. "The grave robbers, the military, businessmen, archaeologists, well, they're all the same to us."

The words have a percussive effect on me. The implications are vast. I can't help wondering if he's lumping us together with the others. I check out Michael's response, and he raises his eyebrows and gestures as if to say, don't worry about it. As if to clue us in, he closes his notebook filled with his glyph interpretations about the runic stones.

"Things happened before you got here," Pedro adds mysteriously over his shoulder as he walks away, "and they will happen after you leave."

It's another triple-carom comment.

What things, I wonder, half-irritated and half-awed by his

stoicism, but I go back to stirring my meal in the pot over the fire, then carry it off to eat alone on the banks of the river. Sitting down, I realize I'm by myself for the first time in days. All around me is a profusion of orange bell flowers. I'm rapt as a shock of blue morphos plays in the falling light. They seem delighted by the way they can move in and out of the shadows so light can catch their wings and turn them into gleaming winged dreams. Further down river a mélange of macaws flies across the river like a scarlet banner. A siege of herons feeds in the shallows.

The enchantment deepens as twilight flickers, and night approaches quickly. The sudden gloom is no mere mirage that dissipates with the morning sun. Far above, in the great webbing of vines and branches, howler monkeys roar like savannah lions in their fight for territory, and bats squeak as they swoop down over our heads. There is a presence here some want cut down to size.

Night is suddenly upon us. I hear Michael's voice call me over to join him for a bracing shot of whiskey around the fire.

"This is the last refuge of real archaeology," he says, pointing up river. "But what really brings me back year after year," he tells me with a click of our glasses, "is this: the glyph-like nature of everything around us: the solitude of the forest, the capriciousness of the river. I never feel more myself than when I'm here. This is who I am, here, not who I am back home."

Lying on his back, he points up at the stars, just now beginning to emerge and coalesce as constellations. "That's called the 'jaguar pelt,'" he says with admiration, pointing up at what we usually think of as Orion's Belt.

"That reminds me of an old Mayan proverb," I respond, "that says all attempts to stop the jaguar's teeth of time are futile. It's like a Central American equivalent of H.G. Wells's quip that history is a race between education and catastrophe. What do you think? Anything to it?"

He deliberates long and hard. The secrets embedded in these ruins, he says, make him think about the deeper reason why the looters may be decapitating the ancient stelae. Besides the obvious need for money could there also be some atavistic longing for the living force believed to run through these ancient stones, or for the enchantment they confer on foreigners? Surely the money would help poor farmers, but there is another impoverishment that can plague a land, an even more pernicious form of looting. There is the loss of access to the *mysterioso* force many believe streams through these ancient stones, the force of life itself.

I ask him if there's anything that can be done.

"There is no easy answer," he says solemnly. "Just the forgotten marvels of the Maya, just a steady leading of people out of ignorance with glimpses of the wisdom that was once here. I never knew there was so much ignorance in the world until I started publishing my papers about what I find here. People believe what they want to believe. Rarely, the truth."

Inspired by his passion for the land and his intractable joy for scholarship that he's been able to transmit to others for eight years on the river, I'm beginning to feel grateful for our friendship and the introduction to the mysteries. Then in a flash I see his words shimmering across the night like quetzal feathers. I'm about to tell him what just flew by when I remember that the quetzal is nearly extinct. What are the odds I just saw one?

Michael rises to his elbow and adds, "I try to tell the people in my groups that they can take the *chu'al* home with them, that mysterious force that everyone feels around the stelae and the temples. You don't have to become a looter. You can be a pilgrim."

An unknown god's dark glove tightens over the forest. The river purls on, moss grows on old stones, and travelers lose themselves in old stories.

Aguatea, Guatemala
March 1992

RAINFOREST

"May you see on the path, may you not get hurt."
—WAYÃMPÍ PROVERB

IT IS TWILIGHT IN the Amazon. The late afternoon steams, turns lime-yellow, and fills with a lepidopterous dream of butterflies, moths, lantern bugs, and giant flying beetles.

In the shade of the chief's hut, village women are pounding manioc in wooden canoes to make fermented beer for an upcoming festival. Kayapao, our muscular river guide, tells us a story as old as the forest. The Wayãmpí were created by God. White men came much later, from white stones thrown into the water. His people learned from their ancestors why butter-flies are indispensable—they fly back to their shores every night and tie down the four ends of the universe to keep it from flying away. They learned that rainbows are the souls of the anaconda, jaguars embody the spirits of dead children, and the souls of demonic conquistadors still chase anyone caught by the rush of dark in the forest late at night.

Over the last two days we have been filming the everyday life of the Wayãmpí in a village "older than contact," as our guide informs us. Our presence is as amusing to our hosts as it is exotic to us. We have come to the rainforest to film some scenes for a documentary on ecological design to help illustrate the natural roots of living in harmony with nature. For that to work we need to personify this ancient relationship by shooting one last series of shots of Chief Kumerei their serenely proud leader, wandering in his favorite part of the rainforest. I ask him through our inter-preters where he feels is the most beautiful spot in the forest.

Leaning against one of the timbered posts of his house, the chief gleams like a polished stone in his deep red *urucu* body paint and brilliant scarlet *kamisa* loincloth. Long strings of yellow and white beads crisscross his chest. A coronet of yellow toucan feathers is wedged into his headband. Ash-brushed whiskers on his face connect him to the jaguar, the stealthiest animal in the forest. He believes they will become one after death, the traditional belief in the exchange of spirit between animals and human. For the Wayãmpí, life is great green continuum.

The chief meets each of our gazes as if judging our courage and our hearts. He listens to our request, nods solemnly. Together with Chief Kumarei, our river guide, Kayapao, Manoles our tribal translator from FUNAI, the Indian Agency, and Henrique, our Portuguese translator, the chief leads us downhill to the banks of what he calls the "canoe path," the Jaguar River. Without a pause, he walks across a submerged log as if walking on water, then squats on the riverbank to watch us thrash around in our overloaded canoe. The chief laughs through his hands like a young boy, which surprises me since I'd heard a chief never loses his sense of decorum. Instantaneously—almost telepathically—his warm smile turns cool. He leaps up and quickly leads us over the *puruna,* the pathless path through the thick web of tendrils, vines, and lianas of the sultry forest. The invisible path disappears behind us with each step as we follow his soft treading over the forest floor, past fantail ferns, dinosaur-pawed ceiba trees, and spider vines that loop and strangle everything within reach.

At a small clearing where the trees have been hacked to stumps, Chief Kumarei calmly shows us the plot he's cleared for his manioc field. We stumble further on through a tangle of lianas past a hundred-foot, red-barked Brazil tree. The chief stops and proudly points out the rubber trees, cinnamon trees, and towering samauma and angelin.

The scent of the forest is an overwhelming mix of life and death, bright flowers and rotting leaves. It is one vast genetic library. I've just glimpsed the first paragraph of a single novel. It would take a lifetime to do it justice.

We stand around, nervously swatting mosquitoes as twilight, "the malaria hour," approaches. Chief Kumarei adjusts the beaded armbands and headband he has worn in our honor. Gazing through us again, he begins to question Manoles, who translates the village dialect into Portuguese for Henrique, who turns the words over one more time, into English, for us.

"Do you have big trees like this?" the chief asks, folding his arms calmly, the *urucu* dye on his dark skin glistening with sweat, the sky-blue beads on his arm glowing bright.

"Not anymore," Henrique replies hesitantly. "Just little ones." He turns to me, somewhat befuddled, searching for words that would somehow explain four hundred years of clearing forests to make room for cities like his own Rio de Janeiro.

Calmly, the chief asks, "Didn't you like them? Why did you cut them down?"

His gaze is unswerving—and unnerving. The moment is as mangled as the vines swarming around the banyan trees that surround the clearing. Every motion seems to squeeze sweat out of our pores. My glasses steam up every few minutes. Our hands constantly swat at insects. Henrique translates, and I say that many of our people *do* love trees and spend time in our forests, but there are many powerful people who feel they need the trees for other reasons. The second the words tumble out of my mouth, I feel ridiculous. Henrique adjusts his steamed-up glasses, and tells him that it's a very complicated matter, very crowded where we live. That people fight for the land, as they sometimes do in other parts of the forest.

Watching the chief's reaction, it occurs to me he understands more from watching us than hearing our groping words. He glowers as he contemplates the fragility of his "demarcated" sanctuary. He can see the light that comes from within trees. He feels the shuddering of the forest floor from fallen trees 1000 miles away. What else has he learned in these cool shadows? I fear we've arrived too late, like Gauguin in Tahiti or Bodmer in Dakota, into a world fading out of existence. Here every word, every path, every story has multiple meanings. How can

I hope to understand in time? Or out of time, for that matter.

"How *many* people?" the chief suddenly asks, enormously impressive in the slanting afternoon forest light. I watch Henrique struggle to convey the staggering numbers of modern urban life to someone who rules over a few scattered families down a remote river in the deep Amazon.

Our deliberations are broken up by the raucous sound of breaking branches, leaves crunching underfoot. It's the rest of the film crew approaching and the laughing of our Indian friends who can't seem to get over how loud and clumsy we are in the forest.

The chief looks away out of embarrassment, and up to the canopy of leaves above us.

"The trees cast shadows here," he says. "So we don't cut them down. Shadows are good when it is hot in the village." He looks back at Henrique and says without any tone of accusation, "We only take what we need from the forest. What do *you* need? What do you take?"

There is no simple answer.

"Tell the chief maybe we're afraid of shadows," I say slowly.

When the chief hears my words he nods, as if understanding his strange visitors for the first time or confirming his gravest fears about us.

At dawn I wake to the sounds of whimpering dogs and shouting. Tumbling out of my hammock, I rush outside to see the commotion—and bump smack into several village kids who've been watching us sleep through the night. A wiry man with tumbling black hair has returned from the hunt. Several women with knives gather around a dead monkey on the ground next to him. He is teaching his son how to string and draw a bow. The father flexes his shoulders, stands to his full height, and fires arrow after arrow into the forest. The boy looks up at him with awe.

I follow the flight of the arrows through the smoke of the morning fires, higher and higher into the forest canopy until they disappear in a mesh of mystery.

Anthropologists, missionaries, Indian Agency agents, *garim-peiros*, gold miners, filmmakers, and politicians are fighting over the eschatology, ontology, biology, cosmology, and futurology of the Wayãmpí. The tribe spends its timelessness swaying in hammocks, making manioc beer, hunting for boar, jaguar, monkey, birds and fish, raising rubber, manioc, cocoa, and cinnamon. They paint black-whiskered jaguar marks on their faces with seed powder, and red paint everywhere else with urucu berries. "They wear their redness because they think it's beautiful," explains the river guide. "They refuse to wear clothes; they don't want to hide the beauty of their redness."

The Wayãmpí say the faces of the new conquistadors are ugly, but, worse than that, the souls of the rubber-tappers, gold-miners, and loggers are ugly because they cut the big red scar of a road through the rainforest to get to the gold, jewels, and women. Wearing a crown of bright yellow-billed toucan feathers, Chief Kumarei proclaims the magical powers of the urucu will protect them as it protected his father's and grandfather's village if they paint their bodies with it. "We were invisible," he boasts. "No Wayãmpí living in their time could ever remember seeing an outsider. We were invisible because of our red paint."

That a color would have so much confounding power is not such a far-fetched idea. Yeats said red is the color of magic. Matisse, Kandinsky, and Renoir thought red revealed the secret of intimacy, the heat of the rising soul, the flushed skin of a beautiful woman emerging from her bath. Who's to say who's primitive and who's the true prophet of passion? What makes *you* turn red?

Tsakeo Wayãmpí, the Jaguar River, Amazonia, Brazil
August 1993

FAVELAS

THE BOY SITS IN the far corner of squalor. He has nowhere else to go. His father abandoned him in this slapdash shack of corrugated tin, mottled cardboard, street rubble, and wire mesh. He holds his head like the heaviest of loads. His eyes are sorrowful and lackluster as he stares down at the sack of cans and bottles he's collected since dawn. It waits to be sorted on the dirt floor in front of him. But he is lost in the endless monotony, the slow descent into numbness, the disintegration of days in shantytown life.

Hearing the racking of a movie camera lens, he gazes through the door to the dirt road outside his shack. The cinematographer on our film team focuses his lens at the boy's rickety cart. He does not flinch. His face quivers only when I turn my own still camera upon him. Our eyes lock.

I ask the boy through our Brazilian interpreter where he will go tomorrow. The question pushes him down the long chute of grief.

Every day is the same, only different, he says. Tomorrow morning he will haul his cart from dawn till dusk across town and back. If he fills it with the ruck of the streets the city will pay him a few *cruzeiros*—the equivalent of a dollar—or trade it for a bag of food. He shrugs, as if suddenly chilled, and says that at least it's a job. Then he adds sullenly he mostly likes the companionship of the other boys who work the carts.

Then, as if we have already left, the boy staggers to his feet and shuffles outside. As he begins to sort the bottles and cans, I wonder if late at night, alone in his tumbledown shack, with rain tapping on the tin roof, he ever thinks about the mad rush for gold in the Amazon, the insane chase they call *a droga,* the drug-like trance that has lured prospectors back into the jungle. Does he dream of catching a ride on a logging truck headed into the forest? Is escape even a remote possibility for him?

Soon it is too dark to shoot any more footage. I pack up my equipment, and as I'm leaving I look back at the boy and feel my scalp prickling. Images slant in on me like a seizure—stories I've read about abandoned kids being murdered by vigilantes, tales I heard in Rio about orphans being force-fed cockroaches or their own feces by police on their nightly sweeps.

I glance back over my shoulder and see something strange and wonderful. The boy is uncannily alert as he pokes around his cart to begin the night-long sorting out of the rewards of a day in the life of the *favelas*—bottles and cans, mirrors, old toys, broken pens, deflated footballs. He is resolutely focused, seeking riches in his jumble of garbage. His face has a radiance I have rarely seen before. My gaze slides down to his hands as they turn over the garbage in his cart as if each object might be hiding something valuable. His fingertips are glowing blue. The air around him crackles.

If you ask me anything more about this, I am not going to answer you.

Curitiba, Brazil
August 1993

Pantherine Dreams

"NIGHT IS FALLING LIKE a dark stone," says João, our one-armed river guide. Alert to the stillness, he listens to the cacophony of sounds of the rainforest, adjusts the cocked shotgun under his stump, and urges us to hurry with our hammocks. Whippet-fast, he moves from one tree to the next, tightening ropes, testing their strength, deftly fastening mosquito netting to the trunks of Brazil trees.

Carefully following his instructions, I'm able to adjust my hammock, and with a long sigh and hearty *obrigado* I plop inside. Slowly relaxing after eight hours of tramping through the rainforest, learning about jaguars, crocodiles, scorpions, chicle trees, gold miners, and conquistador lore, I feel my eyes dilating as I try to adjust to the absolute darkness—and imagine the danger João is alluding to.

For the moment I see nothing, but hear plenty. Horned screamer birds go berserk in the treetops. Giant owls swoop across the wild night. Squeaking bats plunge down over our heads. Getting used to the dark after a day fighting sweltering sunlight is oddly disorienting. But I've come to trust João's every word and morsel of advice and am grateful when he lights a fire in the center of our camp. It means the colorful stories we've been regaled with for five days now are about to resume. I ask him what brought him to the forest while he prepares the *caipirinha,* the sugarcane and lime alcohol that is the traditional spine-bracer for facing the uncertain nights in the jungle.

"To listen to the silence for the rest of my life," he says as serenely as one of the early desert hermits. Expertly, he switches the rifle with a machete, then shakes the bottle of *caipirinha* and takes a long, loud slug. "I came nine years ago, not to escape the city or because of my accident in the logging factory, but to listen to the silence here. That's all."

He listens to the translation into English by Alberto, the riverboat captain from Manaus, and smiles at the melody in the strange tongue.

I ask Alberto to inquire about the shotgun.

"Two weeks ago," João says calmly, "on this same hillside overlooking the tributary, I heard the sound of a creature I'd never heard before. In Manaus you always hear stories about things never heard or seen before—animals, fish, spirits—but I never believe them. The forest does strange things to people, especially if they've spent too much time alone here. But when I heard that sound—that was a sign. I was ashamed. I knew I didn't know the forest as well as I thought I did."

He swore to himself he would be prepared from now on.

No sooner did he mutter that than we heard a cry from the river that sounded like a child being strangled.

"Anaconda," João says in English, without the slightest bit of drama.

My scalp prickles with fear, then my mind recoils with doubt. I don't know if I can believe him. It's hard to conceive of a snake crying forlornly.

Anticipating me, João volunteers, "It's a mating cry. Snakes calling out for each other." He flips on the switch of his powerful flashlight and rakes the darkness.

I manage a weak laugh and say that it's a miracle they can find each other in the dark.

"No, no, no," João corrects me, "That the forest is here is the miracle."

Click goes the flashlight again, leaving us in the loud dark. For a few minutes Alberto and João converse in Portuguese. I stretch and make a move back toward my hammock, relieved that it's just a few feet away, then think to ask how João has been managing to stay up night after night on our expedition down the Amazon tributaries.

"*Tartarugas,*" he says. Turtles. The night he leaves the ramshackle docks of Manaus he always eats turtle to prevent thirst and the need for sleep for the next three days.

Later, I fall asleep thinking the sky has never seemed so close. Never before had I even noticed how it *curves* as it covers us with its fevered stars.

That night came the pantherine dream.

Five black streaks, five panthers striding across the aqua-blue sky of my night mind. A dreamy vision of sleek beasts stalking me across a tangled forest, then lurking in a ceiba tree and trying in a screeching voice to wake me up. Then I switch places and it's me in the tree staring at the five thin shadows at the end of my wrist, crawling across the jungle floor of a white page lit by a sulfur match while I track the beast below....

I wake to a violent shaking and angry shushing. My heart is in my throat as I lash out against my unknown attacker, then realize someone is screaming under his breath, in a strange language.

"Alberto, what the hell is he saying?" I shout as I watch João slip away in the darkness and back into his hammock.

Laughing nervously, Alberto says low and firm, "He says quit making snoring! You make like calling jaguars. You wake jaguars!"

"Very funny, wise guy," I mutter to myself and drift off again, hoping against hope he's joking.

Hours later, I wake again in a cold sweat. The moon is directly overhead—and my ears feel sundered by booming roars. I nearly fall out of my hammock. In a whisper, I ask Alberto, "Jaguar?"

His laughter merges with João's near the fire.

"No, frogs," he whispers back to the terrified city boy. "Frogs, mating."

At dawn I'm roused by a musky jungle scent and the sibilant silence of the forest. I rise unsteadily to my elbows in the swaying hammock, listening like never before in my life, listening as if to the very creation of the world.

Manaus, Brazil
August 1993

145

THE CAVES OF CAPPADOCIA

"A heart that is distant creates a wilderness around it."
—FOURTH-CENTURY DESERT HERMIT

IN THE EERIE VIOLET light of dusk the caves seem as if they've been wrestled into shape by wind, rain, and the hands of god-sparked souls. The saw-toothed cones and pinnacles of tufa rise and fall for miles like mountains of whipped meringue, or candle wax that has dripped for millennia across the ancient villages.

Tonight many of the fairy-chimney caves are lit from within by the flickering light of oil lamps, revealing the shadows of the descendants of the *troglodytes,* the old cave-dwellers who created more than nine hundred hand-hewn churches, and countless shops, stables, and homes out of the soft volcanic rock. Here and there, the honeycombed hills are split in two by the wrenching twist of recent earthquakes. In the medieval villages larks are singing twilight farewells in distant treetops. Axes ring out with the sound of wood being chopped for evening fires. Gypsies are singing plaintively from their black goatskin tents. The cries of the muezzin crackle from the minaret, summoning the faithful to prayer: *Misallah, Misallah! What wonders God wills!* In a trellised café, old men whisper to a passing traveler that he shouldn't stare at the caves, especially the abandoned ones, because they're haunted.

For three days I speak to no one, except when ordering my habitual *meza* plates and Turkish coffees in the cafés. I am feeling invisible but marvelously alert, a walking eyeball when hiking from the village to the distant Goreme valley, which is riddled with solitudinous cells coaxed out of the bizarrely shaped volcanic tufa by the soft hands of hard monks.

On the morning of my final day I seek respite from the handful of loud snap-and-run tourist groups and the farouche backpackers who arrived here this morning from Damascus. I enter in damasked desert light into a cave complex fabled for its frescoes, which I reach by climbing a rickety thirty-foot ladder and ducking inside a dank chamber. In the first room is a stone dining table that stretches the length of the floor. Along the gnarled cave walls are niches for candles and shelves dug for holy books out of the ancient tufa. At the far end is a tiny chapel with a slumped altar. The susurrus of silence reveals the ardor of faith that carved a life of contemplation out of this tormented landscape.

For an hour I sit with my back against the cool wall, listening for the murmuring echoes left behind by the ancient order of desert fathers, Holy Wanderers, Russian recluses, and Irish traders who were infused with faith in what was once called the "hazardous mystical journey." In the depths of their isolation they reported the soul becoming a cosmic echo chamber, a place to pursue the bold experiment with ecstatic vision.

Suddenly, I am overcome by the synesthesia of the moment, the crosscutting of the senses, the turning of the kaleidoscope in the central nervous system. I taste something in the air that is oddly purple and smells *triangular*. The notes of flute music from distant hills look like honey as they flow thickly through the cave. The ancient stone has a metallic taste to it. The crossover of senses here continues to rattle me as I hike through the valley, from cave to cave, utterly absorbed—*though nothing is happening but this*.

Nothing but the contemplation of sadly faded frescoes and the feeling of friction in my soul.

No more than the descent, hours later, into an underground city carved out of solid rock eight levels below the desert floor, as labyrinthine as the world of caves above. In this nightworld city terrified thousands of troglodytes who cowered for months at a time in suffocating conditions, but survived by learning the art of vanishing.

I keep descending down the spiral ramps until I reach the lowest level of the netherworld city. There I find an ancient clay oven and feel compelled to close my eyes and run my hand over the ashes of long-gone fires. Slowly the thinness of the air and the weight of the ground above begin to close in around me like a shroud, and I think of the exiles who waited in dark silence, listening to the rush of blood in their ears and the thunder of hoofbeats in the soft earth all around them. Not knowing if it was the great joy of God's arrival in their souls, or the terrifying Mongol invaders from the cold north steppes who had found the secret entrance to their refuge.

As if they were one and the same.

I feel a shudder—and wonder in that swift hour if it is the cold air or the crimson doubts about my own faith.

Nothing happened but this. Nothing ever does. Except *this*. the strange strengthening of the heart, only this, said the Desert Fathers, the pinprick of time, the sacred speck of this moment

Only this, murmured Rumi, *only this*.

Goreme, Turkey
October 1990

THE SHADOW OF ANCIENT RUINS

*"In Ionia,
the mind hankers after the resplendent past ..."*
—DAME ROSE MACAULAY

I'M REVELING IN THE gallivanting light along the southern coast of Turkey, when a bullet-hole-riddled road sign featuring an unmistakable drawing of an amphitheater beckons me: ANAMUR ANCIENT THEATER.

I brake and turn, curious, the trait that most makes us human.

On the long approach to the ancient ruins, a starburst of astonishment explodes in my heart. After twenty years of visiting ruins all over the ancient world, for the first time I've stumbled upon a nearly intact Roman theater from the first century. The jumbled beauty, the light that brushes the old stone, is a revelation.

Inside, I find tiers of seats, a nearly complete stage and rear walls with statues still in their niches. Climbing the steep aisle steps of the amphitheater reveals sun-spangled light on ancient arcades, colonnades, and friezes. The stage is being set for a concert this evening.

A cool breeze pours in from the azure sea visible from the colonnade that runs across the top tier of the theater. Up here, I can hear the immense whispering of the ancient world and the mournful melancholy that has built up here over the centuries. As I lean against an old arch overlooking the stage, I hear an Italian tourist wave her arm in odd disappointment, saying, "*Sempre pietra.*" "Always stone." So what is the problem,

I want to shout out? What did you expect in a land riddled with ruins?

Sometime later I find myself outside the theater searching for the WC. A lone custodian sitting on a stool points to a wooden shack leaning against the thousand-year-old walls of the amphitheater.

Afterwards, he invites me over to his table for freshly brewed sweet apple tea. As I sit down he lifts a beautiful brass teapot high above his shoulder and pours the tea in a long brown arc, then quickly brings the spout down to the brim of the first cup, then back high into the air and down again to fill the second one—without spilling a single drop.

I'm impressed, even elated. He smiles incisively and offers a toast: Şerefe! Cheers! In companionable silence we drink together, happily listening to the wind in the nearby grove of cedar trees, delighting in the lambent light.

I look up at the great rise of the Roman wall I am resting against. A soft ginger-colored light spices up the stately arches, that act of genius that changed how much stone weighs.

When I look back the custodian's young daughter approaches us in a plain white dress, hair as black as a country night. She offers a plate of sliced cucumbers, olives, tomatoes, and feta cheese. Contented when she sees me pecking away at the delicious lunch, she sits next to her father and avidly watches as he stacks the small Turkish coins of his livelihood, gracefully, with dignity in his field-gnarled fingertips. He takes one coin, puts it to his lips, kisses it gently, touches it to his brow. Closing his eyes, he places the coin into a leather pouch inside his shirt.

Opening his eyes, he sees the utter delight in his daughter's face. She has been watching his every move. Already she knows that beauty reminds us of our wings. He reaches back inside the pouch for the coins and places them inside her hand, closing her fingers over them, then kissing her hand like a blessing.

This is all I ask of my journeys. A single moment that courses through the canyons of my veins to let me know I'm still alive, that simple astonishments are waiting for me in the stolen moments, the unexpected detours.

Drunk at Midnight at My Father's Grave

*"A man who would not love his father's grave is worse
than an animal."*
—CHIEF JOSEPH, NEZ PERCE

THERE IS A MADNESS that calls out for what is lost until
it returns in some new form. After nine bottles of Stroh's and
three shots of Stoli with an old girlfriend in one of your favorite
local taverns, it's on the far side of three in the morning and I'm
leaning against the chain-link fence at Mount Kelly's cemetery
where we buried you.

I hope you're happy now, Dad. It looks like you'll be spending
eternity practically in the backyard of your hero, Henry Ford,
who once owned most of the land around here. It's a nostalgic
touch you would've enjoyed—or sneered at, depending on your
mood. But who knows? Maybe thirty-three years at Ford's
World Headquarters, the Big Glass House, you used to call it,
was enough.

Tonight I'm full of piss and vinegar, as you used to say. As
a matter of fact, I'd like to rip this fence down. Tearing it apart
would be easier than tearing apart my bitterness, the remorse
and anger I still feel about you and your early death. Fifty-six?
That's all you could manage?

Oblivious to the bone-chilling winter rain, I leap the fence
and shuffle through the wet grass to your gravesite. I kneel
down by your army-issue tombstone, and rub my fingers across
the lettering of your name and rank:

STANLEY H. COUSINEAU
SERGEANT U.S. ARMY
1928–1985

I'm searching for a trace of you in this stone—but feel little other than the griefwaves every son feels after losing his father. In a rage I yank weeds from the ground around your tombstone, getting angrier and angrier as mud cakes in my fingernails. I'm fuzzled, confused, and lost. A chill creeps over me. Your presence seems to hover over your gravestone, as you hovered me doing my homework, playing ball down at the park, or when you punished me with spirit-breaking weeks of weed-pulling. My jaw tightens, my neck muscles bunch up, my eyes wince with tears as I recall summer vacations spent paying for your rage over some unnamable problem somewhere else in your life.

Tonight, my old girlfriend cried desperately that she never felt any love from her mother and so felt nothing when she died. Unwittingly, she gave me a mirror image of my lifelong lacerating doubt about your love for me.

Now, on the far side of midnight, it's my turn to moan like Roy Orbison for love and cry out for an end to the corrosive melancholy. Standing stupidly in the rain, I'm afraid I'll bore holes into your tombstone with my fierce gaze, and end up talking to your ghost about how you hated the insanity of the widowmaker war machine, the greed of politicians, the soullessness of bureaucrats, the relentless Michigan winters, and your own loveless father.

Slowly, I feel a phantom touch, like that of a hand on my shoulder. A strange gurgled laugh escapes me when I begin to recall all the things you loved: old Fords, leatherbound books, the paintings of El Greco, voluptuous women combing their long hair, the smell of burning leaves in the autumn, and the music from *Zorba the Greek* and *Never on Sunday*. Scraping the dirt from my nails, I remember how you respected the loamy soil of your rosebushes, people who speak their minds, and any man who takes the time to walk with his kids and his dog through an open field.

Somewhere you are dreaming of me, as I am here now dreaming of you in the vast silence of your graveyard, imagining how different my life can still be if I never forget these things. One more thing, the cruelest one of all. Then and there, in the darkness, I flame with shame when I think that maybe Emerson was right. Maybe it's true that a man never really lives until his father dies.

How terrible, if true.

Maybe that's why you used to yell at me when I was a kid that if I had another brain it would be lonely. You never said what would happen if I had another heart. Is that what you meant when you confessed to me in one of your last letters that you didn't know how to answer your friends when they asked you what I was doing with my life? Is that why you were angry when I said I still didn't know. Is that why you instructed me to never say *I don't know*? "Say, 'I'm going to find out.'"

You died before I had time to answer

I've been trying to make time ever since.

Every story I have told since you died is made-up time so I can answer you.

Dearborn, Michigan
December 1986

VII

"What's yer road, man—holyboy road, madman road, rainbow road, guppy road, any road? It's an anywhere road for anybody anyhow."
—JACK KEROUAC

"Je rôdais, je flânais, je flottais."
(I roamed, I wandered, I floated.)
—BLAISE CENDRARS

"When you get to where you're going—
well, there you are."
—BUCKAROO BANZAI

COUGARS

IN A FUNKY NORTHERN Oregon saloon I hear a grizzled old hunter muttering over a cold mug of beer about cougars. He has the face of a man who has spent his life outdoors, a voice smoky from hundreds of storytelling sessions around seasoned campfires.

At the mention of the sleek cat, his fellow hunters lean closer. The bartender puts his hand out to quiet a loudmouth at the end of the bar, turns down the local country-western station twanging on the radio.

"Did you know," the hunter says, tipping up the front flap of his hunting hat, "that the cougar *can turn off its scent* if it senses danger?"

"W'd'ya mean, turn it off?" scoffs the guy on the bar stool next to him. "Bullshit. Why would it go and do a gol-darned thing like that? Scents is supposed to help 'em during matin' season, right?"

The notion brings a few dirty laughs.

Unfazed, the soft-spoken hunter shakes them off like pesky black flies. "No," he said, "the cougar turns off its scent so it can *disappear.*"

"Disappear, my ass. Don't go fuckin' sentimental on us. Mountain lions are just goddamned predators."

The old hunter's eyes twinkle with curious delight as his friends go on cussing and heckling him. "I've heard tell that one minute hunting dogs are tracking and the next—nothin'! They go nuts!"

"Imagine," he adds slyly, "them good old boys chasing ghosts through the woods."

I sit there listening, sipping suds, nervously fiddling with a coin, flipping it back and forth, over and under my fingers. In my mind I see a timid deer chased by an amber-eyed cougar through a dense wood. Suddenly, the cougar picks up a suspicious scent and realizes it's also being hunted. In one blazing instant—through a fierce act of an ancient will—it *vanishes*.

"Invisible, untraceable. Ain't even got a shadow," the old hunter says in a staccato beat that dissolves my reverie. He stares at me across the rim of his beer glass, shaking his head in admiration bordering on awe.

"Imagine that."

Gold Hill, Oregon
October 1978

The Trunk

THE SPUTTERING NEON SIGN on the roof of the bar across the road from the hospital reads: THE OPERATING ROOM. It's one of those names that makes everybody groan, like a bad jingle you can't get out of your mind. Inside, the regular crowd is lined up four deep for drinks. It's the late 1970s, so they're howling at the disco dancers. For an hour I sip a long, tall, frosted glasses of Stroh's, feeling like a Raymond Carver character moaning Hank Williams songs in an Edward Hopper painting.

Long after midnight, I'm spotted by a couple of leery hometown friends, if playing ball together as kids qualifies as lifelong friendship. It does here, so an extra stool is found for me as the questions swirl about how many years it's been since I've been home. The guys say "home" as if to say no matter where I live now, *this* is the only place that counts in the long run.

Mel shouts, "Well, well, well, welcome home, asshole!" *Nothing's changed*, I'm thinking as he bends my ear as if only ten minutes, rather than ten years, had passed since we'd last hoisted a beer together. Another old teammate, Rick, the bar owner, pulls up a stool and Mel starts in on him, groaning about this, that, and the other. Turns out his wife won't let him get away "up north" anymore, meaning the Upper Peninsula. Rick gives him the evil eye and, distractedly, asks why not. Slow-drawling Mel scratches at the roofer's tar on his hands, then runs them through his grease-clotted hair in a hopeless gesture. "Because she don't ever believe my stories anymore," he says under his breath.

Rick laughs, "Can you blame her?" then slaps the fanny of

a bodaciously flirtatious waitress, and orders another round for us.

"What the hell," Mel says. "Not after what happened last time, man."

"You mean you told her we went huntin' up north? You dumb shit!" Rick bellows. "Now my old lady's gonna ream my ass." He turns to me with an exasperated look that says, "What are you gonna do with this guy?"

Mel's eerie response takes us both by surprise, "I only told her because she *looked,* man."

"W'd'ya mean she *looked*?"

"She was sneakin' 'round the garage lookin' for what smelled so friggin' rank. 'Like friggin' spoiled milk,' she said. Then she started knockin' 'round the car knowin' somethin' was in the goddamned trunk. Couldn't help herself. Pried it open with her nail file."

"You didn't? How stupid can you be?"

"I couldn't think of anywhere else to dump it, man. Got busy with my job. Forgot it was there. She caught me out, man. Serves her right that it was still in there, all bloody, and shit and flies everywhere."

"Mel, you're dead meat, man. How else am I gonna get away up north if I don't have *you* as an excuse anymore? Life ain't worth jackshit if I can't get on the road every weekend."

Rick turns back to me for confirmation. "Am I right, dude?"

I spike my beer and order a round for old times' sake. I've been fond of Mel since I played ball with him as a kid. "Can't imagine life without the road, brother," I say—to an empty stool because Rick's already moved on, moseying over to the waitress. Over his shoulder, he yells, "Mel, you're headin' for the boneyard, man."

"Don't give me no grief," Mel shoots back. For a second the only thing in the bar I can hear is Ernie Harwell's voice velveting the night from the bartop radio. Like the Tigers, Mel is losing, badly. Slowly, he disappears down the long slope of foaming beer glass.

I make some small talk about the whereabouts of the other guys we used to play ball with, but I'm really dying to ask him about the trunk.

As if reading my mind, Mel looks at me plaintively and says, "All this over a damn deer head." He cuffs himself. "How could I have forgotten a goddamn deer head in my own goddamn trunk?"

He stares at the ballgame on television over the bar, and picks at the shreds of roofing tar still in his hair, lamenting the loss of simpler times.

Wayne, Michigan
December 1983

TURTLE BEACH

THE MOTHER SEA TURTLES are coming home. They shudder out of the foamy breakers, one lumbering step after another. Their leathery flippers spray sand as they shuffle across the beach to a quiet place in the gently rolling dunes beyond the tide line. There they squat quietly and go into a glassy-eyed trance, dig shallow holes, and drop their precious cargo. In the next three months, they'll leave thousands of eggs in sand whose temperature will miraculously determine the sex of the baby turtles, as well as the exact moment they will emerge from their brittle shells. Smaller than a human hand, they will peck their way out flippers first, followed by their tiny squirming heads, noses immediately alert for any sign of predators and the plashing sounds of the sea. Only their swarming numbers ensure that their species will survive. For death lurks everywhere. Seagulls, manatees, alligators, and sharks have been waiting for nightfall when delectable, bite-sized turtles scurry to the sea.

Moonlight quivers on the Caribbean for tonight's harsh lesson in natural selection. Along midnight, a 700-pound mother turtle lifts her leathery neck like a periscope out of the surf. Tentatively, she approaches the rock cropping near where I'm lying quietly in the sand, binoculars in hand. In her eyes is a rock-steady faith, rugged determination, tenacity. I feel blessed to be in her presence, and think of my friend who played cello with whales nuzzling his kayak. I sense the timeless man in me.

Satisfied that she has cleverly hidden her eggs from the scoundrels of land and sky, she languorously uses her gigantic flippers to cover them with sugary white sand. Wound up by evolution's crankhandle, she slowly pivots and trudges back into the white-fringed surf, disappearing into the dark sea. Or does she?

Improbably, the sand trembles, the silence is sundered. Soldiers in camouflaged uniforms appear like phantoms in the rude glare of loudly backfiring jeeps. Roaring to a sand-spraying stop, they leap out and approach our small group shining their flashlights like an accusation. They move menacingly among us, questioning.

The soldiers loom over me. Three hulking shadows with machine guns angled on their hips. They beam the flashlight in my eyes. The captain's voice is nearly drowned out by the battering surf. I can just understand enough of his Spanish to realize he's asking me what the hell I'm doing there.

"I'm here to see the *tortugas,*" I tell him.

"Do you have special papers? If not, you must leave. The *tortugas,* they are coming. There has been poaching. We cannot take chances."

I tell them I'm a journalist, and flash a crumbling press pass I once used to keep out of jail in Pamplona. Useless. They scoff at me. The turtles must not be disturbed. If the turtles sense danger they will never return to this beach. Don't you know this?

On the two-hour scooter ride home along the sea road and around the dark forest, I pass by abandoned hotels, Mayan ruins, and 3000-year-old roads. But what keeps reemerging in my mind's eye is the gigantic turtle. She's patting the sand down firmly over her eggs, turning with agonizing slowness, and plodding back into the sea, where she submerges with startling grace and, suddenly weightless, glides through a sea teeming with iridescent night life.

The pang of disappointment fades. A tide of happiness flows through me as I see the lights of the port in the distance and hear the twang of wandering guitar players in the *zocalo*. Tonight, the beer will be cold and fine in the café near the fountain.

There I will reassemble the sharp fragments of the night and try not to cut myself.

Cozumel, Mexico
June 1995

BARRACUDAS

THE WATER IS PRISMATIC. Two sleek streaks of mercury swim together inches below the surface of the sun-frazzled sea. The snorkeler sees them out of the corner of his mask while looking for something else, something lurking in the swirling crevices of red and gold hemispheres of brain coral at the bottom of the blue-green sea. He is pulled toward the unseen, lured by the ecstasy of phosphorescence. When the invader takes a sudden dive and slips through a school of neon fish whose bodies turn and spin, flash and flicker in rays of sunlight, the eyes of the barracudas follow his every move. Does he see something they don't in the shark-shadowed waters of the Caribbean?

This is no twilight hunter. There is nothing to fear in eyes that are hypnotized by the near-vertigo of the indigo-blue sea. He feels lulled by the placid motion of an electric stingray slowly flapping its enormous wings just inches above the sandy bottom of the sea, and the long lines of fish strung together like opal fire. His heart is in his mouth and he wanders far beyond the other travelers he'd rented the boat with earlier that morning. Some are diving, others just lazing in the water. He remembers reading about the sultry beauty of the Palancar Reef as a kid, and always wanting to see it for himself. And now he was lazily floating over the famous reef that drops abruptly 160 feet. He is reveling at the sight of sheer nothingness, absorbing the great silence. He is aware only of the rustle of his own muscles as he swims through lambent light beyond the reef.

He pauses at the watery edge of the great coral reef, feeling weightless and insignificant, and does not see his diving partner signaling frantically at his wristwatch that their time is up, that

The Book of Roads

the boat is leaving for the island ten miles away. Turning in the
water like a corkscrew, he sees his partner pulled up out of the
water into the boat.

Alone now on the edge of the deepest canyon on the planet,
a delicious terror gnaws at him as his gaze falls into the blue
abyss.

The Philosopher of Tulum

TENACIOUSLY, THE IGUANA HANGS on to the slippery rock. His head is poised against the wind, gazing stoically out across the translucent turquoise sweep of sea. He stands sentinel for the 1000-year-old glistening ruins of ancient Tulum perched on the cliffs behind him. His green scales are glinting in the fiery noon sun as he considers the legends of his reptilian ancestors discovering this scorched coast. He sniffs at the salty sea breeze and ponders the epistemology of his forefathers, the cosmology of brother lizards lounging on the stones of the long-abandoned temples. His lidless eyes watch unblinkingly for threats drifting in across the sea.

Each time the wind shifts, his head darts to pick up strange scents; otherwise he is immobile, conserving energy for his contemplative practice. There is nothing in the wind, sand, and sea he does not consider worth meditating over.

Wisdom can be found everywhere if one is alert enough. There are never enough lessons in survival here on this sunblasted shore. One can never be too vigilant. At any moment a wave can whip you out to sea. The tide may sweep away your rock bridge to the sparkling white beach. A hungry Mayan could spear you and grill you for supper. The conquistadors could capture you and take you to be locked away in a wizard's tower back in Seville.

The possibility of extinction concentrates the mind.

This is how a philosopher is born. Here is how one is initiated, trapped on a cliffside boulder through an all-night storm, and discovered at dawn, "Dead, mad or a philosopher."

The galumphing iguana flumps his tail down on the rock

like an old scholar slamming his hand down on an oak desk after an all-night battle with invisible forces. His eyes flare as the tide comes in and explodes on the rocks, like ideas that strike the flint of the heart and set the soul on fire.

The Mysterious Messenger

"YOU'RE THINKING ABOUT life, aren't you?" she says wryly as she sidles up next to me on the stone ledge atop the Temple of the Winds. Her hair is spun gold. She sweeps it out of her eyes like an auditioning 1920s starlet, and surveys the ancient grounds of Tulum.

I can't exactly disagree with her.

I've been staring out to sea and back to the tumbledown ruins of the *Castillo* for the last twenty minutes, clutching my worries while broiling on the spit of the sun. An old nun in high school used to call it *moodling*, as in "Philip, stop staring out the window, stop *moodling*!" As if it were a crime. I tried to tell her I was *thinking*, but she wasn't having any of it. Rapped my knuckles with a ruler and knocked my head against the concrete block wall. Never stopped me from moodling, though.

I'm torn between the extravagance of beauty here—plumeria trees, streaking parrots, capering dolphins, opalescent waters offshore—and the black mood that has simply overtaken me. I'm afraid of committing the cardinal sin of the road—adding on miles for the sake of miles. I can't figure out where this journey fits into the overall scheme of my life. I'm parched, exhausted, and perched on the edge of the hundred-foot cliff. I mop the beaded sweat off my forehead and the steam off my sunglasses, but my brow is still corrugated with anxiety I should have left at home.

"Give it up, leave it for the wind, just let it go," she says haltingly, like an oracle breathing fumes from the netherworld, and dispensing riddlic advice.

Across the old castle grounds now planted with cactus and palms and wild ferns, a man she appears to be traveling with shoots several photographs of her through a long telephoto lens. This in no way prevents her from philosophically flirting with me while posing for him. I can hear the motor drive of his camera as he snaps photo after photo, until she says with a peculiar mix of resignation and provocation, "I suppose 'What does it all *mean*?' is the *only* question for *some* people."

She pauses, and shades her eyes for a moment. Before I ask her *which* question she means, she purrs, "But it's nothing compared to being nowhere else but here, thinking about nothing else but this. Questioning, period. That's the point, isn't it?"

A chevron of seagulls passes overhead, wings perfectly still. They're giving it up, just as my mysterious stranger said we should. With sublime timing, they are leaving it for the wind as they circle over the great ceiba tree in the long-abandoned ruins of the ancient square, the center of the ancient Mayan world, the support of heaven itself.

Charmed by the winged coincidence, I turn back to the woman to ask her about the odd conjunction, but all I catch is the sight of her bare shoulder as she swerves around the slanted corner of the temple, and her disembodied voice saying, "You're a fool to try and explain it yourself." Hearing this, I can't help rolling my eyes, a habit I learned from my father, who claimed he learned it from his. Then I hear her one last time, as if anticipating my rationalizing: "Forget yourself, forget the rest. Blunder ahead as if no one is watching you."

Then she's gone.

Swiftly as last night's dream.

Vanished but for the faint perfume of her gleeful laugh.

Once again, the whirring motor can be heard above the screeching of the scarlet parrots flitting between the ruins and the trees.

And you, what did you think the muse would sound like?

THE LONG BLUE ROAD

for David Darling

ON THIS QUIET AFTERNOON the cellist is traveling down the back roads of the soul in search of the dream of the common music. He is lulling us along with his performance of Bach's cello suites, tugging the curvaceous cello toward him like a lover, drawing the bow steadily across his four-stringed religion until a joyous shout resounds from the nearby cliffs: *Whales!*

Hearing that bluesy noun, he bounds out of the Huxley Conference Hall, carrying his cello as easily as a football, as reverently as a prayer. At the cliff's edge he leans against a wooden plank fence and takes a deep breath of the tonic ocean air as the whales glide by with elegant indifference. His imperturbability is impressive. This cellist knows a secret language, a music the rest of us along the cliff's edge cannot begin to comprehend. So he begins to improvise chords of eerie whale calls to summon them back.

The exquisitely sweet notes fly out from his cello like the utterances of angels in love.

Far below, no small miracle occurs.

The pod of whales pauses for a moment in their great migration down the Big Sur coast to Mexico. Then the great leviathans change direction, turning in water bronzed with kelp. They shoot water up through their spiracles and curl back into the bay where they lurk for a few minutes, flipping their flukes up at the source of what must sound to them like a distant cousin.

Seeing this, the cello player laughs like a rollicking Bodhisattva. He's overjoyed with the wily ways of the plummeting poets of the cool blue sea. Marveling at the never-ending wonders of certain kinds of blessed music, he plays on, sending deep blue whale notes out to sea until long after they've disappeared down the undulating coast.

Back in Huxley, the cellist takes up where he left off, with the Bach cello suites, playing the four-stringed religion that asks of anyone who ever listened in, "Did you get the thing you were looking for? Did you find the thing you mislaid when you were young, the forbidden thing that comes back? Did you find your way down the long blue road of your forgotten voice?"

Big Sur, California
October 1992

VIII

"If we don't change directions, we're going to end up where we're headed."
—REUBEN SNAKE

"Murphy, all life is figure and ground and a wandering to find home."
—SAMUEL BECKETT

"It is a strange thing to come home. While yet on the journey, you cannot at all realize how strange it will be."
—SELMA LAGERLOF

The Columns

NO MOON OVER THE Acropolis tonight. Only a faint silvery spotlight on the eastern columns of the Parthenon. I stand on the roof of the Hermes hotel after a day's exploration of the marmoreal world of classical Athens. A hard rain is falling over me, but I will not move. I need to gaze once more upon the spidery scaffolding and cranes that stand at ease after another day of lifting fallen and fractured stones.

I love these old sites the most when they're deserted. Now, in the slashing October rain, the temple appears to be guarding a majestic secret. Shivering in the blustery winds, I focus on the ingeniously tapered columns. My mind doesn't wander to the gold and ivory statues of Phidias, the magnificent perorations of Pericles, or the epiphanies of Euripides. Not the usual accounts of the glory that was Greece, but to an event recounted in few history books, a night during the 1821 War of Independence.

The Acropolis was held by the Ottoman army, and besieged by the Greek forces trying to regain the very symbol of their civilization. Running out of ammunition, the Turks began to demolish the 2200-year-old-marble columns of the Parthenon so they could extract the lead lurking inside. Fires for the lime-kilns lit up the night sky. Mortified, the citizens of Athens in the labyrinthine lanes below dispatched a messenger. They knew life would be insupportable without those columns connecting heaven and earth.

The runner dashed up the ancient winding road to the Acropolis, and when he arrived at the tent of the commanding officers he fell to one knee. *Don't touch the columns,* he implored them. *We will give you cannonballs.*

The kilns were shut down. That's all we know. Not if the battle resumed or how many Greeks died for beauty for at least the second time in their mythic history. Only that the kilns were shut down, which means the story has veered toward parable, a cautionary tale.

The rain flows down the fluted columns saved by a fathomless love of old stones and the ancient stories they hold within. I gaze out over the rooftops of nearby hotels and private homes. I am not alone. Hundreds of others are likewise contemplating the hypnotic effect of rain and light upon Athena's temple. I can't help wondering, which monuments would I be so horrified of losing that I would give cannonballs to the enemy?

No sense telling me it's only dead stone on that hill—I know it's not. I was dazzled by marble columns long before I was born.

I don't need to know how. I just need to admit it.

READING BOX SCORES WITH PYTHAGORAS

"Number is the measure of all things."
—PYTHAGORAS

I SIT IN SHIMMERING afternoon light in a seaside café on the island of Samos. I'm sipping a cool Pernod and savoring a plate of spicy Kalamata olives. Languidly, I glance back and forth from the front page of the *International Herald-Tribune* to the ancient harbor. The pine-scented air from the nearby mountains fills my lungs. Grapes from the vines of the pergola overhead are so close I can reach up and grab them. The cypress trees around the nearby church are lustrous as they tremble in the breeze. The pastel houses on the hillside glow as if in love with the ancient harbor.

On the docks, old sailors swab the keels of overturned boats with tar brushes, just as Homer described the Greek army doing before the 10,000 ships sailed for Troy. Iridescent fishing nets dripping with seaweed are mended by young men with tough hands and faraway faces. Opalescent light glints off the hillsides where tier upon tier of terraces climb to the sky.

Time in Greece is like time nowhere else. It is a palpable presence, a simultaneity. Many things are happening at once. The ancients used to say that time was the soul of the world. If so, what is timelessness, as this afternoon feels? Here it s still and still turning, and I have the oddest feeling that I can taste it.

At the moment there is a strong sea breeze. I must snap open the paper to reach the sports pages without losing half of it, then quickly scour the box scores so I can get a hit of those transportive numbers set in the sweet clarity of agate type.

Understand, I hate math. I have nightmares of being notified on some remote back road that I actually flunked high school algebra, which means I never graduated and my diploma is being revoked. I don't trust gambling and can't play the stock market. Despite my usual fear and loathing of numbers, my heart flutters when I find entire ballgames compressed into these tiny boxes. Their bold datelines announce the numinous names of green cathedrals: Fenway Park, Wrigley Field, Tiger Stadium. They describe performances with arcane but precise symbols: "ab," "r," and "h," which carry me away with visions of long flights of white baseballs over emerald green fields into dark blue skies. (My gaze plunges down into the cave of numbers, which I swear I can smell. Is it distant memories of the ballparks of my youth, or something more?)

This afternoon I'm thrilled that my hometown team has won. A bold "W" stands next to the name of that mean workhorse Jack Morris, and next to Big Daddy Cecil Fielder's credits I see 2 HRs (36) and 5 RBIs (110). Instantly I hear the roar of the crowd when he crashes two monster homers into the upper deck at Tiger Stadium, driving in five runs.

It's just like FDR said about reading the front pages to learn of man's tragedies and the sports pages to learn of his triumphs, or the great essayist Roger Angell, who wrote, "My obsessively fannish mind can't contemplate a summer without daily box scores."

For this fan, reading the scores and league standings and top ten batting leaders stats is a ride on the time continuum, connecting contemporary players with historical ones, the past and the present. Magical names transmigrate from one era to another. Different uniforms, but the same soul. Mystery plays and performances revealing the music of the spheres being hurled around geometrically perfect diamonds.

In a word, a Pythagorean pursuit. A love of plot and pattern.

If anybody in history would've understood this fascination of mine with the magic of numbers, it would be Samos' own hometown hero, Pythagoras, the most versatile player of his time, a man who played all the bases from mathematician to mystic and musician. Though we know next to nothing about him, we have his stats, his records. According to the announcers of his era, he was the first man to call himself *philosopher,* a lover of wisdom; the first to find a world of harmony and truth, order and elegance, symmetry and soul, in the world of numbers; the first to hear the music of the spheres. According to the mythographers, he discovered the relationship between numbers and harmony while listening to the rhythm of braziers hammering gold in a local shop.

On days like this, in soft lemony light, he taught that the secret nature of the cosmos could be experienced through sacred numbers. The signature of all things, he said in history's first description of an autograph, was drawn in earth, wind, and sky. The world isn't made up of matter, he insisted, as much as music, harmony, and the movement of the soul.

Every day his lessons are reenacted. This afternoon, fishermen's wives are counting the day's catch and registering the magical numbers in tiny scrawl. Old women in black mourning dresses sit quietly inside the shade of curio shops selling musty copies of Greek mythology and English detective novels. A couple of kids on a park bench count the pealing of bells from the white and blue chapel. At the table next to mine, a group of archaeologists argue heatedly about the sacred geometry involved in the construction of Hera's temple in the distant oleander groves.

The last of the trawlers pulls up dockside. The pilot and the boys along the dock are perfectly synchronized as ropes are tossed, tied, and fish gathered up on deck. A Greek Orthodox priest shambles by, hands folded behind him, gazing intently on the old flagstones, muttering prayers about the miracle of creation. Two young lovers curlicue around each other as they wait for a ferry to take them across the channel to Turkey and new adventures.

Everywhere, people find sweet order amidst the sour chaos. That's the task of artists, philosophers, mathematicians, and scorekeepers. All over the world it is the bottom of the ninth inning with the bases loaded and two out.

Every morning we must decide to pick up the bat and stride to the plate and keep our eye on the ball and take a swing and run like the wind—or sit it out. Every night we must decide to run—or not—on base paths that fit the curve of our time's wise rhythms.

On a humble fishing boat docked in front of me two young girls are playing chess. They are my Greek ideal of concentration. They watch the board and the old stone pieces and each other's faces. They have stopped time the best way they know how, and will spend the rest of their lives trying to remember how time stood still while they were young.

"Time," said Pythagoras, "is the soul of the world."

As if suspecting that image might be too abstract he added that time could also be visualized as a child playing a board game.

"And you can look it up," as the immortal Casey Stengel muttered after one timeless ballgame long, long ago.

Samos, Greece.
September 1992

The Magicians of Prague

THE NAME *PRAGUE* MEANS "threshold."

For 1000 years it has been a crenellated city of charlatans and conjurers, mystics and mountebanks, sages and sorcerers. A gothic tracery of a city, surreal under the creeping shadows of its portentous castle.

Long ago, astrologers saw the future in the flight of winged dragons and long-tailed comets. After selling his soul to the devil, the mad alchemist Faust was believed to have been carried away to perdition through a hole in the roof of his house near the old Slav monastery.

The only trees in the old Jewish ghettos were those painted on the walls. The great Czech fabulators tell us that the builder of the fantastic astronomical clock on the Old Town Hall was blinded to guarantee he couldn't duplicate it elsewhere. According to local folklore, a prisoner was once eulogized for playing his bittersweet violin while awaiting sentencing in the dungeon. Violin music, it turns out, is hangman's jargon for condemned men's tortured cries on the rack.

During the Soviet occupation, denounced people were airbrushed out of photographs, erased from history, struck from memory, and Prague was described as more desolate than the ruins of Pompeii. After the invasion in the spring of '68 certain authors were said to have been sentenced to the coal mines for the sin of insulting certain other government apparatchiks.

"It's the light, it's the goddamned light," a journalist tells me late one afternoon as we walk from his favorite tavern to the riverbank. "It's like holding a black crystal up against the moonlight. Sometimes the whole place feels bewitched, under a spell. I know it sounds like a cliché, but you always know that... *it's there.* Every time you walk the streets, your eyes can't help but climb the hill. It *draws* your eyes up there partly because it's so beautiful, partly because it seems like someone's always checking up on you."

After midnight, I wander with Jo through the infernal passages of Old Town. Turning a corner past an old timbered beer hall, we're startled to see the eighteen turrets of Tyn Cathedral looming above the medieval square. The sight is an enchantment. The slate towers seem lit from within, magically transformed by the soft gold light and passing clouds into a reeling vision of flight across the delirious night sky. *A gathering of magicians,* as the poet Nerval described them. Strange presences in the deranged towers seem to be convening to cast a spell over the city, stone sorcerers with the ensorceling power to lift the towers off the rooftops and escape the madness of the last thousand years.

On the walk back to our river barge hotel, the tower lights flicker out. We retrace our footsteps through the dark maze of medieval streets and emerge in the warm light of old gas lamps along the river.

The night uncoils. Restless clouds ramble down from the heavens and along the parapets of the castle. The magic of centuries is distilled. The magicians spread their black-wing capes over the shrouded stones. The castle appears to hover above the moon-silvered river standing watch over the enigma of night. There is something here at once deeply melancholic and ravishingly beautiful. In the wet fog I feel pulled like the puppets that crowd the windows of shops here, and the souls of the Czech people for centuries.

I'm teetering on the beveled edge.

Prague means *threshold.*

Krakatoa: East of Java

THE NIGHT IS SEETHING. The air is sulfurous. Steam plumes up from the dark core of the volcano. Moonlight dashes on and off the island's ash-covered slopes, as if signaling its voyage through the night. Off the portside of the ship the scimitar of moon rises over the jagged-edged silhouette of Anak Krakatoa, as local fishermen call it, the Son of Krakatoa, growing at the center of the caldera. More than a hundred years after the mighty explosion, it is still smoldering here in the Sunda Straits between Java and Sumatra.

We are bathed in the soft blue glow of the radar from the ship's bridge behind us, the ancient fires before us. It is nearly one in the morning. Our friends whisper in hushed tones, stilled by quiet reverence. You lean up against me in your red silk dress, and I hold you close and whisper softly as warm sea breezes blow your raven black hair back across your bare shoulders.

"Tell me again, tell me what happened here," you say. "Tell me *why* you dreamt about this place for so long."

Out at sea, phosphorus glimmers in patches of blue and white. It's like visible music rising from the deep. My thoughts wander to the scrolling pages of an obscure captain's journal. His entries from the time around the cataclysm reveal the strange beauty of disaster. Memory not mine, the great memory linked into because of reading, unreels back to the summer not of the legendary explosion of 1883 but to the summer of 1961.

"You're not going to believe this," I say, "but my earliest memory about Krakatoa is framed by the windshield of a turquoise 1960 Nash Rambler. I was only eight but I remember it vividly, being with my best buddy, Mark, and his family at the neon-ribboned Wayne Drive-In. I can still see the title of the movie flashing on and off around the bright white-and-yellow marquee advertising this awful, awfully unforgettable movie, *Krakatoa: East of Java.*"

I laugh at the long-submerged memory.

"A drive-in theater?" you josh. "C'mon—tell me the truth—"

"Which one, which truth?"

"No, the real truth"

"The real truth or the *reeling* truth? All right, It's one of the first movies I remember. I've been fascinated by volcanoes ever since, reading everything I could lay my hands on. Funny how a little nudge, even a B-movie, can get you started."

"Okay, I believe you. But tell me something *strange,*" you say in the crimson shadows of the volcano. "The *strangest* thing you remember."

"Well, *that's* a tall order," I reply, then scroll through my memory again.

"Did you know," I begin slowly, "that when Krakatoa exploded, lightning bolts leapt from thundercloud to thundercloud, from islands to the sky? Ash and pumice rose fifteen miles high from the raging caldron and formed a black cloud like a huge pine tree with branches of lightning. Pyroclastic flows of magma torched the island before tumbling into the sea, lifting 150-foot-high tidal waves that annihilated 165 coastal villages. Eardrums were shattered for twenty-five miles around the island. Shockwaves wrapped seven times around the globe like a giant cobra trying to squeeze the life out of it. Sonic booms were heard from as far away as the caves of Calais and Istanbul and the spas of Japan. Ash clouds of glassy lava bits circled the globe for two weeks, creating turn-of-the-kaleidoscope sunsets around the world for the next two years that inspired J. M. W. Turner's haunted battle paintings and untold other painters, poets, and lovers...."

"No, stranger than that."

"Well, for years afterwards local islanders told stories about men clutching weird logs as they were propelled miles inland that turned out to be stunned crocodiles."

"No, stranger..."

"Hmm. I do remember that one British captain reported the day after the explosion, 'There weren't even any ruins left....'

"Not even ruins?"

You are strangely silent.

"Not even ruins. Everything pulverized, obliterated, inundated, blown to smithereens in seconds."

An ancient stillness hovers in the night air. Silhouetted fins flecked with moonlight swim in the water below. Thunderheads gather overhead. Far out at sea, a blazing stamp of ball lightning streaks across the blue-black sky. The moment trembles with wild wonder, as if we'd briefly reached into a dark pocket of the past.

Embracing, we turn back to the smoldering island. We learn by being touched by fire. I know you know it is so.

Sunda Straits, Indonesia
December 1993

VERMEER'S DESIRE

I IMAGINE YOU LEANING through the doorway into the room of leather-bound chairs and varnished wall maps. With infinite patience, you wait for the morning sun to pour through the window, to illuminate the face of the woman in the blue dress reading a letter. Imperturbably, you wait until light comes shining through you and stillness descends and a sheer desire shines into the dark mystery of what is longing to be said.

Only now can you see how the woman appears to hold love itself in her hands. Your uncanny attentiveness imagines her *beyond* the moment, hinting at how she will soon finish the long-awaited letter, and reach down to feel the miraculous pulse of life in her gently rounding belly. In this lightly spun moment she dares to dream of her husband's ship far beyond the known world shown on the time-burnished map on the wall behind her.

I traveled all night long from Paris on a yawningly empty train to wander through these crowded galleries in distant Amsterdam, not to admire the virtuosity of one more Renaissance master, but to see how you translated the language of desire. I ventured on clankety old trams across this rain-slashed, cobblestone-souled city built on the wealth of the spice trade, to ask, as James Joyce once did, *Out of how deep a life does the work of art come?*

I'm here in rumpled travel clothes, feeling hungry and ornery, to see how you transformed the calamities of your own world with work of alchemizing tenderness. I'm roving from painting to painting to see how you kept pressing closer to the secret of sudden stillness in women.

Contemplating the exquisite tenderness of the kitchen maid pouring the long cool arc of milk out of the porcelain jug in *Woman Pouring Milk,* the nervous wonder of the woman holding *The Love Letter,* the cool radiance and deep red hues of the *Street in Delft* calms me like little else I've ever known. Yet gazing into your keenly observed world is also disturbing, a strange reminder of the sorrow that laces through all beauty.

I find in the faces of your women the realization that in each of us lives a secret life. You paint what you need others to see: *the real mirage,* the palpable depths below enameled surfaces. You remind us that the world is a canvas of many silences and that the painting of it can be a lonely thing.

Your genius is there, in your palette of crushed pearl light, in your angel-wing whites and lagoon blues that confront the secret wishes of our hearts. No man who wasn't haunted by the riddle of hidden fire could render such compassionate colors out of an unrelentingly gray world. The coruscating light in your work teaches us to peel back the edges of the palimpsest of everything we look at. In your work I can see that ordinary life, perceived with ardent desire, observed closely, retold simply, moves the soul like wind over the sea.

In front of *Woman in Blue Reading a Letter,* I'm imagining your last hours at work on this painting. Sullen twilight has tumbled down across the beetle-browed houses of Delft. You sit down on an oak stool in the doorway to the room of all textures. For the rest of the long gray evening you travel with the fingers of your eyes over the map, feel the fold of blue cloth on the table. You touch the woman's serenely still hands, and read from the cool white sheet of parchment to learn the language of her long mauve sighs.

This work touches me like no other. Knowing that some souls struggle to see the mystery below the surface inspires in me a sudden affection for the whole damned human race. I want to rush back across town and confess to the artist friend I'm staying with on an old houseboat in the frozen Keisergracht canal, *I have seen things today.* He'll nod knowingly, and bring out the warm brandy and stoke the old potbellied stove, and we'll talk late into the night about how your *strange painter's palette,* as Van Gogh described it, could capture the infinity of ordinary moments. We'll debate how you accomplished such *deeds of light,* as Goethe credited you with. We'll argue about how you could have created such *fresh and unique beauty,* as Proust remarked. We'll wonder how you coaxed your brush to conquer the centrifugal force of color the way a bird conquers the gravity of the earth. We'll ask what it was that drew your eyes so far inward, and how the son of a silk worker learned to see through the veil of all things?

We'll want to know how your being an art dealer and innkeeper, one who overheard the secrets of men and women at all hours of the black-tinted night, revealed those secrets on canvas?

Dusk draws down the day. Despite my long vigil I am reluctant to leave the gallery. The museum guard gestures, almost apologetically, at his watch, then holds up five fingers, signaling a few more minutes. I fancy that he sees something is happening to me, to the room that brightens when deep attention is paid.

I turn back to the *Woman in Blue* and feel the haunting of all great art. Something in this is looking at me, reminding me that art is memorable if it watches *you* watching *it*. How is this possible? Who knows, except everyone who has ever disappeared inside a canvas.

Ahem, cough. The five minutes flashed by like five seconds. I glance at the guard, and it's apparent in the sly arch of his eyebrows and shifts of mood whenever his eyes pass over the paintings. He lives with the mystery of painted light, knows that the beauty of a woman's face is holiness made visible.

There are so few places to learn the luminous lessons of tenderness.

Amsterdam, Holland
August 1987

CARVER IN PARIS

for Tess Gallagher

READING YOUR LEAN STORIES and your lank poetry makes me want to drop everything and charge outside to change the air filter on my '82 Mustang. Listening to you tonight inspires me to repaint the patio furniture, go fishing with a down-and-out friend, write seven poems about something I stopped seeing a long time ago, or describe a waterfall to a blind man.

Reenter the real world, as you'd say. Do some truth-telling.

That's what I heard you talking about when you talked about love in the rain-loud Paris bookstore back in the summer of '87. That's what I saw behind that home-from-hell look on your face that late afternoon when you followed your friends Richard Ford and Jonathan Raban to the front of the room and shyly read your poems. Your shyness took me by surprise, though not your wistfulness. You played the crowd like a jazz man, syncopating the moment itself. Ford's stories had been stiletto-sharp, especially the one about the guy who saw a bear catch on fire. Raban was coyly ironic when he regaled us about bumping into Paul Theroux in a small village along the coast of England—where their rivalry kept them from divulging anything about their journeys to each other.

But you broke open the game. In your poems you were as clear as a trout stream. You spoke as if love were the only force on earth worth talking about, our only chance to defeat death's hammerlock on our lives. You read as if the long slow alchemy of your recent life had changed life's wicked disappointments into something else almost palpable—the possibility of transcendence. You described "stupendous changes" as the only thing worth writing about. In a room where the tension of literary anticipation had frozen us unnaturally in our seats, calm soon ruled.

Then you read. Your stories. Trembling.

You kept flicking your hands, to stop them from trembling, or in a kind of phantom memory flicking away ashes from past cigarettes. We were there with you. On your quest for the real lurking behind the phony, in your world of fractured fables, your stories penetrated the darkness. In those bleak tales of characters gazing over their shoulders, the long slow suicides in faceless suburbs, the seedy menace of things in rustbelt factories, the forlorn world of sawmills, truck stops, diners, and bars, I heard the warning bells from life's dangerous railroad crossings. But I also saw hope for love's redemptive touch. I imagined changed expectations about shattered lives. I felt the heart's unruly ways.

Who knows why we do what we do, you humbly reminded me that afternoon, as I listened from the top of the staircase. Who can tell why we carry on after our hearts are splintered? Or why "I'm sorry" are the two hardest damn words to pronounce, and sometimes never make any difference anyway? Or why it's agonizing to give up the shot glass on the bedside table?

I heard your words as valentines to the utterly lost, messages in a bottle to places where passion was lying low, but lurking just fine behind the FOR SAIL signs advertising old boats on the curbs in front of boarded-up laundromats in the drizzly Northwest. I heard an ardent belief in the possibility of epiphany for the emotionally collapsed out there on the asphalt roads of America. I heard that poems and stories should stretch us, as when the inconsolable grief of the unfound dream is finally surrendered, and forgiveness and love begin to thrum in the heart, that there is always a chance for momentary redemption.

These were moments that got past my defenses.

"Get in, get out. Don't linger," you recommended to a

young Danish traveler that evening who asked for a little advice. "Endow things with immense, startling power," you said to another earnest poet, then gently reminded her of the necessary fire, for a story with lasting power. "Poke through the ordinary details of life," you urged to a note-taking professor from the Sorbonne, the worthwhile details of life to be found in the ashes of our lives. We must convince the reader that our characters "have seen things," as you said softly, with stop-breath sweetness, and the Paris rain purled down the window glass. "That's the soul of the story," you said, quoting Chekhov, your voice ringing with laughter and surprising me with your choice of the old touchstone word.

That's what I heard that night, from my perch next to the bookshelves featuring International Fiction, along with the accents from a United Nations of readers, and the steady pinging of rain on the Paris rooftops. The bookstore was jammed with backpackers, scholars, even waiters from nearby cafés. All of us listening intently to your "wordmusic," as Tess would say later on, words that revealed your "perfect pitch in the soul and spirit department." Plain and simple music that expressed your forgiveness of the world's wicked disappointments.

To the last question, the one all true writers disdain, about the purpose, if any, of stories was, you replied, "Stories are something glimpsed only for the – "

Then your voice trailing off at the end, drowned out by thunder.

Eight years later, I'm reading you again. By the time I finish your story about the blind man describing a cathedral, I'm feeling cleaved in half. A long-buried question slowly emerges, the one at the end of your reading that night at Odile Helier's *Village Voice Bookstore*. As if it were yesterday, I recall how we all strained to hear your answer through the guttering rain. I go frenetically searching through my undermemory of yellowing notebooks and journals, piled and stacked in the basement. Finally, in an old French blue grid notepad marked "1987," I find, at the bottom of a coffee-mottled page, the jumbled half-answer. But the last word is indecipherable. Flabbergasted, I squint and try to focus, then shift the notebook under a bright light.

"Music? magic? nuance? numinous?"

I can't make it out. I feel like a fool.

What's the word, Ray? What were we supposed to glimpse? What's the last word on stories?

I read the sentence out loud again: "Stories are something glimpsed only for the—" I reread it for the rhythms, the lunge forward into hidden meaning. I close my eyes and recall that afternoon with its exquisite melody of coffee aroma, pastry smells, and the burbling sound of rain on cobblestone that pervaded the room. I visualize the wolf-like gaze Ford cast toward you, and the owlish wisdom that danced across Raban's face. Moments that reenter the skin.

Then, as if foaming to the surface from a deep river, a word comes to me: *marvel*. I check it against the scribble on the notebook.

Somehow it fits: "*Stories are something glimpsed only for the marvel.*"

The sentence clicks in, the idea makes its way home, as if along "the new path to the waterfall," that you described that evening, as if in a dream we were all dreaming together on our last night on earth.

Paris, France
September 1989–August 1997

The Night I Drove Kerouac Home

*"Anyway, the time has come to explain
the Golden Eternity..."*
—JACK KEROUAC

THE AMBER LIGHTS FLICKER past as we slip across the long stretch of the Golden Gate Bridge. The twin towers loom above us like colossal sentinels. Foghorns moan across the bay.

Jan stares mournfully at the *neon redly twinkle* of the *white city of San Francisco on her eleven mystic hills,* as her father described it on the long roll of butcher paper that became the notorious runaway novel.

I tell her how much I was moved by her story at Gerry Nicosia's dinner party of how she came to read her father's work. Through the haze of her fourth dialysis treatment of the day she had described how she was twelve years old and in the hospital for her problem with alcohol. Her doctor noticed the name "Kerouac" on her medical chart. On a hunch, he asked if she was related to the famous writer. She shrugged. He asked if she'd read any of his books. Petulantly, she shook her head no. A few minutes later, he returned with a copy of *On the Road,* which he handed to her, saying, "Read it. It might help."

She had told us all this with a tang of regret. "I was up all night," she'd said with end-of-the-world weariness. "By the time I finished I finally understood why my father was never around while I was growing up."

As we pass under the mighty towers of the bridge, I confess I didn't get around to reading it until I was twenty-two. I was lost and languishing in London, working for a professor of literature who thought I needed a jolt to get me, well, on the road again. From his library he pulled down a leather-bound edition of *Seven Pillars of Wisdom* by T.E. Lawrence, a history of the English Secret Service—and a first edition of her father's *On the Road*.

"Your dad's book was a kind of hurricane for me," I tell her. I plunge ahead into No Man's Land, trying to convey the way I felt when all those wind-blown words and bebopping rhythms helped catapult me around the world. Emboldened, I tell her how his *holy goof zany lunacy words* helped made me want to write.

A wry smile crosses her face. "Everyone remembers the first time they read that one," she says with sudden childlike exuberance. Her eyes flash with momentary delight. Then she asks, "But where are they *now*?"

Her fingers drum nervously on the window molding of the car door. She seems ravaged by the mean mix of health and literary problems—the struggle to finish her third novel, and the bitter fight over the literary estate. She looks as if now she's only longing for the quiet anonymity of her motel room.

Jan's attention drifts away, as she gazes out at the silver wake left by a ship far out at sea. Her sad face is cast in an eerie silhouette that slowly shape-shifts into the spitting image of her father.

For one phantasmagorical moment he's leaning back in the passenger seat of my knockabout '82 Mustang: peripatetic, poetic, and beat, to paraphrase the playwright. Jack ever-lovin' Kerouac, slick and slack in his brown leather jacket, the original coolhunter, wistful in his world of hurt, caught in some dharma bum time-warp between love affairs, tumbledown motels, ramshackle bars, and the long, loping back roads of *bluer than eternity Wildamerica*.

In this *one crazy Roman candle* instant he's staring across the dark bay, longing for the loony locomotion of the open road, digging the long blues line of the distant lowing foghorn on Alcatraz, marveling at the glorious memories of driving with his bud Neal Cassady, the holy goof himself, in an old juddering jalopy under a night-gliding moon, past *groves of lonesome redwood trees,* over boundless plains and beyond the great lakes, listening for the bone-deep cries of jazzmen who might *raise men's souls to joy.* All the while they're reading from the bluesy manuscript of night like a couple of Zen lunatics, mad-dashing into the heart of strange roads at the crackling of the blue dawn.

Go moan, go moan for man, go moan, I hear in the jeweled weirdness.

Her smoky voice lures me back. "So I guess my father wasn't around because he was roaring back and forth across the country, driving like a madman, then sitting in a room for months writing about it. He didn't seem to have time for anything or anybody else. Even me. When I figured that out I was finally able to forgive him."

I ask if she has any other memories of him. With disarming shyness she says, "I remember him coming into my room when I was a little girl and whispering '*Shush*' to my little sisters so he wouldn't wake me. But that's all, that's all I remember until my only other visit with him when I was in my teens.

"It's not much," she seems to conclude with a dash of her father's *doomtragic* inflection, "but I'll take whatever I can get."

I downshift for the toll booth, and root around in my vest pocket for some change.

"I'm so tired," Kerouac's daughter says with her father's *end of the continent sadness.* Her voice is stretched on the rack of night. "I don't expect to be around forever, you know."

Her voice seems to catch in her throat, as it did earlier in the night at Nicosia's when she told the story of the time she visited her father's house in Florida in 1994. She seemed frail and vulnerable in the telling, but strengthened when she said she felt "at home." After serving tea, the new owner, a relative of Jack's last wife, asked if he could get her anything else, and in her inimitable way she said exactly what was on her mind and in her eyes. She said she'd love to have her father's roll-top desk.

"That's the way the cookie crumbles, Jan," was the mocking response.

She owned virtually nothing of her father's. She was crushed then, and now, in the retelling, still reeling from the stolen time.

Remembering those words, I thought that she had come to live by her father's *go moan for man* words as if they were mad prophecy.

We pass like phantoms through the toll booth, and drive on through the marbleized mist shrouding the Presidio, past the darkly floating boats of the Marina. Her father's words came back to me, summoned by the force of his daughter's loneliness: knowing how *happiness consists in realizing that it all is a great strange dream,* and by the city that inspired *a thousand dreams of zest,* as we suddenly reached the bright and garish lights of the Holiday Inn on the Wharf.

I drop her off with promises of looking her up in Albuquerque someday. She nods grievously, then vanishes into the *motel, motel, motel loneliness* her father knew all too well. I imagine *locomotives wailing all night long* as she closes the door behind her.

Go on, press on, regardless. *Everything depends on those who go on,* I want to say through the window. But I let her go, remembering her old road man father's words: *But, no matter, anyway, the road is life....*

San Francisco
June 1995

Les Voyageurs

"Not long ago on a far trail I dared to roam…"
—TRADITIONAL VOYAGEUR SONG

IT'S BEEN A LONG time since I spent a night underneath the stars.

After thirty-five years I'm back on the lake, reclaiming a lost piece of myself, and attempting to understand one that is unfolding into the future. I haven't been here since 1960, when my father drove the family up from Detroit in the family Falcon, the air frosted with the silence of a feud. The two-week trip was supposed to be a relaxing summer vacation, but also "instructional," as Dad used to say. "Family heritage time," he called it. He was adamant that his children should know how he spent his boyhood. Working on my great-grandfather Charlemagne's farm up in Verner, Ontario, meant sixteen-hour days tending to the vast fields of oats, barley, and potatoes, baling hay, milking cows at dawn. If Charlemagne was in a good mood, Sundays might mean fishing for bluegills and sunfish or gathering buckets of blueberries on giant glacial rocks frequented by brown bears.

Back then, the journey took two days. Our only stops were in Windsor to have our photographs taken in front of Cousineau Street; Stratford, a mecca for Shakespeare lovers; campsites where explorers Hudson and La Salle camped; and a few battleground sites from the war of 1812. It was summer school all the way to Lake Nipissing, with a little family sing-along of *Frère Jacques* and *Alouette* tossed in for comic relief.

Once there, we stayed in a log cabin perched on an enormous

glacier boulder overlooking the pristine lake. We caught so many fish Dad couldn't keep our lines wormed long enough to cast his own. One time he forced my brother Paul and me to watch an old friend of the family sever the neck of a snapping turtle. It plopped loudly into a bright white porcelain bowl, followed by a sickening green gush of the turtle's recent meals of small fish. Dad thrust a steel rod into my quavering hand and the slimy, severed head *snapped* its jaws right around it. I screamed to high heaven, and my little brother burst into tears. The sudden lurch scared us out of our wits, but my father and his friend found it uproariously funny.

Now it's the summer of 1995 and Dad's been gone ten years. I'm paddling a canoe with Jo across fifty kilometers of the French River and down into Lake Nipissing. Along with seventeen distant cousins in nine other canoes, we're reenacting one arc of the "settling" voyage that my great-great-great-grandfather Cyril Monette made by paddling seventy-five miles a day from distant Quebec. Once there, he set up his farm on land he found with help from his Indian river guide, Mosquito, and married my great-great-great-grandmother Odile, who my father told me was half-Indian. Our Canadian Gothic archive contains a photograph of them together in front of their log cabin. Cyril is long-bearded and implacable, Odile an upright and fearless-looking soul.

The first night, we camp on one of the lake's innumerable boulder islands. Before the cooking fire, Michel, who is paddling with his sixteen-year-old son, Marcel, patiently helps me piece together the family saga. Cyril and Odile's twelve children sired another seventy. One of them, Olive, married my grandfather, Horace. One century later there are 64,000 descendants splayed out across Canada, America, and Europe.

"Long winters, long nights, eh?" he winks.

I ask how many there were in his family.

"Oh, I'm one of twenty-nine," Michel says nonchalantly. "Several sets of twins. But my parents didn't like odd numbers, eh? So they adopted one more baby to make an even thirty."

On the second night I spend some time around the fire

with my distant cousin Raymond Guy, who with his wife Louise founded a French-American school in Sudbury. They're passionate canoeists, glad to pass on the old traditions of the river. From them I learn that "calm-nerved voyageurs" paddled fifteen to eighteen hours a day in handmade birch canoes, could carry 400 pounds of goods on their backs, read the smoke wreaths sent up by Indians along the river while canoeing, dance on their hands, and were fabulous fiddlers. They often sang to synchronize their strokes, and they kept time with their paddles.

The next day we weathered a fierce open-lake storm. That night, after my fellow *voyageurs* have gone to bed, I read the old chronicles in front of the fire and I learn that my ancestors wore red feathers in their hats and kept "sprightly French conversation," and during the long winters in the forts gained a reputation for being "an effervescent race of men." As one chronicler wrote in the eighteenth century, "No portage was too long, fifty songs could I sing." I also learn that my father's fondness for origin names may have been hereditary, after all. According to the book, these wayfarers had a tradition called *the namings.* They were great wordsmiths, describing everything they came upon in the vast and mighty land, from lakes and rivers to beetling crags, mountain peaks, and strange land formations, "labeling everything that came within their ken," as another pen of the day had it.

On the last night, Jo is alternately flushed and pale through our campfire dinner. We huddle together by the fire to stay warm and talk about the day's voyage through the lightning storm, but she is tiring quickly and she excuses herself, saying she needs to sack out. I hug her and kiss her and promise to follow her as soon as I get in a little stargazing. My eyes follow her shadowy movements inside our lantern-lit tent, and my heart feels the inscrutable tides of love pulling me toward her.

But I need time alone on this sacred rock.

Stoking the fire under the skies of my ancestors, I begin to feel the immensity of my connection with this land, this water. The constellations rotate in the dark heavens above. I imagine my great-great-great-grandfather Cyril camping on this same boulder, before claiming the remote and recently burned land no one else wanted.

Over the lake flashes a reddish-blue streak of lightning. From afar comes the anguished cry of a loon. Staring into the fire, I think I see the face of my great-grandfather Charlemagne, then see him rolling cigarettes with one hand, setting forth across Ontario in his canoe and setting fur traps here on his way north to Thunder Bay. Peals of thunder echo in the night. I remember my grandfather Horace's stories about running the rails clear to British Columbia, working the winters there as a dynamiter in the mines, then returning to marry and spend his summers here grilling the catch of the day for his five sons and daughter. Then my own father's face appears in the fire. He's all of thirty-two years old, still young and handsome, wondering where his life is headed, trying to name the unlived life in his soul, longing to imagine his own adventures in the footsteps of Lewis and Clark.

It's a splendid night. The moon glimmers overhead. Shooting stars skate across the strangely familiar Canadian night. I feel luxuriously alive. An uncanny feeling glides through me like a perfectly stroked oar. It occurs to me for the first time that I am the son of land-and-lake-forged men and women.

Now I am moving into an unknown world with a sweet woman at my side, whose hands lightly rub the curve of her belly where a new life has been growing inside her for the last five weeks, cell by cell, synapse by synapse, heartbeat by heartbeat.

I am listening hard for the name of the journey the three of us are embarking upon, the grit and feel of the unfolding future.

I am talking to my ancestors who camped here long ago, and I am praying for courage on my next voyage, and his.

IX

"The light from the oncoming train focuses the mind,"
—BRUCE SPRINGSTEEN

"A ship in port is safe; but that is not
what ships are built for."
—GRACE HOPPER,
COMPUTER SCIENTIST
AND U.S. NAVY REAR ADMIRAL

"Dreaming while I drive
Dreaming back to another time
We all live so many lives
I'm dreaming while I drive."
—RB MORRIS

The Way That Is No Way

BY THE TIME THE old sage turned 160 years old, he'd grown weary of the corruption of the ruling class in palace life. No one listened anymore to the wisdom of the old ways that he had spent a lifetime preserving in the archives. They scoffed at the wisdom he'd winnowed from the most venerable books left behind by the ancestors. Wearied of the vanity of court life, he knew there was only one thing that would bring him peace of mind. Like the Taoist masters before him, he had to leave the velvet cage of the Middle Kingdom and spend his remaining years in the hardscrabble mountains far to the west.

The old philosopher quietly left late one night under a sceptered moon, riding in a rickety chariot pulled by a lumbering black ox. This would be his last journey. He rolled on for many days through the dangerous trail called the Han-Ku Pass. When he finally reached the last border gate he was unceremoniously stopped by a young soldier named Yin His, who was called the Keeper of the Pass, and who claimed to be less than surprised by his arrival. The border guard had been reading the signature of all things in the clouds, watching the flight of birds, counting the rainfall. The omens predicted everything.

"You are about to withdraw yourself from sight," the Keeper of the Pass said to the Keeper of the Archives. "I pray you compose a book for me."

The wizened archivist pulled at his white beard, adjusted the reins of his chariot, biding his time. He had not expected this. He had disciplined himself to take refuge in *not* speaking, having written that "Silence is a great source of strength." Sometimes speaking was the way, sometimes not. He was tempted to say that "Those who speak do not know; those who know do not speak."

But that would have been less than compassionate, the virtue he believed in the most, next to simplicity and patience.

Of this hinged moment he knew that whatever he said would not be the way, that the way of the world could not be said. *Have faith in the way things are,* he wanted to say. *The way is the way of* wu wei, *the way of not doing but being.* It took him 5,000 characters to not say so, in a work compiled by the Keeper of the Pass, later called the *Tao Te Ching*, and credited to the "Old Man," Lao Tzu.

The old sage could not *not* have known this. He shrugged his shoulders, adjusted his courtly robes, and left for the farthest reaches of the west, rolling where there was no where there.

The Keeper of the Pass told those that followed that the old man's chariot wheels left no tracks, no way, no how.

Night Train

THE MIDNIGHT MOON WAS full, lighting up the slick iron rails as I stepped across the tar-blackened crossties, reveling In my boyish escape plan, far from the furies unleashed at home when my father returned from the strip bars near the Ford Rotunda smelling of J & B and trouble.

I'm twelve going on eighteen, longing to prove myself to myself. I'm dying to take a running leap into the gaping door of a boxcar, as I've seen dark-hooded hoboes do a million times, usually at dusk. I've seen them counting the seconds on their fingers — one, two three —as they calculated the lunging speed of the rattling freight train before they made their dangerous leap, believing the risk of severed legs and skull-cracking yard goons was worth it for the ride to freedom.

The night air trembles as the train slows down for the Howe Road traffic crossing. It rattles past the Minnesota Mining factory, the green dream of Little League fields, and the yard of rusting school buses. I look up in time to see a lone hobo clambering over the roof of a refrigerator car, his shoulders shaking with mischievous energy, his sneaky road-wise, rail-worthy, risk-defiant smile hinting that my time is coming, that I too can get away before every place becomes the same place.

I time my jump as the train chugs down the tracks. I leap through the open door and onto the wooden slat floor of the boxcar.

Terrified, alone, exhilarated.

We pass over the crossing, I see the flashing red lights and hear the warning bells. I'm beside myself with excitement but disappointed that I'm all alone. No friend to elbow and give a boyish thumps-up and shout with glee. I pace back and forth over the rumbling floor as the train picks up speed, passing the old grain store, the Wayne Drive-In, and the old Willow Run Ford Plant, which my Uncle Don helped retool to build tanks and planes for the war. The train reaches the sprawling fields outside of town, and the fear of the unknown world stretching out before me becomes too much. The creaking train slows down for another crossing. I leap off, falling on my shoulder, rolling over and over like I've been tackled on the 40-yard line.

The pain is delicious, the taste of my first adventure.

Dusting myself off, I turn to walk home and notice the glint of a smile on the face of another hobo hiding in a shadow-fretted boxcar. His expression is as mysterious as the strange marks of hobo code he and his brothers and sisters leave behind on trees and fences. This one signals something like, *All you need to know, kid, is the secret schedule that reveals the key to your dream of escape. You can hear it in the lonesome call of the train whistle for who knows where, who knows how. You can see it in the blur of wheels clacketing along the tracks for the meetings with the unmet friends. There is another world, kid, you can bet your sweet ass there is another world.*

Crossing over the front lawn of the house of my growing up, I slink past the porch down the driveway and sneak in through the back door, careful not to let it slam behind me. Finally in bed, the sheets feel cool and crisp. My heart is pounding like one of those pneumatic hammers I've seen the railroad workers use on the tracks. I am happy to be home, but already planning my next escape.

For the rest of the night, I listen for the lonesome whistle of the mystery train bound for nowhere and everywhere. I look for the signal of another life flickering over the bruised-boxer sky of my hometown. The moment blazes like a steam loco-motive's firebox, glows like a lantern swinging off the back of a wobbling caboose, fades to a vanishing point.

It's all happening at once — the past, present, and future — and it's still happening all at once, even now, the long, long now.

A Parable about Lamplighters

"DURING THE SEVENTEENTH CENTURY," says the old bookstore owner, "this building was a Latin Quarter monastery with a curious custom. The most eccentric monk was named the official lamplighter of the *quartier*. Every night he lit the lamps so those who risked a menace-fraught night walk might survive. Every morning he extinguished them with a copper candle snuffer."

The face of the owner of The Rag and Bone Shop of the Heart is as burnished as the leather-bound volumes of Joyce, Proust, Miller, and Nin he keeps in the rare-book room on the second floor. But George Whitman doesn't think of himself as a writer, though he likes telling beautiful young girls who flock there he's the lost grandson of Walt Whitman.

When pressed George describes himself as a guardian of a sanctuary, poised halfway between heaven and earth. He thinks of book lovers not as strangers, but as angels in disguise; not as customers, but as unmet friends. He is what Malraux called *engagé*, fully committed to the struggle against a future without books.

The wobbly sounds of a French accordion waft up from the cobblestoned plaza. Slivers of lively late afternoon light dance across the leather bindings of the books surrounding us in the fabled Writer's Room, where Anaïs Nin, Laurence Durrell, and Henry Miller once lived. When his assistant asks for a rare book, George leaps to his feet, pulls a red-bound volume from a sagging shelf near the mullioned window. He caresses the bindings and bounds downstairs with the leather-bound ball of light in his hands.

"I'm like that monk," he says with hang–dog sadness. "For the last fifty years, it's been my job as a bookseller to bring a little light into the world. My books are luminous. Their purpose is to gladden the heart."

Smiling, he disappears down the worn wooden staircase, as if expecting a host of angels who've appeared with an order for an illuminated volume of the "Song of Solomon."

So they'll have something to read for the rest of eternity.

The Dangers of Reading All Night

WHEN OLD MR. LYNCH reached the top rung of the ladder he saw the book he had been searching for wedged between the towering stack of books he was leaning against and the rafters of his grandmother's roof.

The ladder swayed precariously as he stood on his tiptoes and reached for the book. He tugged gently, and as he pulled it out he dislodged a dog-eared copy of Hawthorne's *Twice-Told Tales*, which fell and thumped on the floor far below. He tugged again and watched as a moldy edition of Macaulay's *Lays of Ancient Rome* and a rare volume of *Prehistoric Guernsey* fell from their perches and bounced off the ladder on their way down to the floor of the attic. One last time he pulled, and out flew a copy of *Look* magazine with the fetching photo of Marilyn Monroe on the cover. Foolishly, he lunged for it and nearly toppled over.

Damn, he thought. *I've been looking for that magazine for years.*

Clouds of book dust billowed around him. The ladder swayed dangerously, and he felt a wave of nausea roll through him. Relieved, he steadied himself and held up the book that he had been lusting after for years so he could read the title on the leather binding: *The History of the Decline and Fall of the Roman Empire, Volume VI*, by Edward Gibbon. The gold letters gleamed in the faint light. His heart pounded with anticipation. Over the years he'd read the first three volumes of Gibbon's masterpiece, but then he'd lost track of the final one with the English historian's controversial conclusion. But he couldn't find it for the life of him, like so much else in the sprawling mansion.

This is why you never throw anything out, he said to himself.

You never know when you're going to have to know something.

Mr. Lynch clutched the book in his hand like a long-lost friend.

Slowly, he made his way down the ladder, trying not to knock over anything else, which was easier said than done. All around him were towering piles of books, newspapers, magazines, pamphlets, telephone books, old Rudy Vallee LPs, horseracing forms, baseball and football yearbooks, Sears Roebuck catalogs, and car repair manuals. They were haphazardly stacked from floor to ceiling in the shadow-strewn attic. He could hear the cooing of pigeons on the roof above him, the scritching of mice underneath the floorboards below, and his own throat-clutching breathing.

When Mr. Lynch reached the bottom of the ladder he turned his body sideways so he could thread his way through the labyrinth of books to the pull-down stairs that led him back to the main part of the house and his puce-colored overstuffed reading chair.

Standing in the hallway, Mr. Lynch had to catch his breath before navigating his way through the cramped passage into the night-darkened parlor. If he squinted, he could just make out the light from the Tiffany lamp. Here, there, and everywhere were books, books, and more books. They rose from the swaybacked hardwood floors to the flaking plaster rosettes on the ceiling. He sucked in his ample stomach and slithered down the hallway, his face brushing up against the loose-leafed magazines, and yellowed newspapers, and hundreds of read and unread books.

Each unread one felt like a reproach.

Someday I'll make a list, he vowed, *so I can find them when I want them and want them when I find them.*

Sharp slants of light shot across the house, revealing the lost world of books he'd been hoarding since his grandmother died. He glanced around the room and felt a riot of emotion roiling in his heart. It was the thrill of books to remember mixed in with the dread of books already forgotten.

The air was thick with dust, bird droppings, and mold from

the thousands of books he'd been hoarding since he was a kid. Somewhere he'd read that he should be careful about mold growing on those old books, but he'd never gotten around to dusting, much less cleaning everything with vinegar and water, which was supposed to be the only solution.

Twenty more yards, he calculated. *I know I can make it.*

With a grunt, he shoved aside several unopened boxes of God-knows-which books. Each box was a reminder of the long walks he'd made all over Oakland and Berkeley, to every library, bookstore, and Salvation Army outlet. Finally, he was able to creep the last few yards into the musty parlor, where his reading chair waited for him, the last gasp of empty space in the boarded-up mansion where he had been hiding for years. Nine square feet of freedom where sat his overstuffed reading chair. Smiling wanly, he changed his old loafers for his thread-bare slippers and allowed himself to fall down into the chair. He never wanted to get up again. Here was his home within a home.

A single blade of amber light slanted in through a hole in the wall next to the front door. That was the tell-tale sign that the street lights in front of the house had flickered on. It was at least nine o'clock. The soft light landed on a pallet full of his grand-mother's antiques he couldn't bear to part with. He looked long-ingly at her old Victrola, the Singer sewing machine, a Detroit Electric stand-up radio, a pallet full of steamer trunks, and books, books, books, and more books. The room was starting to look like one of those barns that sold antiques he'd once seen in West Marin when he was a kid. Maybe he should have a yard sale? He could use the money to buy the 1933 second edition of the Oxford dictionary he'd always wanted. No, then people would want to start poking around inside the house, looking for more books, and this and that. Not worth the trouble.

All I want to do is read, he muttered to himself as he settled down into his trusty reading chair, a puce-colored piece of furniture only a grandmother and a book-hound could love. Mr. Lynch stared at the heavy tome in his hand and quickly calculated the number of chapters he could read before dawn.

Now this is heaven, he thought. This was what he lived for, the anticipation of a languorous night of reading.

Smacking his lips with glee, he cracked open the Gibbon book and began to revel in Rome's slow descent into madness.

Near dawn, the hour of the wolf, *le temps du loup*, as his French-Canadian grandmother used to call it, he was startled by a loud creaking sound. *The house settling in*, he thought, annoyed that his reverie had been broken. Moments later came a muted roar.

Probably another stack of newspapers falling down.

Out of the corner of his eye, he saw the fifteen-foot-high pile of *National Geographic*s that loomed over him bulge and shift. He considered ratcheting his old bones out of the chair and rearranging them, but his eyes were drawn back to his book by the centripetal force of the story he had been dying to read.

Near dawn, Mr. Lynch awoke from a dream-addled sleep. *The Decline* was open to a passage in Chapter LXIX that he tried to read through bleary eyes: "Vicissitudes of fortune, which spares neither man nor the proudest of his works, which buries empires and cities in a common grave."

A common grave?

Was that where he had left off?

Where was I? he wondered. He riffled through a few more pages to Chapter LXXI and read, "All that is human must retrograde if it does not advance." *Ah...*

His last riffled thought was, *One chapter to go. Tomorrow, I'll finish up.*

He never knew what hit him.

The first to topple were the *National Geos*, then the six volumes of Proust's *In Search of Lost Time*, then twenty-two books out of the 108 that his boyhood hero, Ray Bradbury, had published. Each pile that fell triggered a paper avalanche. A history of paperweights toppled over, followed by an analysis of the drinking habits of the French *voyageurs* in the Yukon. The avalanche continued.

A wooden crate marked STROH'S BEER was filled with his collection of Topps baseball cards, which his mother had told him she'd thrown out when he didn't go to the prom in his senior year of high school. When the box hit the arm of Mr. Lynch's reading chair it broke open and out flew hundreds of baseball cards, like a magician's doves released from his stovepipe hat.

Strangely, the very woman Mr. Lynch used to refer to as a "Nosy Parker" was the neighbor who smelled something putrid coming from his house and took the time and trouble to call the police. When Officer O'Reilly from the Oakland police department arrived at her house he jotted down a few routine notes and nodded wearily at the ramshackle Victorian mansion next door.

"Okay, I'll check it out, Mrs. Garvey," he said. "Probably just a dead skunk under the house. You did the neighborly thing by calling us."

Stepping onto Mr. Lynch's front porch the officer yelled out his name. No response. He tried to jimmy open the front door, but it wouldn't budge. He found an axe in the truck of his police car and used it to claw an opening large enough to reach the inside handle. When he coaxed it open, the door burst off its hinges and he was

knocked off his feet by a deluge of books. He shook his head in disbelief and pushed his way through the door and was flabbergasted to see the mountains of junk. He used the axe to hack his way through it like a tunneling miner, advancing slowly in the direction of the God-awful stench in the center of the parlor.

An hour later, he found Mr. Lynch buried with his nose in a thousand books. One by one, Officer O'Reilly pulled them off the bewhiskered old man. With no little disdain, he tossed aside bestsellers and obscure works, old copies of *Sports Illustrated* and scattered volumes of the *Encyclopedia Britannica*, cartons of *Popular Mechanics* magazines from the 1940s, and a Manhattan phonebook that felt heavy enough to be a wheel stop for a 747.

Five days, more or less, Mr. Lynch had been rotting there, the coroner said later. When the media got a whiff of the story, Mrs. Garvey told the reporter who knocked on her door that the saddest part of the whole sorry episode was that the "old hoarder," as she called him, had never returned all those books and magazines to the libraries where he'd borrowed them.

"Imagine the late fees Mr. Lynch piled up," she added mournfully. "If he'd paid them, our local library could've stayed open. Word on the street is that he just kept telling the librarian he lost the books. She must have felt sorry for him."

The reporter politely asked her if she'd ever been inside her neighbor's house. She said no. Why bother? I can't read." She didn't think they had anything to talk about.

Berkeley, California 1989

BLUE PEARL

I'M RIDING MY BIKE back and forth, up and down East-lawn, the shadow-strewn street in front of our house, when I hear my dad yelling, "Get in here. It's the Apollo 11 mission. They're landing, they're landing on the moon! Get your ass in here. This is history."

"Okay, okay," I mutter. No sense arguing when he's in one of his historical moods, telling me to read this, read that, look at this, look at that, remember this, remember that. I leap off the bike, fling it down on the front lawn, bound up the steps onto the porch and dash inside the house, slamming the screen door behind me. Usually, my parents would yell at me for banging the door, but not tonight. I'm just in time to see a barely visible Lunar Module setting down on the moon's surface, just in time to hear Neil Armstrong say in a static-stricken voice, "Houston, Tranquility Base here. The Eagle has landed."

The old Philco television glows in the dark living room. I feel like I'm walking into church just as mass has started. My mom and dad and Gramma Dora are leaning forward in their chairs trying to make sense out of the weirdly out-of-focus picture on the TV set, but it's hard to know what we're looking at.

Seconds later, another voice comes on, this one clarion clear, from Mission Control, in Houston, "Roger, Tranquility, we copy you on the ground. You got a bunch of guys about to turn blue. We're breathing again."

As they breathe, so do we.

Quietly, I flop down on the carpet and flip my baseball cap in the corner. Hours go by. My mom serves us TV dinners. We play a few games of scrabble. Finally, we hear Armstrong saying he is going to open the hatch of the module and step outside. Now we watch him step out of the hulking safety of the space capsule and edge down the ladder of the space module, and wait to hear the first words from the first man on the moon.

I know I'm supposed to watching history in the making, as my dad's been telling me all week, but to me the picture on the screen looks like an old negative that I saw at a photography exhibition with him down at Greenfield Village in Dearborn.

"Listen, Philip, listen," he insists. "This picture is coming from—" His voice catches, he tries to regain control, then adds, "From 240,000 miles away. Imagine that."

There is wonder in his voice as he keeps muttering to himself and sipping from his glass of J & B; he is more reverential than I've ever seen him, even in church. I'm only sixteen but I'm restless. Part of me would rather be riding my bike. I'm trying to listen like a good son, so I focus on the screen despite the grainy image and the crackling tinfoil voices, and the tension in the room. I am curious what Armstrong will say. Everybody's wondering. We even talked about it in science class.

Letting go of the ladder, Armstrong steps onto the moon.

"That's one small step for man," he says, all gravelly, "one giant leap for mankind."

The far-flung words the whole world has been waiting for, the first words spoken on another world. And I don't have a clue what he's talking about.

I'm about to ask my dad what the astronaut meant when my gramma clucks her tongue and whispers something to my mother, who is hovering near the kitchen door.

"It looks like a big, blue pearl, doesn't it, Rosie?"

Blue pearl? I'm lying on the rug, leaning on my elbows, staring at the TV, wondering what in heaven's name she's talking about. I want to shout at her that if anything the moon looks like a big, white pearl hanging there in the sky. But I hold back, remembering my mom telling me that gramma's losing her marbles. Mom folds her arms and puts her forefinger to her lips to warn gramma to be quiet for another minute.

My father shushes them, pointing to Walter Cronkite who

has come back on the screen. "Listen, listen..." he repeats in his reverie.

The person regarded as the most trusted man in the country leans across his desk, takes off his black horn-rim glasses, and gleefully rubs his hands together. "Man on the moon!" he says, his voice cracking. "Oh, boy!" He pushes himself away from his desk to collect himself, repeats Armstrong's words, "The Eagle has landed," as if to reassure the entire world that America has landed safely on the moon, so we can stop worrying. That's what uncles do; they reassure us. Uncle Walter turns to Wally Schirra, an early astronaut and now a TV analyst, "Wally, say something. I'm speechless."

My dad's all choked up. "Rosemary, can you fill my drink? Three ice cubes. And can you bring Philip a bottle of Hires root beer?"

"Rosie, Rosie..." my grandmother whispers.

To me, she's acting like she's in the confession booth down at Sacred Heart in Dearborn. My mom slips back into the room like a maid, carefully holding my dad's favorite whiskey glass with the usual three ice cubes, and sets it on the TV tray next to his armchair.

Strangely, Gramma Dora says louder than anything she's said all night, "It must be like touching the face of God, Rosie."

I'm about to say something smart-alecky when my mom responds to my gramma's unexpectedly philosophical comment, "That's sacrilegious, Ma."

Then I see my gramma's chin trembling. She doesn't really support the space program. "I just don't believe in it, Philip," she said earlier that day. "If God meant us to fly he would've given us wings." But she seems caught in the moment like the rest of us. I've only seen her like this at mass, during communion, her eyes glazed, raised in prayer.

An out-of-this-world image resolves on our eerily glowing television. Armstrong bounds across the Sea of Tranquility and into the ocean of legend on humanity's first moonwalk.

My father says, "Up there no one knew if his foot would sink—or not—in the soil of the moon."

Together, we watch Armstrong bouncing on the trampoline surface of the moon. I'm getting goose bumps watching Armstrong and then his flight mate, Buzz Aldrin, following behind him, edging down the ladder, saying, "Beautiful, beautiful, isn't it? Magnificent flight, magnificent desolation."

I can barely believe my ears. These guys sound more like poets than pilots.

Gramma chimes in, "Stanley, Rosemary, if you think this is a good thing to have our boys prancing around the moon like this, you've been euchred by all those fancy-pants scientists."

My dad rolls his eyes in exasperation. It runs in the family. I've seen my uncles do it, my grandfather Horace do it, and even my great-grandfather Charlemagne do it. It's the patented Cousineau eye-roll.

"Haven't you been watching, Dora?" I'm praying my dad doesn't start lecturing her. He adds, "No, no one knows if they'll make it back."

Now I get it. He's not reprimanding her. He's actually worried. His voice rumbles, reminding me of the turbo-charged engine he loved in the '69 Mustang Mach 1 that he drove when he took me around the Ford Test Track. We are wild about engines in our family. We know that the more powerful the engine, the faster the getaway.

"Ma, you can't stop progress," says my mom. "No one says you have to like it."

I watch the whiskey sloshing around the ice cubes in my father's glass, and notice as if for the first time how he scratches his left bicep when he's nervous. That's where, on a drunken dare while he was in the army, he had a red heart tattooed, with the word MOM inside the heart pierced by an arrow.

And then the strangest thing happens.

The tension is broken by the sudden whitening of the window behind the television. The moon is rising over the rooftops of the houses across the street and silvers the living room.

"Moonmilk," my grandmother says.

"What?" my dad asks, astonished at a word he doesn't know.

"Moonmilk," she repeats. "That's what my grandmother used to call it." At first I have no idea what she is talking about, then the marvel of the word hits me. She's describing the moonlight coming through the window.

"So you do appreciate it, after all," dad says. He raises his glass of whiskey, and says, "Cheers." Then he adds, "Remember what my grandfather Charlemagne used to say, 'Stone by stone, a cathedral.' Well, I say, rocket by rocket, the moon."

"Oh, fiddlesticks," Grandma Dora mutters.

"Stanley," mom says, "leave it be."

By then my dad is drifting away from the rest of us, floating in his own space, like the third astronaut on the spaceflight mission, Michael Collins, who hovers above the moon in the Command Module. Years later, I will read that he called the Eagle "the weirdest looking contraption I'd ever seen in the sky."

It's been a long night. I want to slink away to my room but as I make my move to excuse myself my father insists that I stay for another minute to listen to the avuncular Cronkite sign off for the night. At first I only him hear say something about how what's happened will be indelibly stamped in the history books, that we will forever remember July 20, 1969 as the day man reached and walked on the moon. And then he ends the evening's long broadcast with words that my dad would repeat to me for years to come: "Aldrin, Armstrong, Collins are the best of us and they've led us further and higher than we ever imagined we were likely to go." Why, why did he ask me on all my trips back to Detroit if I remembered that night in front of the TV watching history unfold, and if I ever thought about what Cronkite meant by some heroes being destined to lead us beyond what we were capable of? What was he trying to tell me?

Safely back on earth, Aldrin and Armstrong will be asked what the mission meant. Their responses will be elliptical as their flight pattern.

"Only that we're no longer confined to earth," Aldrin will answer.

"The unknowns were rampant," Armstrong will say.

★ ★ ★

By the time my dad clicks off the television I've changed my mind about disappearing into my room. Instead, I follow the moonlight and step out onto the front porch with the screen door banging once, twice behind me.

The cool night air rustles my hair. I crane my neck to look up at the moon. It seems different now. The screen door opens and closes with a bang as my dad joins me. He hands me a cold root beer, and clinks his glass with mine.

Together, we gaze at the moon, shoulder to shoulder. There is nothing to say, but everything to look at. Far above us looms the moon, the stars, Venus and Mars, all of which my dad points out wordlessly.

Up and down Eastlawn, the crickets keep chirping, the lawn mowers keep purring, the telephone lines keep buzzing, as if everything is the same as it ever was. My mind wanders and I wonder what the earth looks like from the moon, and then it hits me: it must look like a blue pearl. How could Gram have known?

My dad puts his hand on my shoulder.

We keep looking up at the moon.

It seems closer.

OPENING DAY

IT ALL BEGAN SO well. It was his first one-man show, at a hipper-than-thou gallery in Baltimore. He recognized several folks who'd driven down from New York, including a feared art critic from Philly furtively draining the good Scotch behind the bar. Unexpectedly, Cal Ripken Jr. bought three of his American Impressionist paintings of bohemian life in Paris, then slipped him two box-seat tickets to the next Orioles game.

Then the gorgeous young art student arrived, dressed to kill in a black felt beret, tight red sweater, and lacy black nylons. He watched with wry amusement as she did a hip-hop version of Art Buchwald's five-minute Louvre routine, dashing through the exhibition, her head swinging side to side so she wouldn't miss a thing, determined to race ahead and see it all. Before she could parry and thrust with the art crowd she spied him across the gallery, and gave him the once-over-twice, checking his profile against the photo in the catalogue. Without missing a beat, she bee-lined for him with her heart's most ardent question, oblivious to his negotiations for his next show.

I've arrived, he told himself. *My own show, Cal Ripken, box seats, a drop-dead beautiful art student about to ask me about my painting, my work, maybe even my theories about light, color, and American Impressionism—*

"How long you been painting?" she asked, bluntly, hand outstretched, waiting for the crash course advice, the one-minute solution.

"Oh, about forty years," said the forty-year-old painter, feeling sideswiped by cliché. He was hoping the irony would sound hip, his quickness be interpreted as the bravura of wit.

She pulled a face. She took the news well about as well as a rent increase.

He changed tacks. "I'm inspired by John Constable," he said, hoping for an opening with her, or at least that she would notice parallels with him, or at least one of the Impressionists.

"Monet? Or do you mean *Manet*?" she asked, seriously. "Monet, Manet. I've heard it pronounced both ways. Biting down hard on her ruby red fingernail, she grimaced, then purred, "Forty years? I think I'll do abstracts."

Miniatures

*"What is seen is comprised of things
which seldom appear."*
—EVAN CONNELL, JR.

FOR TWENTY YEARS, I wasn't sure if I had actually seen what I thought I'd seen that night at the Los Angeles County Museum of Art. The memory was as ambiguous as a fever dream. What I'm fairly certain about is reading an article by a local art critic in the *L. A. Weekly* about an exhibit called *Worlds Within Worlds* that focused on the curious career of an obscure Armenian American musician and microminiaturist named Hagop Sandaldjian whose specialty was carving works of art out of single grains of rice that could fit into the eye of a needle. The article recounted Sandaldjian's gallery of rice grains he had carved into a miniature Mount Ararat, a Snow White, Napoleon, and even a ballplayer with a bat on his shoulder.

Was it real or, as Ella Fitzgerald crooned, was it Memorex, a copy, a facsimile?

Impressive, if true, but possibly an urban legend. For years, I'd been as haunted by the evening as I'd been by a nightmarish dream I'd had over the years where I was in the family Ford Falcon with my dad driving deliriously fast in pea-soup fog, careening toward a cliff outside of our town until my dad slammed the brakes and the car skidded to a perilous stop with its front wheels dangling over the edge, spinning in the air like Wile E. Coyote's legs in a Chuck Jones cartoon.

While the back wheels clung to the gravel.

The unsettling dream had taken on a kind of granulated reality over the years in my memory box, but the trouble was that there were no cliffs like this in the town where I grew up, and my father thought I was a moron when I asked him if he remembered the night we almost drove off a cliff.

And what about the fever dreams of speaking in French with my great-grandfather Charlemagne about his years as a *voyageur* while we were canoeing in the Yukon? The trouble being I've never been in the Yukon.

I've been to scores of art exhibits, but what I remember of what I saw that night comes up gauzy and unclear, a half-submerged and impersonal, as if it was something only read about in a musty *National Geographic* during the gauzy moments before sleep?

First, came a pugnacious memory of the phosphorus smells from the nearby La Brea Tar Pits when I parked the car that night. Then the memory of the unusual Thursday night museum crowd, mostly the usual culture-vultures at the L.A. County Museum, cacophonous with cadaverous art students and immigrant Russians could distract him, Russian and Armenian immigrants murmuring in the long line, strange syllables from beneath the known world. An old friend from my time on a kibbutz in Israel, Helen, had accompanied me but was restless, asking why we couldn't have just gone somewhere simpler, with fewer people, like McCabe's for some music. Wasn't Kenny Rankin playing? Or a long walk on the Santa Monica Pier? Wasn't there supposed to be a full moon tonight?

Undaunted, I gushed over the description I'd read in the *Weekly* that morning, after my classes at the American Film Institute, about the exhibit. "Hey, I thought it might rekindle your travel fire," I half-joked to her, remembering how she'd recently confessed a longing to travel again.

"Actually," I'd said, "there's something else, something the art critic wrote that got under my skin. He said that a visitor would be guaranteed to see something *peculiar* —that's the word he used—something you never thought possible."

"Peculiar?" she echoed. "What do you think he meant?" She furrowed her brow while I maundered on about the phenomenal popularity of Russian and Armenian miniaturist art. Shrugging, I put my arm around her shoulder in trust-me fashion and admitted that the work stymied me. I wasn't sure why I cared, but trusted the strangifying feeling that the word *peculiar* had on me.

"Call it a hunch," I said, managing a slight smile as we inched along in line, handed over our tickets, and approached the first glass-covered wooden exhibit tables that contained articles about the artist's work that I'd read about in the catalog. They were curious but not completely captivating, and most of them weren't even in English. One photo captured the miniaturist huddled over an atomic force microscope, which made my own eyes dilate in excitement.

"I think that's why we came, Helen," I said and pointed to the next exhibit table where six high-powered microscopes were on display, available to visitors just like us, and why the line was inching along so slowly.

"Oh, wonderful," she said sweetly.

When it was my turn at the first microscope I bent down and gazed into the viewing piece. At first I saw nothing but the reflection of my own eyelid. Blinking, I homed in on the first image, the miniature artwork that had caught my attention in the paper that morning. As I did, the room closed in on me. My head felt like smoke, my hands like clay as I tried to focus the microscope, impatiently groping for the focus knob on the column of the microscope. Nothing but shades of darkness and the occasional flare of light. The eyepiece felt constricting, angering up my blood, as the old ballplayer Satchel Paige used to described it.

Suddenly, I had the right eyes, as Rilke described Cezanne's breakthrough. I'd read the news today, oh, boy, about a lucky man, an Armenian artist who conjured art out of rice grains. On the wall were photographs of the rice grain artist's gallery of art, including birds, letters, musical notes, miniscule sculptures, and a ballplayer. He was a minor leaguer you might

225

say, lingering on deck, painted red with a yellow cap, his hips twisted like Ted Williams after a perfectly balanced swing. The rice grain art was a revelation, a glimpse of beauty and care on a microscopic level I'd never dreamt was possible.

Reassured, I leaned over the eyepiece and turned the focus knob. I became oblivious to anything but the uncanny sight of a single grain of rice resting on a glass mount. According to the exhibit catalog, it had taken Sandaldjian thirteen days worth of intricate carving with a diamond sharp scalpel to create his beautiful cameos with their stupefying detail. And still I wasn't prepared for what appeared. Splayed out on the glass mount underneath the microscope was a boatman on a raft with a barge pole in his river-strengthened hand. I watch the boatman gazing across the riverbank, perhaps for a waiting traveler, and feel the urge to see more. Despite the grumbling of the crowd behind me, I adjust the focus knob again so I might divine the face of the traveler.

"You okay?" Helen asked. "*What do you see?*"

"Uh, yeah, no problem..." I said, covering the white lie. There was a problem. I couldn't move. I was paralyzed for reasons reason does not know. Time passed that was no time, time, "that other labyrinth," as Borges wrote.

The restless culture vultures lined up behind me grumbled for me to move on. "W'd'ya' waitin' for, Christmas?" bellowed one blowhard. "Can't wait all day, buster," snarled another. I could hear the restless pawing on the floor tiles, but wasn't motivated. "Boy, some people think they're the center of the universe. You writing a term paper or something?" "Hey, Narcissus, you lose your Echo?"

A sense of wonder washed over me like warm rain on a cool evening. So precise was Sandaldjian's work he was able to reveal an otherwise invisible Achilles' fabled shield during the Trojan War, intended by Haephaestus to reveal the entire universe. This gasp of life took my breath away.

Two microscopes! How could the museum have prepared so poorly for the opening? Two microscopes for thousands of people?

Frantically, I twist the focus knob again and this time the

boatman begins to transform. At first glance he had been riding a raft, a barge pole in his river-strengthened hand. As I focused, I could make out the riverbank, a waiting friend, an oak tree, a horse, a cloud. It's still not enough—and I don't even know what I'm looking for.

I squeeze the concertina of my imagination and can make out an expression of serenity on the boatman's face. Neither a copy, nor an act of fugacious cleverness, the image is so precise on the grain of rice that it seemed to pulsate with a preternatural life of its own. I'd never known such patience, such devotion.

I hold my breath and turn the knob once more. In that gasp of infinity I had the sinking feeling, the accusation of long self-deception, the suspicion that I never done anything with the precision revealed by the artist's hand. Only fire and ice, piss and vinegar, as my English friends used to joke. Disappointment stung like a paper cut.

When I pull myself away from the microscope a museum guard is hovering over me whispering very loudly that I have to move on. I can barely hear her. I'm staring at Helen and thinking about the farmer in Albania (or Japanese soldier in the Philippines) who had been alone so long he needed to be convinced by passing travelers that he wasn't a ghost.

Remembering the legend about Japanese calligraphers waiting for the moment between heartbeats, I imagine the maestro of miniatures leaning over the rice grain with his diamond-tipped tools, like Blake's God with divine calipers, creating a world of order, detail, and precise beauty. When the moment comes, you better be focused, I think, seeing himself carving a grain-sized Charlie Chaplin leaning on his cane, learning to wear his sorrow with dignity.

Taking her turn at the microscope, Helen looked flummoxed, frowning, as she fiddled with the focus knob. I picked at some spackle still crusting my fingernails from another long week of house painting up north. Waiting, I became self-conscious of the smell of turpentine that was reeking in my clothes. Bitterness stung my heart. I was ashamed of my own hands, my hair, my body, despite the bravado I often trotted out about how many Victorian Ladies I had painted in San Francisco. "Is that all you have to show for your years in San Francisco?" asked Jim, one of my fellow housepainters,, as if deliberately trying to puncture my romantic self-image. "You say you're a writer—but what have you published?"

I hated to admit it but he was right. I had lost my focus, lost my capacity for attention, forgotten about the beauty of the world, despite all the facades I had painted. My ability to be lost in the present, like the Armenian artist, had been reduced to a world far smaller than his, reduced really to the wood grain of the window sashes I had learned to sand and spackle and repaint. Day-by-day, hour-by-hour, house-by-house, I had sold my soul for a few hundred bucks. Travel money, I rationalized. Biding time was more like it. The great thief Procrastination had stolen my time, as Ben Franklin had warned.

Somewhere I've read that real art looks back at you. Vermeer's woman, Rembrandt's self-portraits, Van Gogh's night skies, all have the peculiar power to gaze at you while you are gazing at them.

For two or three minutes, one luminous night at the L.A. County Museum, one of the strangest works of art in art history looked back at me. It stirred me in the sense of the ancient Greeks who defined beauty as that which *provokes* you to think, to act, to feel, to see yourself. That minute grain of rice told me, if that's the word, that I had lost the part of me that dreamed of crossing the turbulent river to the other side of my life, that *I* was the phantom boatman, the anonymous traveler, in the rice-grain, the ghost in the grain, who had been stuck in the mud, looking for a boatman to take me across the river. Until now I couldn't see his face because it had been mine all along.

That night an old Armenian, proud to see the artwork of one of his compatriots in such a famous American museum, was the only one in line who understood why I had been riveted by Sandaldijian's work, the only one I saw who equally descended into reverie.

As I was leaving with my friend Helen, he took me aside, and said as quiet as a spy, as if there were guards listening in,

"My mother knew him well, and said that he would time his motions to come between his heartbeats, thus maximizing his control of his fingers. She said that those who saw Sandaldjian at work said that they could not tell when his hands moved."

The old Armenian shrugged, then asked plaintively, "If his hands weren't moving, how could he move me so much with his art? It's a miracle, a miracle."

The Chauffeur

THE HOTSHOT MOVIE STAR'S long, cool, white stretch of limo is there to pick me up at the arrival curb at LAX, right on schedule. The chauffeur's sporting a black satin hat and white patent leather gloves. Leaning against the car, he holds a white placard with his boss's name in oversized block letters: MICKEY ROURKE, and mine in miniscule and misspelled letters below: PHIL CUZINOW.

Inside the cool ride, the man makes no small talk, needs just one question from me to set him off on a smooth riff about life in the fast lane. I mull it over a second and then ask one he hadn't been expecting: "Hey, bro," I say, in my best streets-of-Detroit style. "This pretty cool for me, but I'm wondering, what would be an exciting ride for *you*?"

His face in the rear-view mirror is startled. "Nobody done ask me that before."

He hums to himself for a moment, something that sounds like an old Jimmy Ruffin song, then adjusts the rim of his hat. "Since you asked, man, let me tell ya. Exciting for me would be *Patti LaBelle*. I swear, Patti LaBelle."

"Why her? You've got to let me have it straight, man."

"I just dig her music and her vibe, man," he says. "I would pick her up in *my* stretch—ya gotta understand, man, this is *my* ride, and I'd help her into the backseat and serve her champagne and take her anywhere she wanted to go. Hell, I'd drive her to Vegas, if that's what she wanted. That would be tops for me. That would be the best."

"And then what?" I ask, half-dreading something bawdy, kicking myself for the very thought that he had something salacious in mind.

"And then, and then, I'd ask her to *sing* to me."

As we pull off Lincoln and on to the 405 heading north to Wilshire, I let that sink in.

"Just hearin' Patti LaBelle sing to *me*, me alone, in the back of *my* ride, well, I can't imagine life getting any better than that. Going down the road with Patti *LaBelle* singing to me. Anything I wanted to hear—"If Only You Knew," or "My Love, Sweet Love," or, man, maybe "Over the Rainbow." You ever hear her version of that? If you had, *you'd* be over the rainbow, man."

The limo slows down in the rush hour traffic. Dinner with Rourke is scheduled for eight at Spago's, but suddenly I'm in no hurry.

My main man sighs like a weary man dropping down into a warm bath. Unselfconsciously, he turns up the AC, glancing straight ahead, far down 405. I hear him murmur to nobody in particular, as if I weren't even in the back seat, "Ride all night, me and Patti *LaBelle*, ridin' all night."

He's all roundhouse smiles, and he catches me in his rear-view mirror, smiling back. "What's up?" he says. "I say too much?"

"No," I say, shaking my head, "not at all. I just love hearing a man talking about his dreams."

"Right on, right on, right on."

"So she's your dream ride," I say as we snail along on the freeway, then wanting to nudge the conversation along, add, "Out of all the stars you've driven around who has impressed you the *most*?"

A taxi cuts us off and he hits the brakes—but doesn't panic, doesn't blow his top. "Glad you asked, man. Drove Mr. Lou Gosset once, and when I picked him up I did what I probably shouldn't have, but I poked him in the chest with my finger and told him, "I pay hard-earned money to see you, dude. I like what you do, my man. You make me *proud* to be black, brother."

"Hey, that's cool," I say, trying to imagine the tough guy gunnery sergeant in *An Officer and a Gentleman* being poked in the chest.

"And then there's Mickey," the driver says. "For Pete's sake, you haven't done ask me about Mr. Rourke. Mickey's a great guy, despite losing tons of money standing up for himself. He's got the *swag*, brother, you know, swagger. I kinda admire that. Reminds me of my own dad. I don't care what *Variety* and all those rags say, he's a man of principles. A man not ruled by money, like most cats in this town. Yeah, I admire that." We pull up in front of front of Spago's in Beverly Hills for my script meeting with Rourke, who's just back from filming a steamy thriller with the gorgeous Carré Otis, in Argentina. A friend of mine has set up a meeting with him to talk my writing a political who-done-it in Northern Ireland, an IRA film.

The chauffeur hustles around the front of the limo and dashes back along the curb to open the door for me, making me feel more helpless than famous. As I step out, he holds the door and strikes a quick, crisp bow. I haven't seen a gesture this elegant since watching the Pullman porter's at the Michigan Central Train Station in Detroit.

Smiling to beat the band, I step out of the limo. Looking into Spago's I feel my stomach churn. How the hell did I get into this? I don't really want to write a movie about Americans fighting with the IRA, but I do want to hear the pith. Suddenly, a phalanx of bug-eyed tourists and sniggering photographers leap in front of me, snapping photos and asking for my autograph, and when they don't recognize me, as one they lean down to peer into the darkness of the limo, looking for somebody famous. The chauffeur isn't intimidated or impressed. He pushes them back like Jim Brown throwing a forearm as he storms through the front line of tacklers. I manage to shake his hand and tell him how much I enjoyed the ride—*his ride*—and realize I never asked his name. I feel a hot flash of shame and ask him, but my voice is drowned out by the screams of the crowd who suddenly see Mickey Rourke, in a shirtless black leather vest, showing off his burnished South American tan, arriving on his Harley-Davidson. Seated behind him, in a lime-colored, low-cut dress is his girlfriend, the green-eyed beauty, Carré Otis. She's bleeding beauty to the sharks in front of the Spago's.

It's a bloody feeding frenzy of fans. The chauffeur tilts his head toward the restaurant door, suggesting I avoid the melee.

A half-hour later, Rourke and Otis arrive at our table. Throughout the meeting, script ideas are tossed out and shredded like confetti. Flimsy proposals are made like the air kisses blown across the restaurant from table to table. Any momentum for solid script ideas has been lost. It's one interruption after the other, cell calls, autograph hounds, arguments with the agents at the table about other impending movie deals. Over several shots of Jack Daniels and swipes of chips and salsa the boss regales me with anecdotes about his boxing career.

"Hey, man, I hear you ride," he says. "Got your ride with you? We could ride up One to San Francisco." He's disappointed when I say my ride is at home, and then sniffs a little when I tell him I've been riding a Yamaha 850 for the last few years. "If you think it can make it," he says, "I could meet you in the city and we could ride up to Mendocino and get a motel and then we can really get serious about the story."

As we talk, they start nagging him again. His agent, a personal assistant, and his girlfriend's entourage break into our conversation with industry gossip and stock market tips. He tries to navigate between all of us, but finds it harder and harder to focus. My mind drifts back to the nameless chauffeur and something he said moments before we pulled up in front of the restaurant. "It's the road, not the load," he had said. "That's what counts on this cat's roadmap. It ain't about what's outside a man. It's about what's inside."

With that he had coolly swerved into a spot in front of Spago's, "Hey, bro, before I get out, tell me your name."

"Don't need no name," he said. "Just call me the luckiest cat in the world, the cat who's been waitin' for Patti LaBelle all his life."

The chauffeur paused and added, "And my parents called me Harold. So can you."

WHO STOLE HER ARMS, MAMA?

FALL, 1997. PARIS. For one startling moment I am alone with the most voluptuous woman in the world. Alone in a room that was teeming with tourists only moments before. She has stood like this—sentinel-silent—for over 170 years. I gaze at her in reverie, seeing her in person for the first time, after gazing for years at a framed photo of her above my father's silver-painted workbench in our basement.

The silence snaps in half.

A wisp of a girl comes skipping into the gallery with her mother right behind her, calling out to her to *shush*, in a lilting Irish accent. When the girl sees the famous statue looming in the center of the room she stops within a few feet of it, as if a large pane of glass has suddenly come between them. She turns and asks her mother in the wispiest of voices: "Where are her arms, mama?" The girl's mother says again, slightly embarrassed, "*Shush*, sweetheart." Tenderly, she puts her forefinger to the girl's lips. "We're in a *museum*."

Leaning against the back wall of the gallery, with my sketchbook tucked under my arm, a smile saunters across my face, reflecting the happiness that has lit up the room. The girl's sweet insistence touches me; the mother's hushed-breath reverence moves me. There is a mystery looming here that needs little explanation, just attention, just time.

Her mother's unusual pronunciation of *museum* is a marvel. She lingers on the *muse* in museum in a way I've never heard before. She utters the word with the awe of a medieval visitor to a Cabinet of Wonders, who points out to a fellow visitor, "Look—dragon bones!" Her murmuring emphasis on the first syllable—*muse*—brings home the origin of the word like none I've heard before, like an echo of a very old fascination with the "house of the muses." Her dulcet tones send me back to a time when it was believed that museums housed the nine forces that inspire, *in-spirit*, the arts. Still, the girl frowns, crosses her arms, and insists again, "Tell me, mama, tell me *why* her arms are *missing*!" Strangely, her insistence and her cadence reminds me of the missing lines from the first edition of James Joyce's *Ulysses* that were recently discovered among 6,000 other errors, "Tell me, mother, the word known to all men."

Something is always missing, some of it is even found again, some not.

Together, mother and daughter approach the two-thousand-year-old statue as if entering a church. Then as kids will do, the girl breaks away and skips around the statue, as if it's a maypole, never taking her eyes off it, never losing her delight. Her mother watches, eyes ablaze with pride. The girl returns to her side as if pulled by the centrifugal force of love and clutches her mother's hand again. The mother turns silent, furrows her brow, tilts her head in wonder, and tries to determine what happened to the famously missing arms. "*But mama, who stole them?*" the girl asks again, not petulantly, but dispirited, in the way of a child who has been encouraged to express her curiosity. "Who stole the arms of the Venus de Milo?"

Her mother shakes her head, shrugs her shoulders, and admits, "Sorry, love, I just don't know."

My scalp prickles with nervousness. I'm afraid the mother notices me noticing them. But she surprises me.

"I don't think anybody *stole* them," the Irish mother says reassuringly. "She's still beautiful, *anyway*, isn't she? Even without her arms, she's beautiful." A whole world swings on that subtly chosen adverb.

Now, it could have been sheer museum fatigue since I'd been meandering the halls of the world's vastest museum for several hours. My mind goes as blank as a newly stretched canvas. It's humiliating because I practically grew up with the Venus de Milo, at least with reproductions of her in my father's art magazines, postcard collection, and history books. At that moment I'm struck mute, as silent as the hundreds of other statues that stand like sentinels in the Louvre's Greek and Roman sculpture galleries.

Watching them, I think about something Walter Benjamin wrote after a visit here, "For what one has lived is at best comparable to a beautiful statue which has had all its limbs knocked off in transit, and now yields nothing but the precious block out of which the image of one's future must be hewn."

A plangent silence hangs over the gallery. The Irish woman and I stare at each other awkwardly, brought together by that strange intimacy of art. And yet I have the awkward feeling she is hoping I might say something that will satisfy the girl's curiosity.

"What do you think?" she asks.

At that moment, as so often happens to me, words I love come back to me, Joyce's missing response to the missing question, long left out of the novel that meant the world to me when I was in my twenties, alone, lost in Dublin, unable to go home to Detroit, unsure about how to move forward into the life that was waiting for me.

"Love, the word known to all men." My head is reeling, my heart roiling from so many memories and reflections compacted into what John Updike called "eternally ramifying moments." Gazing at the voluptuous goddess, then turning back to the Irish woman, I say, "Beautiful, *anyway*."

The moment stretches like a canvas. Our short exchange hovers above us like a word balloon, a wall caption to a painting, an inscription carved in an old stone.

Then come the little girl's plaintive words, "Maybe, but I *still* miss them."

To explain this enigma would explain what is still missing in my life.

THE BULL CATCHERS

"The true fight is with the duende."
—FEDERICO GARCÌA LORCA

THE HERALD BLARES HIS bugle to announce the seventh and final event of the *tourada*, the great "taurine spectacle," as the Portuguese press calls bullfights at the Campo Pequeno. Six black slumps of bull have come and gone. Six times the *cavaleiros*, wearing their "suits of light," riding on their powerful Lusitano horses, plunge their *bandarilhas*, or small javelins, into the backs of the bulls, not to kill them, as in other bullfighting countries, but to stun them into submission.

A thrilling day, but I've been to bullfights before, in Spain and Mexico, and even in the Central Valley of California. What's passed today is but prelude for the event that brought me out of my seclusion in the tiny village of Penedo, out on the Atlantic coast. I'm here for the *pega de caras*, literally the "face catch," which I heard about over a glass of port at a local bodega. I had said a few sputtery things about searching for the "soul of Portugal" to a painter friend named Anxo, who humored me by saying in his usual staccato accent, "Two things you must do—listen to live *fado* music and witness Portuguese-style bullfighting."

And so it was that I found myself a week later in Lisbon, crisping in the hot sun and gaping at the two-part spectacle. Traditionally, Anxo had told me, the first half of the event is the eighteenth-century pageantry of the *cavaleiro,* which features the *cavaleiros* fighting the bulls from horseback, and the second half is the *pega* featuring *grupo de forçados*, literally, "bull grabbers or catchers," That's all I knew, and I had no idea how little it was or what any of it meant.

The red *toril* door to the corral slides open with an unnerving clank. The last of the furified bulls charges out into the center of the bullring, snorting, clawing at the ground, spinning around like a living corkscrew, looking completely disoriented.

And so begins the last movement of the "liturgy of bulls," as Lorca called it. The Spanish poet compared the *corridas de touros*, the bullfight, with the fight with *duende*, the blood surge, the spirit of the earth, the almost unendurable fever pitch of emotion, the necessary reminder of death. *Duende* is, as Lorca wrote, hand-to-hand combat with death.

The *black thread*, as I've come to think of it, runs through art, music, poetry, dance —and bullfighting. And I need to see it if I'm ever going to understand this strange land. I have been hearing about the unique Portuguese form of bullfighting for months in the *bodegas* of Lisbon, Sintra, Colares, and the village of Penedo, where I've been living for a few months in an old stone cottage.

And now the *cuadrilla* gate shudders, the sound rippling across the arena. Out march the *forçados*, the team of eight young men who intend to catch the bull with their bare hands. Nothing between them and the bull. No javelins or daggers, no shields or even capes to distract the bulls. They are dressed flamboyantly in damask and velvet, flared red pants and ruffled white shirts. They are barehanded and might as well be naked. Hands on hips, heads erect, defiant, the *bull catchers* form a tight line for the ritual *pega de cara*, the "face catch," which means grabbing the bull by the horns and wrestling it to a standstill, to stillness, to submission.

The *forçados* are out to prove something other than their ability to kill, as in Spain or Mexico; they are here for something subtler, even more archetypal. I don't know what it is, and I need to know.

Down in the arena, the *peões* is shouting to distract the bull. He twists away from the bull and leaps the wooden fence behind him. The great beast is alone and bewildered. Out of sheer annoyance, it charges the boards, which shudder with an impact that reverberates around the arena. Satisfied, it snorts in contempt at the sight of the cowering *peões*, a kind of provocateur, behind the protective fence, then turns and glowers at the near mirage of unarmed *forçados*, the bull catchers, lined up one behind the other, like a dart aimed straight at its heart, and mine.

Unswervingly, they march to their fates, which may be why it's often linked with *fado* music, which refers as well to the fates, but also like the young boys and girls who were sent every year from Athens to Knossos to be sacrificed to the bloodlust of the Minotaur. Those victims were resigned. These *forçados* are anything but resigned.

Step by stuttered step, as measured and ritualistic as flamenco dancers, the brace of bull catchers march in single file into the center of the ring, although *march* may be too strong a word. They are trying to lure—not trick—the bull into charging them. Of course, it looks utterly insane to me, even from my safe perch in the stands. Would a diver try to lure a white shark, would a hunter poke a grizzly bear in the eye, a beekeeper deliberately rile a hive? Never!

And yet that's what the *forçados* are doing. Not defying death like a testosterone-fueled teenager driving drunk after midnight on a dark country road, or dancing with it, like those engravings of the *danse macabre* in medieval Europe. Not even like the cliff divers I once saw on Easter Island, climbing higher and higher to deliberately dive off the most dangerous peak. There is an entirely different level of confrontation here that is revealed with the first steps of the *forçados* toward the bull.

And then just as it seemed like sheer lunacy for the eight defenseless men to provoke one steaming bull, the *cabo*, the head of the line, the front man, as he's known, breaks way away from the relative safety of the group and takes *five, six, seven, eight* steps into the abyss between him and the bull. There, he digs his heels into the sand, watching with the fierce focus of a sniper every move of the bull. The bull paws the ground like some Warner Brothers cartoon animal, snuffles and snorts—and thunders across the arena straight at him.

The cabo backs up three steps, digs in his heels to absorb the impending impact—the deafening noise in the arena stops and becomes dirge-quiet. I half expect to see the *forçado* explode like soldier hit by a hand grenade, or at the very least see an artery severed by one of its horns, the blood spurting across the arena like a swoosh of red on a Picasso canvas. My mind reels forward as I imagine the death-defying kid impaled and flung in the air to a ridiculous death.

But at the last conceivable moment the cabo times his jump perfectly, seizes the lowered horns of the hurtling bull, and hangs on as the bull tries to gore him. With majestic grace, it snaps its head upward as violently as a medieval catapult.

Emboldened by his ability to hang on to the whiplashing bull and by the teamwork of his fellow *forçados*, the front man tightens his grip long enough for the second kid to leap on the other side of the contorting bull's massive head. In the under-gloom of the long Lisbon afternoon, the hulking bull shakes its shoulders, trying to free himself of the bull catcher, but the kid will not let go, not now, not ever. He seems possessed, trying to turn a nightmare into a dream, trying to survive, but not caring if he dies a noble death before this frenzied crowd.

Once they see the front man clutching the head of the bull the other seven *forçados* pile on, leaping on its bulging back in a manic effort to slow it down. The rampaging bull manages to fling off one of the young bull catchers, who bounces off the shuddering sideboards. The eighth *forçado,* the *trabajador,* is the last to leap onto the bull, but he grabs its tail and is dragged in the dirt as the bull bucks and snorts and tries to fling off its tormenters.

"Ee-yah, toro!" he shouts as it lunges at him, slides through the dirt, stops near the boards. He holds on to its tail with blood-stained hands as he's dragged from the sun-drenched to the shadow-fretted side of the arena. Man and beast spit blood at the same delirious moment, sending the crowd into an even more fevered dream. They stand motionless, mere feet from each other, they can smell each other's blood. He stares into the death-black eyes of the bull. He is unflinching, knowing this is the moment he can break its spirit.

Outraged, it bellows and stomps around in a circle, pulling the brazen kid behind him, leaving a body-wide groove in the sand. Contemptuously, the bull carries all seven *forçados* a good twenty yards, pauses like a locomotive changing tracks, then bolts for the boards, throwing off one kid after the other to the ground that seems to shudder with every tumbling body. The bull shakes off six of them, but not the seventh, the very first. He has been gored and his shirt is bloodied by the twisting horns, and somehow he still holds on until the bull charges the boards again in a raging effort to pin his nemesis against them. At the last second, the bull catcher lets go of the horns and falls to the ground, and the bull crashes into the boards with a sick, thudding sound.

Motionless, they stand in an epic confrontation, darkened by the gathering shadows in the corner of the arena. The bull catcher who will not let go, the bull that cannot believe he has been caught. Unable to intimidate the *forçado*, unwilling to stomp around any longer, unworthy of its own anger, its shoulders ripple in some faint gesture of surrender or indifference, and it staggers away to the corner of the arena.

The emotion in a stadium is a tremulous thing, moving in waves from fan to fan, lifting everyone out of their seats, in admiration for the confrontation of man and beast, but also for the spectacle, the evidence of tenacity. It's as if the veil has lifted on a scene that transpired 100,000 years ago between early hunters and the hunted. We are in the arena, but we aren't, we have been flung hundreds of centuries back in time and gotten a *glimpse*, no more, no less, of the terror of raging animals, and the tenuous grip our ancestors had on survival. It was there in the fury of the beast, but also in the fury of the young bull catchers holding on for dear life.

A joyous—almost berserk—*Ole!* rises from the crowd.

Whoever said the bullfight was the "indefensible but irresistible" got it half right. The wag who said this must have just returned from a *pega*, the kind that moves an entire crowd to undulate like a swallowing snake. And now, with the magnificent bull catching its own breath in the darkest corner of the arena, the roguish bull catchers conclude the ritual with a swaggering circuit around the bullring. This is the traditional *vuelta*, sheer preening, breathing defiantly, not unlike the bull they were trying to catch. Am I seeing things? Or is their march a miming of the thing they admire most? Was their catching of the bull an effort to absorb the great beast's strength and nobility? They swagger around the ring, as bouquets of flowers rain down on them, along with hats and shoes, black bras, red panties, and business cards. The bull catchers soak it all in, not ones to suffer fools gladly, or fans inelegantly. The first *forçado* files past us, death-drenched and proud of it. And yet something is different about them, as if some great force has passed between them and the bull, an ancient force, a fierce strength, a tenacity. Did it pass when they subdued the great animal—or because of it? Did the bull surrender the great force? Is this what the Paleolithic artists were trying to capture when they painted bulls on their cave walls, or the fresco painters in the Knossus Palace on Crete?

"The *duende* then is a power, not a work," Lorca wrote. "It is a struggle, not a thought…. Everything that has black sounds in it has *duende*." There is a black sound here, and black-pooled eyes sweep the stands searching for anyone among us who has the courage and tenacity—or is it lunacy—to test fate the way they just did. "Which of you can stand up to death and wrestle it to the ground as we just did?"

His eyes lock on mine, as I saw him do with the bull minutes before. I feel split in half like cordwood, exposed, and half of me claps in admiration until my hands burn, like the rest of the crowd, and the other half of me quivers with doubt. His glance almost seems unfair as it asks the quickening questions: *"Could you have held on? Would you have flinched? What role have you played in the drama of death? Do you hold your ground even now?"*

CATCH AS CATCH CANNES

"Tout est le chemin."
(Everything is a road.)
—FRENCH FOLK SAYING

AT A CANNES FILM Festival party press conference at the Hotel d'Albion, I'm pressed between a shrivel of movie critics, a deal of agents, a panic of producers, and a lone English actor, Jeremy Irons. As one of two stars, along with Robert DeNiro, of *The Mission*, which we've all just screened at the Grand Palais, Irons is here to field questions about the rigors of filming in the wilds of South America.

The press release gives us the overstory, the facts of the film, how it is set in 1750, a benighted time when Spain and Portugal were carving up the world between them. The pope had his cassock in a twist because the rival countries were demanding that he sacrifice his missions in South America. The schizophrenic situation is personified in the character of Father Gabriel, played by Irons, the spiritual leader of the remote but fabled Guarani mission. This was the center of the infamous "Jesuit Republic," whose paradise is threatened by both politics and the mendacious slave trader, Rodrigo Mendoza (DeNiro), who is seeking redemption for his profiteering from the "red gold," the Amazonian Indians.

The screenwriter Robert Bolt wrote in his press notes, "Supposing there had been a pair of Jesuits, one with the old time skill of bearing arms, and the other with the simple skill of doing Christ's work, when asked to by the natives under his care, the Guarani, what then?"

Still gaunt, bearded and beaded from his time in the tropics, Irons is first asked by a reporter from *Variety* what it was like to work with DeNiro, his American costar. With startling honestly for a press conference, he said that at first there was a bit of a conflict of styles. But overall, he added, it was an honor to work with the star of *Taxi Driver, The Deerhunter,* and *The Godfather.* A reporter from *Le Monde* followed up with a convoluted question in the academic style of one of the old film magazines like *Le Cahier*, something about why he chose a *religious* project.

Coolly, Irons replied that Bolt's script was the finest he had read in "quite some time," then added that he also wanted to work with the director Roland Joffe. Why? Everyone wanted to know. "Because I felt he was a director who understood me. I thought I could hand myself over to him. In the past I was guilty of...preserving myself...holding back. He helped me with the self-consciousness that has restrained me in other films."

More star-struck questions followed. The special correspondent from the *San Francisco Examiner* asks Irons what impressed him the most about his latest role. It's so different from the rake he played in *The French Lieutenant's Woman*, or the Polish activist in *Moonlighting*, or the moody lover in *Brideshead Revisited*. Irons mulls over his response, then says, "It was the combination of physical and spiritual challenges, like climbing the rockface of the treacherous Iquazu waterfall."

Drolly, he adds, "I insisted on doing my own stunts. I much preferred that to the peril of the deadly boring sideline game of waiting, or being fanned by an assistant director."

A reporter from the *Baltimore Sun* asks if he faced any particular challenges playing a Jesuit priest, a question that gives him pause. Insouciantly, he draws on his cigarette, like an eighteenth-century gentleman on the Grand Tour. By then it's too late. A publicist dashes in to announce the press conference is *over* because "Mr. Irons has to attend another screening at the Grand Palais."

And just like the room is evacuated.

I watched the gaggle of reporters and movie critics scramble away to grab the first seats in the Palais. It was a chance for me to take my time to finish my notes. But the last question lingers in the air like the smoke from one Irons's Gitanes. After viewing forty-four movies in twelve days for *The Hollywood Scriptwriter*, ranging from Sam Shepard's melancholic *Fool for Love* to the goofadelic *Dr. Otto and the Riddle of the Gloom Beam*, I'm in no mood to chance another egregiously bad film like the one the night before about the woman who fell in love with an orangutan. Excuse me, the proper phrase here would be *un coup de foudre*, as one French reporter insisted on correcting a fellow American reporter.

On my way out of the room I'm accosted by a French critic whose tape recorder is still whirring. Oblivious to my increasingly foul mood, he asks me tauntingly, "You American writer! What happened to all your John Waynes?"

Weirdly, he's referring to the American boycott of the film festival because of the international disputes over the Chernobyl disaster. In inimitably Gallic fashion he is referring to Sylvester Stallone and Arnold Schwarzenegger and others who stayed away in droves because of terrorist threats.

Before I can construct a reply, I am saved by the legendary press agent Renee Furst. She snags me away and gives me a tip that Irons might be available for a brief one-on-one interview. I immediately agree, seeing it as a chance to catch the *understory*, the mythic undertow of Irons's experiences in South America.

What a coup—*de foudre* or not.

Five minutes later, I'm shuffled off back into the conference room where tea is served again and Irons arrives, tugging once again at his Gitane. Sporting sunglasses and a betel-nut necklace presented to him during filming in the Amazon, Irons squeezes the Gitane between his fingers, sips tea, ponders my question. The actor drops his grandiloquent theatricality as I begin personably, with a confession, that I too was "down and out in London," as I'd heard him say he was during the press conference. Looking for some common ground between us, I made small talk about busking around the cinemas of Leicester Square and cleaning flats in the West End during the mid-seventies. About the only thing we shared in common. He laughs easily with me about our common apprenticeship in the arts.

"Of course, I'm fascinated by how you prepared for your roles in the past," I say. "But how does anyone prepare for the role of a spiritually tormented seventeenth-century missionary? How do you research someone like that? Did Father Berrigan help you?"

I was referring to the famous Jesuit activist priest who had been recruited by Roland Joffe for a bit part in the movie.

Suddenly, it was as if the pane of glass between us was lowered. The determinedly distant actor became the essence of presence. He took a pensive sip of tea, lit another cigarette, and locked into my gaze.

I was terrified by what he might say.

"Actually," he began, uncertainly, "I spent five weeks traveling through the rainforests of South America with Father Berrigan. We sat for hours together, Daniel Berrigan and I, picking each other's brains. He asked me about acting techniques, and I asked him about spiritual life. I virtually went into retreat with him. I learned that he was similar to the character I was playing, Father Gabriel."

His description of the famous activist priest, and, even more, his delivery, reminded me of something that Berrigan later wrote in his own book-length account of the movie project, in which he described Irons as a "wise, clear-souled" man who moved around the set "like a liquefied leopard."

The actor paused, extinguished his cigarette, and allowed me time to ask my next question, as if he somehow had decided to trust me, or at least to wing it.

I went for it. "How did you reconcile the ambiguous political nature of religion in those days with the demands of a modern film, which might not take those religious issues as seriously?"

His malachite eyes hardened, then stared off for a moment at the tall French windows of the press room, and out over the palm-laced, Rolls-Royce-lined Croisette to the sea beyond. He seemed transfixed by some significant memory from the filming in what he called the "sweatbath" of the Columbian jungle.

"You know," he began tentatively, "I don't consider myself a religious man. I grew up without religion. So what I had to do was find his *humanity*."

I sensed he had Berrigan with what he said next. "Any man who believes in God and sees the errors of the world must have moments of doubt. I wanted to embody that."

My pen hovered above my hand–sized spiral notebook. "How can you build that...negative space, for lack of a better phrase...into a character? That sounds nearly impossible."

Irons flicked his cigarette into a nearby ashtray, then said slowly, with great orotund vowels, "I listened to his *soul*."

Taken aback, I followed up, "And what did Father Gabriel's soul tell you?"

Without hesitation, he said, "That we were closer than I had anticipated." He laughed. "I found to my surprise that we share a sense of moral torment and rebellion. But I also found myself talking to God, particularly before a difficult scene. I told him that if I fucked up it would reflect on *Him*!"

An awkward laugh burst out of me, and I asked, "How do you put the fear of God into God?"

"Now *that's* one of the best questions I've ever had to field," he laughed again. "So good I dare not answer it."

Rather than try to answer it, he lit another cigarette. "Okay," I said. "I'll let that go. But did working on *The Mission* have any impact on your own spiritual life?"

He grinned devilishly, shrugged. "Well, now I see that religion has been a good governing principle. It can guide our wild instincts. One can then ask oneself more important questions than 'How do I get richer?'"

His entourage hovers near our table, their ears sutured to their mobile phones, while his agent eavesdrops on our conversation. Annoyed, Irons asks for more time, and contemptuously waves her off.

"Ten minutes of them is an hour too much," I say, reviving a snide line that I'd once heard in London

"Anyway, what can an actor hope to learn from native people like the Guarani, who played their own ancestors in the movie? What did *you* learn from them?"

"Oh, my God, the Guarani taught me so much, especially how to channel the wild instincts that an actor must harness. As a matter of fact, they were better than any extras I've ever worked with, because they were so marvelously spontaneous. No self-consciousness. I found myself asking, 'Why am I looking at them this way? Why do they look at *me* the way they do? What do I see when I look at them? What do they see when they look at me?'"

This was the most thoughtful thing I'd heard from anybody in the movie business during the entire film festival. I chanced a possibly too obvious question: "And what did they see in you?" I was particularly interested in how they endured the final scene. Irons nodded at my reference to the excruciatingly realistic finale in which the European artillery slaughtered 1400 Guarani who were calmly marching out of the cathedral they had built with their own hands, under Father Gabriel's tutelage, carrying no weapons, only banners, crucifixes, and holy icons.

"I think they were able to relate to the reenactment by way of their own oral traditions, their own storytelling," he said, wincing at the memory. "They seemed to view it as an extension of their own inner theater, the acting out of a ritual or myth that has more to do with fertility, virginity, war, and so on. It was really quite extraordinary."

"Did you ever consider hanging around, remaining in the jungle after you wrapped?"

The actor vigorously shook his head. "No, I never thought of staying. No, not at all. I didn't like the food, the aimlessness. But I suggest that *you* go there. It's one of the last unexplored places in the world. Go without any plans. It's one of the last great adventures."

Once again, his hovering publicist gestured to me that I had the privilege of asking one more question. I had to think quickly, and asked the only thing still pressing on my mind. "What can actor hope to learn from working with tribal people, those practically untouched by Western civilization?

Taking a long draw from his Gitane, he said, "There's no apology about them, just a childlike quality that is vital for an actor to maintain contact with, the thing that allows one to just be. I've always tried to use that as my working principle, for it allows you to be as you are and recognize the same thing in others. For example, I don't know you, do I? I don't know where you come from, who you really are. But that's part of the mystery, isn't it, the wonderful journey of getting to know another human being. I've never been interested in people who just lay it all out there for you."

His thoughtful response brought to mind a line from the movie that had stuck with me: "It is on such twists of fate and conscience of men that the plans of the mighty often founder."

"Yes, I loved that line," Irons said.

The publicist was finally exasperated with us both, and she stretched her strangler-vine arms all over him.

Irritated, he said, "You must simply make the journey to the rainforest while there's still time. There's so little real mystery left anymore, except for the mystery of getting to know other people, other cultures, other times." His eyes blazed like a fire when a handful of spice is tossed in. "That's what acting's all about. That's what the journey of *life* is all about. That's our real mission, not this, not this."

With that soulful suggestion emerged the real Jeremy Irons, if such a protean actor can be reduced to such a singular role, which is that of the troubled intellectual with a fractious emotional life who redoubles his intense search of the truth about himself.

With a grand flourish, he gestured to all his handlers, arched his eyebrows, grimaced, and reached out to shake my hand, sighing, as he got up to leave, "God, I miss it, the dignity of it all."

Cannes, France
1986

THE END OF THE ROAD

"COUNT BACKWARDS FROM A hundred," the anesthesiologist suggests. "Okay, count along with me now. A hundred, ninety-nine, ninety-eight, ninety-seven..."

The operating room is cold as the devil's own heart. I'm nervous about going under the knife for a quadruple hernia operation. The surgeon says he's done doubles and even triples, but never a quadruple, laughs and asks if he can write up my case for the *New England Journal of Medicine*. He's trying to put me at ease. I smile wanly, and begin harmonizing with the anesthesiologist, my voice hoarse, then squeaking: A hundred, ninety-nine ..."

Never got past ninety-nine.

Out of the squeeze-box of memory comes a newsreel of twenty-five-year-old images of my '73 Capri, the pride and joy of my college years, exploding, burning, much of it even melting on the side of the road, along Otis Redding's dock of the bay, in Berkeley.

I thought I had made friends with fire. I thought I knew it, literally and figuratively. I've been in Vulcan's own foundry, the fire-belching bowels of the River Rouge Plant, outside Detroit, where my father led school groups, famous movie stars like Gene Kelly, Van Gogh's nephew, and entire baseball teams like our own Tigers, on tours. I've walked in smoking sneakers across the burbling lava beds of Kilauea. I've felt the blistering heat of houses burning in the marina during the '89 San Francisco earthquake.

And then my damned car burst into flames and I had to learn about fire all over again.

I've also read the poets like Sappho and William Blake, memoirists like Gretel Ehrlich and James Salter, who all beautifully evoked the primal fire, about our hearts on fire and burning down our days.

I didn't know half of what I thought I knew, which was less than nothing.

Forty-eight hours after I finished repainting its faded metallic copper body, outfitted it with four brand-new radial tires, and filled the gas tank for the return trip across the Bay Bridge—after lavishing all that attention on it my fifteen-year-old Capri had the gall to die during rush hour. Smack-dab in the middle lane of the sky-high curving approach from 580 to 80, leading onto the gorgeous span across the bay. Which is to say, it sputtered, hissed, coughed, juked, and gnashed its gears before grinding to a dead halt. Stupefied, I felt the car rocking and rolling in the fierce winds of the passing cars and trucks. All I could do was stare dumbly at the odometer, which was frozen forever at exactly 186,542 miles.

On the cold slab of the operating table I have the gauziest sense of being asked by a nurse, a doctor, the anesthesiologist—who knows?—how I'm doing. When I try to speak it feels like somebody has been spoon-feeding oatmeal to me—a nurse, my grandmother, Rita Hayworth?—and all I can do is make pitiful whining sounds.

My car died. Did I say that already? Did I mention that it was the end of the road for the car my dad bought me my senior year in college, the car I drove eleven times back and forth across the country, the car I took to the Wayne Drive-In to see *2001: A Space Odyssey*, the car I took camping up to Algonquin Provincial Park in Northern Ontario and down to Mardi Gras, to seventeen ballgames down at Tiger Stadium, and then cross-country from Detroit to San Francisco to begin my new life.

My damned car died. I'm not sure if I mentioned that. It flamed out. It was consumed by hellfire. It was torched, it gave up the ghost, it defied three humungous hoses pulled by the Berkeley Fire Department.

★ ★ ★

Are you okay, sir? Do you need more painkillers? Who's talking to
me? You talking to me? Who's talking to me? I can't place the
voice. What do you mean, am I okay? I just escaped a burning
car—and I'm trapped—can't escape, can't stay.

Thousands of cars are careening past my own, leaving me
lurching in the slipstream. Not a single one dares to stop, not
one person stops or even slows down to offer help. They're
whizzing by like Indy 500 cars racing the clock at the test track.
I'm stuck in a burning car that's exploded in the wind tunnel
that is the off-ramp. I don't dare get out of the car. There—
can't you see him? The truck driver slowing down and flipping
me off? Stop him! He's taunting me and now he intentionally
grazes the door handle of my moribund car.

I'm fading in and out like images in the 1920s Abel Gance film
on Napoleon, my narrative dissolving under the anesthetic
into nine screens at once. Lying there on the operating table, I
come in and out of consciousness, remembering random things
like flicking on the car's red flashers, checking the odometer
to see how many miles I've racked up, thinking *I'll never get to
200,000 now.*

Carefully, I edge my body out of the car, holding tight to
my satchel, which contains my manuscripts. I try to flag down
one of the careening cars, but they're all in bat-out-of-hell
mode, trying to get home before the next guy. I'm disappointed
in the lack of common decency but now I've got to take care
of business.

Finally, a daredevil in a bright yellow VW bug slows down
and stops behind me, shouting, "Do you need a push?" She's
offering to push me bumper to bumper down the off-ramp and
onto the shoulder of the road. I'm surprised by her offer—a
Good Samaritan's act, if there ever was one. Gratefully, I hop
back into the car, shift into neutral, feel the gentle bump of
her fender against mine, and steer down the ramp and out of
danger. Then she drives me to the nearest station so I can fill up

my gas can. Minutes later, I'm jogging back to my car, ready to do what I've done several times before, fill an empty tank, in summer, spring, fall, and winter. But when I climb back behind the wheel and turn over the engine this time something under the hood explodes and ferocious clouds of black smoke bulge up from beneath the hood.

I think he's waking up. Oh, no, we lost him again. Are you sure he's okay? I think he's talking in his sleep. What's he saying? He's mumbling something about fire.

Through the windshield, I can see the fire down below working its way through the space between the hood and the car body. The flames start licking their way menacingly toward the windshield, begin to move underneath the car, toward the gas tank. An explosion seems seconds away. I grab my old leather satchel with its precious cache of manuscripts, then leap out of the car and am nearly side-swiped by a semi roaring by. Leaping out of the car, I toss the bag to the shoulder of the road, hoping against hope that I can extinguish the fire.

Like a maniac, I scoop up fistfuls of gravel from the side of the ramp and toss them onto the car, trying to at least prevent the flames from spreading. My antics are futile against the ravaging fire. My hands dripping with blood from the broken glass embedded in the dirt I'm scraping from the roadside.

Phil, we're here, you're okay, how are you feeling?

I want to say *I feel like death*, but don't want to upset her, but there is death all over—can't she see it? I'm back on the side of the road, feeling wind-whipped by the passing cars. I think someone stops and asks if he can help, then shakes his head and says he'll call the fire department for me at the pay phone just up the road.

Twenty frenzied minutes later, I collapse in defeat on top of my satchel and watch numbly as fire devours the plastic radiator grill that I had patched up only weeks before, watch the bronze paint that I had just redone mottle, split, and arch like a cat's back on the hood, and listen and smell the burning rubber as my four brand-new radial tires explode one by one. Then the engine block cracks from the fire within.

Moving around to the front of the car, I flip up the viciously steaming hood, the new paint job glistening, then alligatoring, the metal hood rippling. I'm confused, unable to risk pushing it alone to the side of the road. Standing there on the shoulder, I'm stricken with the thought that the fire was my fault. I didn't tank up, I hadn't had a tune-up in too long, I had missed my car's vital signs, the kind that guys raised in the Motor City were supposed to notice. Disgraceful. Wait, no, it couldn't have been, right? I had looked at the gas gauge, thinking, hoping I had neglected to fill it, and the real reason it died was because the tank was empty, the dreaded needle on "E." Maybe there was a leak in the gas line? Who knows, I could have been leaving a trail all the way from Oakland, where I had spent the morning.

By the time the fire truck arrives and the water hoses are unspooled and two firemen lamely try to squelch the fire, it's all over. Never had I really seen fire until now. It had devolved into a mythological symbol, a literary trope, a poetic reverie, a mystical sign in the lives of hermit saints and sages. It hadn't occurred to be that the great fire that had helped forge cars at the River Rouge Plant could also be the elemental power that could devour them years later.

"Looks like it started in the carburetor," the fire chief says to me, a little too nonchalantly. "It's half-melted." When I lean underneath the smoking hood, the carburetor looks like big glob of slithering mercury. As Zorba said, *the full catastrophe.*

Easy for you to say, I want to respond, *You've seen a million fires. I haven't. Has your car ever caught on fire? I doubt it.*

Of course, I say nothing out of respect. I act grateful, though I'm not. I'm steaming mad, at him, at myself, at the car, at *fire* itself. A startling hatred creeps up my spine, a wild rage with nowhere to go.

"Goddamned shame. A good car is hard to find. We're all

looking for that 2500-pound buddy. It can be a family friend, right?"

Well, maybe the guy's all right, after all.

Strange, as we're talking I can see my burning car reflected in his sunglasses. Words seem pathetic in the face of that fire. The second tire explodes, the front window steams and cracks, then the third tire, then the fourth. The images of burning rubber, rippling metal, iguana-finned flames began to fill my bones.

When I swim back to the surface of consciousness I'm groggy, finding it hard to focus on my wife and son and the attending nurse. They want to talk about the operation and ask about my pain level on a scale of one to ten, ten being excruciating. I am about to ask about my car, whether they called a tow truck, or the insurance company, or was she able to save it. But I'm confused. Nobody seems to be upset about my dead car except me.

"How are you feeling?" asks the nurse.

"I'm burning up."

"Don't worry, it's all over. You can go home tomorrow."

"No, it's the end of the road," I said, not sure where the words came from or where they were hiding for so long.

"What do you mean? Now you're just being silly. You're fine, it's not the end," she insists.

"No, it's the end of the road. Can't you see it? Can't you read the odometer?"

And then I tumble down the log flume of sleep, trying to forget all about the fire, which burns in me still.

Berkeley, California,
October 1988

LAST EXIT BEFORE PARADISE

"The journey itself is my home."
—MATSUO BASHŌ, JAPANESE POET (1644-1694)

THE OLD PHILOSOPHER'S EYES are encrusted with sleep. He blinks once, twice, and shivers, as Ngodup, his Tibetan assistant, nudges him and whispers that he has a visitor. Slowly, he turns to me and tries to focus through gauzy eyes. He looks at me, through me, beyond me, his gaze, as always, fixed on eternity. It is the look of someone lumbering toward the other world, unsure if he wants to return to this one. It is unnerving. Since I first met him twenty-five years ago I've been struck by the oracular scholar's piercing blue eyes, partly because of the kindness that poured through, partly because of the gravitas that suggested he was focused on this and only this moment.

Now, the blue has faded, and the eyes are sad. Huston's brow furrows as he tries to place me, anxious that he isn't being plagued by another stranger tramping in to visit him in the old guest room of his home in Berkeley that hospice has converted for him. The last time I visited him I was forced to wait an hour because four complete strangers had barged their way past the housekeeper and stomped into Huston's room, claiming that they had driven all the way from Texas because, as they told the entrapped professor, "Your books changed our lives, and we want to thank you."

Later, his wife Kendra told me through clenched teeth that Huston was too confused to tell his intruders he had no clue who they were, and he was too kind to ask them to leave.

Remembering this, I say nothing, manage a smile, and grip

his skeletal hand. Once as firm and strong as his ideas, it is now wispy, the loose skin thin and transparent as filo dough. If I don't hold on tight, it seems as if his hand could float away like dust motes.

Clearing his throat, his eyes fluttering, trying to get used to the bright light after the long darkness of his afternoon nap. The reflex reminds me of one of his favorite parables, Plato's Cave, which he used to illustrate for audiences how foolish it is to mistake shadows for reality, and how painful it can be to see the sun for the first time.

Finally, his eyes widen in recognition.

"Anyone," he says in the familiar lilt, "would know we are good friends by your smile and handshake."

His sing-song cadence is an echo of the Chinese he grew up speaking as the son of missionary parents in Soochow, China, near Shanghai.

"Hello, Huston," I say slowly, "Jo and Jack send their love."

He nods numbly without real recognition. Not even the cochlear implant he has endured for years can help him anymore, his wife had recently told me. He is reduced to reading the lips of his visitors.

Ngodup knocks on the door and peeks in. "Dr. Smith, do you need anything?" he asks with an air of touching tenderness. Huston shakes his head and smiles. Ngodup nods, turns to me and points to a large yellow law pad on the night table next to the bed. I pick it up, fold back the pages written on by a half dozen previous visitors, and scrawl my name with a black magic marker in big block letters to nudge his old friend's memory. Recalling that Huston has a few other friends with my first name, I quickly scrawl the names of my wife and son, which I'm hope he'll recognize since he married Jo and I and is Jack's honorary godfather.

"Huston," I whisper, "Jo and Jack send their love."

The venerable historian of religion, author of spiritual classics that have sold millions of copies in dozens of languages, and one of the great voices for tolerance and cross-cultural understanding in our time, stares at the message on the yellow law pad, as if the letters are indecipherable, ancient cuneiform, a long-lost script he's examining in the moldering archives of the Bodleian Library. But he's not deciphering ancient mysteries. He is no longer rummaging around in the stacks on his lifelong search for the wisdom literature of the ages.

He is simply trying to comprehend the moment.

He is like the stranger in a strange land he used to lecture about, a man returning from a long journey who is not recognized and cannot recognize the world that has gone ahead without him.

For ten excruciating minutes, his head bobs up and down as he tries to read my scrawl. His eyes are barely visible through the slits of his eyelids. He tries to fathom the mysteries of our three names with the same determination he used to understand the arcane truths of Plotinus, Meister Eckhardt, or Frithjof Schuon.

Still, his tenacity shows through. He is unrelenting, his scholarly stubbornness still serving him. Now his eyes dilate with recognition. We both smile. It is one of life's delights to see and be seen. His eyebrows ratchet upward with every degree of increasing understanding. Something resembling awareness returns from his fathomless depths. He enunciates the words until his forehead corrugates with a new thought and response.

Looking up, he says impishly, "Please send them my love—*with interest!*"

Satisfied with my laughter, he knits his eyebrows as I'd seen him do on stage with me countless times, a master at playing the crowd, and intones, "Wonderful...*but who are YOU?*"

"Phil," I remind him. I'm grateful for what appears to be the return of his gnomic sense of humor and launch another volley of laughs—until I realize it wasn't a joke after all. His face sags with shame and confusion. The name seems to mean nothing, just four disconnected letters, having nothing to do with the face before him.

So much for being recognized.

I feel foolish. I want to make amends. I lean across the bed and slide the yellow pad away from him so I can circle my name at the top.

"*Phil*," I repeat, reaching across the abyss.

Suddenly, his scrutiny turns fierce. He grabs the pad back and studies the circle and the name inside it and then nods and hands it back with profound relief and satisfaction, an expression I recall seeing on his face when he worked on the galleys of his illustrated edition of *The World's Religions* at his dining room table.

"Oh, *Phil*," he says, finally, smiling.

I'm oddly relieved, feeling recognized, even vindicated for my visit.

Scrunching up his mouth, his voice descends into a stentorian tone, as if addressing an amphitheater of students at one of the myriad universities where he taught, he demands to know, "*Which one?*"

"Phil *Cousineau!*"

"Oh, *that Phil*," he purrs, as he falls back to his pillow, smiles, and meets my gaze. "Phil *Cousineau, as I live and breathe!* How are you? Does Kendra know you're here?"

He has returned from the Back of Beyond.

Satisfied, his crusted eyes close again. I sense him falling a great distance into the meditations he learned in the cold, distant Japanese monasteries of his youth. Instead, he begins to sing—actually sing. A melody gathered somewhere on the back roads of his globetrotting past, one of the ten times he "girdled the earth," as he loved to remind me when he compared (fairly competitively) his world travels to mine. I get the haunting feeling he is listening to a distant spectral memory. Minutes later, as the music fades, he opens his eyes and turns back to me, saying, "What a *friend* I have had in you."

Huston enunciates like no one else I have ever met, as if every word he utters *matters*, a constant source of consolation for me over the years. His pronunciation of the word *friend* sounds like a benediction. It's as if he has sanctified the room. Ever the teacher, he allows the words to linger like incense in the Blue Mosque, as if to ensure I understand the enormity and tenderness of what he is saying.

I have barely fathomed the emotion of his paean to friendship when he broaches the subject that is sitting on his shoulder like Odin's raven of death.

"You know, I am never going to get out of this bed again."

He says this like a pronouncement from a lectern.

"After traversing the world, I have not moved out of this room for six months. I don't expect I ever will again."

This is a philosopher's way of talking about how the end is nigh, without using the word, and not because he is squeamish about the subject. Far from it. He is allaying my own fears, as Kendra has told me he has been doing with his closest friends, telling us, lest we forget, that he is at peace, that he has no fear about "the end of the road," as he puts it.

"I know, Huston, I know. I'm sorry—"

He snaps, "I don't want pity. I'm in no pain, I'm at peace."

What I hear him saying reminds me of the last two lines of D. H. Lawrence's poem, "The End, the Beginning," where the great poet describes the *need* for utter darkness, oblivion, and forgetting means that it's better that we might experience the numinous:

> *"But dipped, once dipped in dark oblivion*
> *the soul has peace, inward and lovely peace."*

How could I be so stupid? Huston is trying to tell me that his soul has already been immured in the dark oblivion of terminal illness, and you know what, I am at peace, my friend, I am enjoying "inward and lovely peace."

Chastened, I can hear my dad's voice now, in one of his sterner moments, "How thick can you be, Philip?"

I am witnessing what Huston once described to me as the "equanimity" that is achieved after a lifetime of practicing—not theorizing—one's deepest beliefs.

I am tempted to ask, "Practice *what*?" Stillness, compassion, kindness? No, not quite. I sense that there is something else that he has been practicing all along, something more elusive, something more essential. I need to know.

Then it comes to me, I can hear it in my third ear, a Dopplering echo of a conversation we had while working together on the second volume of his memoirs, *And Live Rejoicing*, where he was determined to render his conclusions after some fifty-plus years of studying the world's great wisdom traditions.

"I'm not afraid because I *know* we are in good hands," he had told me with an unassailable sense of confidence, "and for that knowledge we should be grateful."

What he has been practicing all along is *praise* for the miracle of life. Not sappy flattery, but gratitude in the spirit of Rumi, who said, "He who does not praise daily is a thief." That depth of praise.

I never pushed him on the point, never asked him *whose* hands. I didn't have to. It was beyond debate. He believes in a personal God, not some amorphous force or Great Spirit. For him, God is a lived truth, an *encounter* with the Divine, and that is enough.

Never a self-dramatist, his words had emerged devoid of self-pity. "But that's all right. I feel no pain. Tell our friends I'm in no pain."

The wizened philosopher takes a deep breath, allowing for the dramatic silence that had served him well as a professor of philosophy and religion for decades, the ellipsis between word and thought that is at the heart of peace.

Watching him close his eyes and gather his strength for a few more minutes of conversation, he appears preternaturally calm, like a white heron on the banks of a lake, a preternaturally calm image of peace in the very shadows of death.

"And *you*, have you been traveling?" he asks. "I was telling Kendra you travel more than anyone I know."

I'm taken aback by the thought that in the last hours he would waste a single breath talking about me with his wife, but quickly recall their evening ritual of reviewing the events of their day over dinner and occasionally a cocktail. The ritual seemed to sanctify their marriage, to use one of his favorite verbs, by giving a name and lending a story to their daily encounters.

"Yes, for the last three months—Greece, Turkey, the Midwest, and India," I say tripping over the words, anxious that the list may sound like boasting to the old globetrotter in his bedridden state. As he often has over the years, he detects my misgivings about my peripatetic life.

"Don't try to *bump* that out of your life!" he shouts. "It's a deep part of you."

The choice of word—*bump*—is so odd that I rip off a page from the law pad and write it down to later retrieve a few strands of our conversation, and quickly add: *interest, friend in you, no pain.*

I am trying to magnetize our conversation with the floating filaments of words and images.

He notices and files it away for future discussion and says slyly, "I've also told Kendra, 'That Phil, he takes more notes than anyone I've ever met.'"

Without warning, he grabs my hand again with a steely grip and adds, "*Don't stop*, don't hold back."

I'm unsure if he is referring to the bump or the notes, but let it go. It hardly matters. I just know that the insistence is curious. The words have the tinny echo of someone speaking to a ghost of himself from long ago. Weariness rises off him like heat waves over a desert road.

I feel a pang of guilt that I'm overstaying my welcome, dreading Kendra's discovery of me lingering here after promising her I that would only stay for five minutes. Am I deluding myself that he needs this visit, these reminiscences, or is he enjoying the company?

"Huston, old friend, I need to go now so you can rest."

"Rest, that's *all I do!*" he bellows again. The words are throttled by a choking attack. Still, he goes on. "At least you didn't say, '*You look great!*' That's the kiss of death for all old people. *Of course,* I look great—all I do is rest."

At that he coughs into a hand towel, the color leeching from his face.

"Yes, I need to collapse now."

Gasping for air, he dabs at his teared-up eyes, a gesture that betrays his self-consciousness about his weakening body. To counter the embarrassment, he makes a feeble joke about hospice care.

For a moment, I'm afraid that he is afraid. But what on earth could he be afraid of now? He is ninety-five and lived the good life, seemingly one without regrets.

"Before you came, the technicians were working me over for three quarters of an hour." To illustrate the point he pokes at the air like the nurses poking at his bedraggled body with needles and probes. He cries out comically, "I don't know what they were doing! What could they be looking for now? There's nothing left of me to fix. I'm *a...mess!*"

He is valiantly trying to make light of the dark moment. But his emotions are turning him inside out, revealing a vulnerability I'd only seen once before, when we met a few days after his granddaughter was murdered on her boyfriend's yacht in far away Tahiti. His voice comes back to me like the sound of an agonizing adagio coming through an old radio: "I-I never thought anything could be worse than the loss of one of your children, but this is worse, the loss of a grandchild." His voice crackled, but he found his equilibrium, and asked me in a reverential voice, "I would like to keep working with you on our book, *The Way Things Are,* two hours a day, while I plow through this grief. Life must go on."

Then he hung up.

Voices. Where are they stored? In some great vault in our brain? In the attic of our souls? So many images, so many voices, in so few minutes. And then where do they go? Into what Carl Sandburg once called the "forgettery"?

Suddenly, the hospital bed trembles as Huston is hit with a jolt of pain.

What does it matter now? I try to convince myself that I'm overstaying my welcome because I'm somehow strengthening his spirit with our conversation. Instead, he is weakening with the effort to speak. I make an attempt to stand up and take my leave. He stares at me nonplussed, swivels his attention around the spare guestroom, where his hospice bed has been placed. The room is filled with the cold truths of hospital paraphernalia, in harsh contrast to the warm souvenirs of a lifetime of travels and scholarship in his living room, where we had met for the last two decades. There, we were surrounded by a lifetime of travel souvenirs, Buddhist statues, Hindu paintings, a portrait of His Holiness the Dalai Lama, and my favorite, the Huichol yarn painting he bought from a medicine woman named Dona Lupe when we worked together in the remote mountains of Mexico on our documentary film, *The Peyote Road*. That image jogs a memory of Huston's indignant voice from my interview with him for that project, "Calling peyote a *drug* is like describing the wine at mass as *booze!*"

Closing my eyes, I call up the image of the Huichol artwork that now seems auspicious, a kaledeiscopic vision of the journey of the soul into the afterworld.

Again, a tumble into reverie.

On our last night in Mexico, under a jaguar belt of stars Huston remarked about the peyote pilgrims who had gathered with us for four days to entrust us with the making of the film about their ancient way of worship.

"These people seem to be permanently in the hypnagogic state," he said, "prolonging the dream until they can't tell it apart from being awake. Perhaps it is a deeper state than waking, the very ground of being, the very heart of heaven."

A handful of his books line the shelves, right in his eyeline, as if to give him a daily dose of reassurance. His eyes rest on a copy of *And Live Rejoicing*, sitting face out. He smiles at the memory of our collaboration, and I wonder if he recognizes himself on the cover. Then his voice rings out, "How many *slim* books did we do together?"

Again, the deliberate enunciation. It's a curious question, but consistent with the tradition of the mentor feeling he needs to put the student in his place every once in a while. Am I being overly sensitive, or did he stress the diminutive word *slim*? I'm mildly offended then reproach myself that it can hardly matter now.

"Oh, let's see," I say, "one, two, three, four, four books, plus, we can't forget the five American Indian documentaries we worked on together with Gary Rhine, and James Botsford, and Vine DeLoria."

Huston nods the nod of the gods, not just a chinwag of approval, but an affirmation from on high about the work we've done together. He pauses again, measuring his thoughts, parsing his words like no one I've ever known, out of comfort with silence and a devotion to language. I think of it as the long deliberation, an intensity of contemplation I've appreciated in him for twenty-five years as we worked on his essays about the verities of the perennial philosophy, or the need to recall and respect the "forgotten truths," or the tragic neglect of indigenous religion, and the importance of teaching in a world where elders abandon their responsibilities to young people.

Finally, he musters, "Yes, those days were important. We've been down many roads together and done some important work."

He stares off into the other world for several orbiting minutes.

His expression spurs a memory of the answer he provided when I asked him what he had been trying to convey to his students over the fifty-plus years of teaching religion and philosophy. Without hesitation, he replied, "I tried to give them a glimpse of another world, and a better one."

An elliptical remark. The kind he has always reveled in. Decisively chosen words that leave room for contemplation and invite conversation. The summation of his long teaching career also reflected his fierce belief in transcendence, and a reminder of one his bitterest regrets, the loss of that confidence in modern times.

"Huston, that's why I described you in my introduction to *The Way Things Are* as being more of a metaphysician than a philosopher, or even an historian. It seems to me that your true focus has been on the invisible realm so that we might better understand the visible one."

With that Huston appears to fade back in time, as I imagine the desert fathers retreating into their caves in remote Egypt and Turkey.

"Yes," he intones, "I recall that essay. It's true, I'm a metaphysician, not a philosopher. At best, I am a reluctant historian of religion. Even I did not realize that until I read those words of yours. I am grateful for the distinction. You were the first one to point that out. I believe that what is most important is invisible because it stands behind and supports the visible. And if you want to understand the visible, you must look carefully into the invisible."

Lacing together the beautiful string of words leaves him breathless. Where did the strength come from for such an outburst of conviction?

Now he grimaces like a runner crossing the finish line, slowly closing his eyes as if ready himself for the long goodbye. I take advantage of the fugitive moment to grab the law pad which is lying on the bed covers and scribble a few more chance words—*slim, books, memory, films*—to spur my memory later.

Of course, he notices.

"I like you, Phil, but you take more notes than anybody I've ever known," he says, repeating himself. But this time he adds, "And that worries me."

He lifts the yellow pad again, reading the runes, asks, "*And Jack?* Your son Jack. You said he's been accepted into nine colleges. Good. And he has finally decided on purchasing which course of studies?"

"Cal State Monterey Bay, Huston," I begin. "He'll be pleased you remembered. He has a wonderful young…friend… now, Huston, and she has been reading your books on religion."

As I wait for a reply, I realize he hasn't understood a word I've said. He blurts out, "I have a hearing aid somewhere. Over there, I think."

I rustle around on his side table for the newfangled hearing aid and hand it to him, saying,

He smiles sweetly as I repeat my message about my son, but he is light-years beyond flattery about his readership. Instead, he simply reaches out for my hand and fumbles with our grip until we are locked in a vigorous soul-brother shake.

"If I had had a son, I would have wished him to be like Jack. He is a good boy."

He looks long and hard at me, and then beyond, over my shoulder, into the infinite world beyond me. Not worriedly, not nervously, but contemplatively.

If this is Death, this is how I want to die, at peace, without bitterness about the longest road of all.

Coming back, he double-clutches and returns to the topic of my son.

"I've known only two people who have completely transformed their lives—and Jack is one of them."

His acknowledgement of my son's bouts with illness over the last few years stuns me, considering how he is teetering at death's door. I'm also mystified who the other person might be. Ram Dass? Aldous Huxley? Krishnamurti? His wife, his daughters, one of his grandchildren? Who might he be referring to? I'm dying to ask him but am stymied. It feels inappropriate to ask him now. I.file it away as a question later on for Kendra.

"Thank you, Huston, I will be sure to let him know. He will be glad to hear that. He loves you. For now, I'm sure you want to rest, okay? I should really go."

His eyes rain tears.

He does not want to let go of my hand, of life itself.

Twenty-five years flash by like an old newsreel. I see him at a publisher's party where we first met, Christmas, 1989. He's seventy, I'm forty-seven. He's updating his classic, *The World's Religions*, which has sold two million copies. I've just finished my first book, which has yet to sell a single copy. What do we possibly have to talk about? Fortunately, Stanislav Grof steps in and engages him, then Richard Tarnas, Sam Keen, and Maya Angelou. I was struck by how ramrod straight Huston stood, how his eyes seized mine, and he asked me a serious question, treating me as if I were the only one in the room: "What are you working on now?"

I hesitate before replying, "I'm writing a book about famous last words."

"Ah," he replies, "that is an important topic."

The acknowledge was the first of many times he revealed himself to be the embodiment of Confucian *chun-tzu*, the ideal gentleman, the scholar with a deeply human heart who teaches by moral example and no little kindness.

His smile triggers a kind of movie lap dissolve in my mind. It's the late 1990s. We're driving in a rental car in circles around Santa Barbara, trying to find a theater where we're scheduled to appear as part of the prestigious Mind & Supermind lecture series. I look at my watch. We're supposed to be on stage in twenty minutes. I pull off the road, high in the hills over-looking the city. I fumble with a map to get back on course. I've been so immersed in our far-ranging, gallivanting conversation that ricocheted from our work with American Indians, to another book we want to propose to UC Press, to baseball lore and his love of tennis in college, to a dramatic revelation about him driving around with Martin Luther King, Jr. in the mid-sixties. The talk is an adrenaline rush for a conversation junkie like me. I'm reeling with the excitement of the here and now, dizzy with the moment, and he is unflappable about the fact we are supposed to be on stage in ten minutes.

"I'm lost," I say woefully.

"We're never lost, if we're with friends," he says, kinder than he needed to be. I pull off the road and look at the map provided by the rental company.

Rather than being annoyed, he pats my arm and says, "Don't worry, *I* got lost here once. I think it was 1957. I was about your age and driving Mr. Huxley to a lecture for this same series in the very same hall. Don't worry, they can't start without us."

"You mean, *Aldous* Huxley," I mutter.

"Yes, Aldous," he said, smiling. "A fine man with a keen mind."

Letting go of my hand, Huston slowly but triumphantly clenches his own into a fist and lets it hover in the air, as if inviting me to meet halfway for a fist-bump for the first time in our long friendship. Where he learned that gesture I'll never know, nor if he had planned the fist-bump as his way of punctuating—or celebrating—our last visit.

Not to worry, I want to say to my old friend, *death is nothing more than a bend in the road of life.*

Wisely, I keep it to myself, realizing how ridiculous it would be to philosophize with a real philosopher, or should I say, split infinitives with a real metaphysician?

"Huston, sorry, one last thing," I say. "I'm going to be meeting with some filmmakers who are working with your old friend, the Dalai Lama. They want to know if you have a message for His Holiness?"

The wizened professor sighs, waits, his eyes wet, his lips moving as if articulating a thought, out of reverence for the question.   "Yes, tell him I think he is the world's peacekeeper. You know the story of how his disguise hid him in the fields and helped him escape from Tibet? He was 4 or 5 years old, and it was a cops-and-robbers tale. A blizzard came and disguised his path of escape that helped drop the boy across the Indian border."

Once again, he takes a deep breath, coughs into his hand, then says with steely strength, "Tell him that I vividly remember his oracles told him when he was but a boy that he was going to live a long life.

Tell him, I pray that the oracles are valid."

And now we both know it is time for me to go.

Huston pats my hand, and smiles to beat the band, as my own grandfather used to say, then plays an unexpected, even melodious grace note. "Phil," he asks, "do you remember our good friend Reuben Snake, the Winnebago Road Man? He once told me that life is a long road and the best thing we can do is to walk in arm-in-arm down that road with our brothers and sisters. He was a wise man."

Catching his breath, my old friend adds, "I'm certainly glad I didn't miss out on meeting you."

For me, those will always be his famous last words.

Berkeley, California
December, 2014

X

I stand under a slate gray Connemara sky
slashed with rain
and ask the old sheep farmer the nettled question,
"Where does this road lead to, Mr. Keaney?"
He leans against the drystone wall,
hand-built by his grandfather,
gazes up the clabbered road leading to the bog,
whistles for his faithful sheepdog, and sighs,
"To the end, lad, to the end."

Notes on the Photographs

Page ii, Frontispiece: The Road to the Findspot of the Venus de Milo, 2008

Page v, Dedication page: The Road Through the Rice Terraces, Banaue, Philippines, 1996

Page x, Introduction: Stone Bridge, Hydra, Greece, 2014

Page xiv, I: The Streets of Assisi, Assisi, Italy, 2012

Page 24, II: Burnished Streets, Montenegro, 2011

Page 46, III: Road Across the Prairie, Saskatchewan, Canada, 2013

Page 64, IV: Chartres Labyrinth, France, 2010

Page 96, V: The Pilgrim's Road, Clonmacnoise, Ireland, 2009

Page 116, VI: The Great Red Scar, Amazon, Brazil, 1993

Page 154, VII: The River Road, Lake Nipissing, Canada, 1995

Page 172, VIII: The Appian Way, Rome, Italy, 1993

Page 200, IX: Ephesus, Turkey, 1993

Page 270, X: Famine Cottage Mural, Inisboffin, Ireland, 2003

Page 272, Notes on the Photographs, The Sacred Way, Akropolis, Athens, Greece, 1995

Page 274, Acknowledgments: Angkor Wat, Cambodia, 1996

page 278, About the Author: Author Phil Cousineau, on the Royal Road to Knossus, Crete, 2014.

Answers to all the riddles on page 47: a road

PASSING THANKS

FIRST PUBLISHED IN A fine art edition under the guidance of the brilliant Berkeley book designer Richard Seibert and published by Sisyphus Press in 2000, *The Book of Roads* is a satchelful of travel stories written over the last three decades. For several years since the book sold out its first two printings I have been at wit's end about how to revive it and found some solace in the old chestnut about the intrepid Kentucky explorer Daniel Boone. The legend goes that he was once asked if he was ever lost in the woods. His reply was crisp and honest, "No, but I was bewildered once for three days." Fortunately for me, whenever I became bewildered about the direction of the original book I had savvy guides who helped me find my way through the dark forest of writing over the course of the nine years it took to compile the original stories. The person most responsible for this second expanded and revised edition and to whom I am deeply grateful is my long-time friend and publisher, Brenda Knight of Viva Editions, for granting me the opportunity to repave my earlier road stories, and add a dozen more roads to the map of memories. Without her belief in the worthiness of these travel stories, this new edition would not have been possible and I am grateful. Likewise, her team at Viva Editions has proved friendly and encouraging throughout the process and I would like to call out Kara Wuest for her keen editorial sensibility and unflagging devotion to smoothing over the bumps in the road of publication, perceptive copy editing of Kitty Burn Florey, Scott Ideleman/Blink for his striking cover design, and, Frank Wiedemann for his road-worthy text design.

This freshly minted edition would not have been feasible

without the careful retyping of the original manuscript by a fellow traveler, Lou Ann Granger, whose love for the road—and road stories—is equaled only by her professionalism. Special thanks to our fellow pilgrim, Joan Ishibashi, who generously offered her time and keen eye for another pass of copy editing, as well as the original editing guidance provided for the first edition of the book by the lynx-eyed Valerie Andrews, and savvy work of Steve Anderson.

This second edition has also been given some roadside emergency help by the unstinting support of my friend Erin Byrne, who has been using the book in her own writing classes and helped keep the interest alive in it, the Delphic wisdom of Alexander Eliot, who has been a staunch supporter of my travel writing for decades, and the continued championing of the stories by one of the most perspicacious travel writers of our time, Pico Iyer. I couldn't hit the road with this new edition without acknowledging the roistering support of the roadster Mort Rosenblum, and my friend over the course of many projects exploring the Red Road of American Indian issues, the lawyer-poet, James Botsford, my Canadian cousin Raymond Guy and his wife Louise for helping me explore the river roads of Ontario, Canada, and special thanks to my mentor in living with joy in this world, Huston Smith, who often reminded me how proud he was to have "girdled the globe ten times."

A special doff of my Irish tweed cap to my friends at Book Passage in Corte Madera, California, especially Karen West and Elaine Petrocelli, for the opportunity to read these stories and display many of the photographs that accompany them at their annual Travel Writers and Photographers Conferences. Bountiful thanks as well to the sharpshooter, photographer Chris Franek, who took the cover shot of the author on what is reputed to be the oldest road in Europe, the 2500-year-old paved stone road leading to the Palace of Knossos on the island of Crete, in September 2014, and to our buddy, the rambunctious road dog, Patrick Duffy, for his unswerving support for this new edition.

Final thanks to my road manager, Jo Beaton Cousineau,

for clipping out a *Far Side* cartoon by Gary Larson that says, "And as you travel life's highway, don't forget to stop and eat the roses," and posting it above my writing desk. It shows that she understands my moodling habits more than anyone, as well as the truth of the old Irish proverb that is the final motto for this project: "The longest way around is the shortest way home." I'd drive all night just to be with you and our young roadman, Jackie Blue Cousineau.

North Beach, San Francisco—Hydra, Greece
November 2014

ABOUT THE AUTHOR

BORN IN AN ARMY hospital, Fort Jackson in Columbia, South Carolina, on November 26, 1952, Phil Cousineau was on the road two days later, driving north with his parents in their 1949 Hudson to the Civil War era town of Wayne, Michigan, down the road from Detroit. His peripatetic career was launched during his time as a sports writer and photographer for his hometown newspaper, *The Wayne Dispatch*, his journalism studies at the University of Detroit, and the four years he toiled in a Detroit steel factory. Over the course of his post-college Grand Tour around the world he worked as a harvester of date trees on an Israeli kibbutz, construction worker in London, housepainter of forty-four Victorian Ladies in San Francisco, screenwriting teacher at the American Film Institute, adventure tour leader, teacher, documentary filmmaker, photographer, editor, anthologist, creativity consultant, and youth sports coach. His many books include *The Art of Pilgrimage*, *Deadlines*, *The Hero's Journey: Joseph Campbell on His Life and Work*, *Stoking the Creative Fires*, *The Blue Museum*, *Wordcatcher*, *The Painted Word*, and *Burning the Midnight Oil*. Along with his twenty-plus documentary film credits, many of them shot on the back roads of the world, since 2008 Cousineau has served as host and co-writer for *Global Spirit*, which airs nationally on PBS and Link TV, and is currently a guest host on New Dimensions Radio, the longest running interview show in radio history. For the past several years, he has appeared frequently as an on-camera commentator for Warner Brothers DVDs on the mythology of movies, and for Major League Baseball (MLB.com) and the

National Football League on the mythology and iconography of sports.

Cousineau lives in North Beach, San Francisco, with his wife Jo Beaton Cousineau, and their son Jack, his favorite travel companions.

Author Photo: Chris Franek

Books by the Author

The Hero's Journey: Joseph Campbell on His Life and Work, 1990

Deadlines: A Rhapsody on a Theme of Famous and Infamous Last Words, 1991

The Soul of the World: A Modern Book of Hours (with Eric Lawton), 1993

Riders On the Storm: My Life with Jim Morrison and the Doors
(by John Densmore with Phil Cousineau),1993

Soul: An Archaeology: Readings from Socrates to Ray Charles, 1994

Prayers at 3 A.M.: Poems for the Middle of the Night, 1995

Design Outlaws: Frontiers of the 21st Century
(with Christopher Zelov), 1996

Soul Moments: Marvelous Stories of Synchronicity, 1997

The Art of Pilgrimage: The Seeker's Guide to Making Travel Sacred, 1998

Riddle Me This: A World Treasury of Folk and Literary Puzzles, 1999

The Soul Aflame: A Modern Book of Hours (with Eric Lawton), 2000

The Book of Roads: Travel Stories from Michigan to Marrakesh, 2000

Once and Future Myths: The Power of Ancient Stories in Modern Times, 2001

*Coincidence or Destiny: Stories of Synchronicity that
Illuminate Our Lives,* 2002

The Way Things Are: Conversations with Huston Smith, 2003

The Olympic Odyssey: Rekindling the Spirit of the Great Games, 2004

The Blue Museum: Poems, 2004

A Seat at the Table: The Struggle for American Indian Freedom, 2005

Angkor Wat: The Marvelous Enigma (photographs), 2006

Night Train: New Poems, 2007

The Jaguar People: An Amazonian Chronicle (photographs), 2007

Stoking the Creative Fires: 9 Ways to Rekindle Imagination, 2008

Around the World in Eighty Faces (photographs), 2008

Fungoes and Fastballs: Great Moments in Baseball Haiku, 2008

The Meaning of Tea (with Scott Chamberlin Hoyt), 2009

City 21: The Second Enlightenment (with Christopher Zelov), 2009

The Song of the Open Road (photographs), 2010

The Oldest Story in the World: A Mosaic of Meditations, 2009

*Wordcatcher: One Man's Odyssey into the World of Weird
and Wonderful Words*, 2010

Beyond Forgiveness: Reflections on Atonement, 2011

Shadowcatcher (photographs), 2012

The Painted Word: A Treasure Chest of Remarkable Word Origins, 2012

And Live Rejoicing: Chapters in a Charmed Life
(by Huston Smith with Phil Cousineau), 2012

The Soul and Spirit of Tea (with Scott Chamberlin Hoyt), 2013

*Burning the Midnight Oil: Illuminating Words for the Long Night's
Journey into Day*, 2014

Who Stole the Arms of the Venus de Milo? [forthcoming]

AUDIO BOOKS

The Art of Pilgrimage: The Seeker's Guide to Making Travel Sacred, 1998

Once and Future Myths: The Power of Ancient Stories in Modern Times, 2001

The Way Things Are: Conversations with Huston Smith, 2004

A Seat at the Table: Struggling for American Indian Religious Freedom, 2005

Wordcatcher: An Odyssey into the World of Weird and Wonderful Words, 2010

*The Painted Word: A Treasure Chest of Wonderful Words
and Their Origins*, 2012

*Burning the Midnight Oil: Illuminating Words for the Long Night's
Journey into Day*, 2014

The Book of Roads: A Life Made from Travel, 2015